"In this deliciously gripping book, the editor: highly readable and deeply enlightening tour o. the creative and bold pioneers of psychoanalysis in Hungary, not least the achievements of Michael Balint and his first wife, Alice Balint. Beautifully researched, incorporating much previously unpublished data, this groundbreaking volume offers not only extensive historical wisdom but, also, reminds us of the ways in which the work of Balint and his Budapest colleagues can enhance contemporary psychoanalysis."

Professor Brett Kahr, *Senior Fellow, Tavistock Institute of Medical Psychology, London, and Visiting Professor of Psychoanalysis and Mental Health at Regent's University London, and Honorary Director of Research, Freud Museum London*

"In a period when the idea of 'correct technique' was becoming crystallized around language, Michael Balint explored the 'gulf between patient and analyst' like no other, taking care to acknowledge the fractured balance between the individual and the environment, while teaching us the importance of becoming 'unsolid'. Nowadays we are, perhaps, more ready to appreciate the sensitive, profound, and elegant way he rethought the basic grammar of the analytic experience. This collection of essays and original documents on *Michael Balint and his World*, illuminates a variety of less known aspects of *The Budapest Years*. It is an engaging invitation to revive his inspiring legacy. I strongly recommend it."

Carlo Bonomi, *Ph.D., training and supervising analyst of the Società Italiana di Psicoanalisi Sándor Ferenczi Network (ISFN), associate editor of the* International Forum of Psychoanalysis, *and Founding President of the Sandor Ferenczi Cultural Association*

"I hear with pleasure and emotion that the book about Balint and the Hungarian analytic society will soon be available. The list of contributors is impressive. Much thanks to them."

Judith Dupont, *Psychoanalyst, Translator, Author and Editor, Member of the French Psychoanalytical Society, Founder of the psychoanalytic journal* Le Coq-héron, *and Literary Executor for Michael Balint*

Michael Balint and his World

This fascinating collection explores the life of renowned psychoanalyst Michael Balint in his native Budapest. With a Balint revival in mind, *Michael Balint and his World: The Budapest Years* brings together the work of psychoanalysts, social thinkers, historians, literary scholars, artists and medical doctors who draw on Balint's work in a variety of ways.

The book focuses on Balint's early years in Budapest, where he worked with Sándor Ferenczi and a circle of colleagues, capturing the transformations of psychoanalytic thinking as it happens in a network of living relationships. Tracing creative disagreements as well as collaborations, and setting these exchanges in the climate of scientific, social and cultural developments of the time, *Michael Balint and his World: The Budapest Years* follows the development of psychoanalytic thinking during these critical times. The book recalls the story of several "lost children" of the Budapest School and reconstitutes Balint's important early contributions on primary love. It also examines his little-known relationship with Lacan, including the extended discussion of Balint's work by Wladimir Granoff in Lacan's first public seminar in Paris in 1954, published here for the first time.

This important book provides a fresh perspective on Balint's enormous contribution to the field of psychoanalysis and will interest both scholars and clinicians. It will also inspire those interested in clinical practice and the applications of psychoanalysis to the cultural sphere.

Judit Szekacs-Weisz, PhD, is a bilingual psychoanalyst and psychotherapist. Born and educated (mostly) in Budapest, Hungary, she has taken in the way of thinking and ideas of Ferenczi, the Balints, Hermann and Rajka as an integral part of a "professional mother tongue". Living and working in a totalitarian world sensitised her to the social and individual aspects of trauma, identity formation and strategies of survival.

Raluca Soreanu is Professor of Psychoanalytic Studies in the Department of Psychosocial and Psychoanalytic Studies, University of Essex, and psychoanalyst, member of the Círculo Psicanalítico do Rio de Janeiro. She is the project lead of *FREEPSY: Free Clinics and a Psychoanalysis for the People: Progressive Histories, Collective Practices, Implications for Our Times* (UKRI Frontier Research Grant).

Ivan Ward is former Deputy Director and Head of Learning at the Freud Museum London, where he worked for 33 years. He is author of a number of books and papers on psychoanalytic theory and the applications of psychoanalysis to socio-cultural issues. He is an Honorary Research Fellow at UCL Psychoanalysis Unit.

History of Psychoanalysis
Series Editor
Peter L. Rudnytsky

This series seeks to present outstanding new books that illuminate any aspect of the history of psychoanalysis from its earliest days to the present, and to reintroduce classic texts to contemporary readers.

Other titles in the series:

Karl Abraham
Life and Work, a Biography
Anna Bentinck van Schoonheten

The Freudian Orient
Early Psychoanalysis, Anti-Semitic Challenge, and the Vicissitudes of Orientalist Discourse
Frank F. Scherer

Occultism and the Origins of Psychoanalysis
Freud, Ferenczi and the Challenge of Thought Transference
Maria Pierri, Translated by Adam Elgar

Sigmund Freud and the Forsyth Case
Coincidences and Thought-Transmission in Psychoanalysis
Maria Pierri, Translated by Adam Elgar

A Brief Apocalyptic History of Psychoanalysis
Erasing Trauma
Carlo Bonomi

Theories and Practices of Psychoanalysis in Central Europe
Narrative Assemblages of Self Analysis, Life Writing, and Fiction
Agnieszka Sobolewska

For further information about this series please visit https://www.routledge.com/ The-History-of-Psychoanalysis-Series/book-series/KARNHIPSY

Michael Balint and his World

The Budapest Years

Edited by
Judit Szekacs-Weisz,
Raluca Soreanu and Ivan Ward

 Routledge
Taylor & Francis Group

LONDON AND NEW YORK

Designed cover image: Diana Ghyczy

First published 2024
by Routledge
4 Park Square, Milton Park, Abingdon, Oxon OX14 4RN

and by Routledge
605 Third Avenue, New York, NY 10158

Routledge is an imprint of the Taylor & Francis Group, an informa business

British Library Cataloguing-in-Publication Data
A catalogue record for this book is available from the British Library

ISBN: 978-1-032-31451-8 (hbk)
ISBN: 978-0-367-85777-6 (pbk)
ISBN: 978-1-003-30982-6 (ebk)

DOI: 10.4324/9781003309826

Typeset in Times New Roman
by codeMantra

Contents

Series Editor's Foreword   *xi*
Preface   *xiii*
About the Editors   *xv*
Acknowledgements   *xvii*
Contributor Affiliations   *xix*
Editors' Note   *xxi*
Chronology of Michael Bálint's Life   *xxiii*

PART 1
Budapest trails   **1**

1   **A brief introduction to the Balints and their world:**
    Object relations and beyond   3
    JUDIT SZEKACS-WEISZ

2   **Michael Bálint, his world and his Oeuvre**   9
    ANDRÉ HAYNAL

2a   **Remembering André Haynal (1930–2019)**   16
    JUDIT SZEKACS-WEISZ

3   **The problems of education and society in the Budapest**
    School of Psychoanalysis   18
    FERENC ERŐS

3a   **Remembering Ferenc Erős (1946–2020)**   30
    JUDIT SZEKACS-WEISZ

4   **"I look into a room through a round gap". Alice Bálint's life,**
    work and diaries   32
    ANNA BORGOS

PART 2
Creativity and primary love   53

5   Therapy, object relations and primary narcissism:
    Metapsychology in the early works of Michael Bálint   55
    ANTAL BÓKAY

6   Primary harmony: Baby observation on infantile hopes
    and quiet states   64
    JULIANNA VAMOS

7   Human links   71
    ANTONELLA BUSSANICH

8   Michael Bálint and the Budapest School of Psychoanalysis on
    the importance of creativity   74
    ZOLTAN KŐVÁRY

PART 3
Lost children of psychoanalysis   89

9   Lost children of the recent history of psychoanalysis:
    Tibor Rajka MD, 1901–1980   91
    JUDIT SZEKACS-WEISZ

10 Remembering Dr István Székács-Schönberger   99
    GÁBOR FLASKAY AND ZSUZSA MÉREI

11 My debt to Michael Bálint   109
    KATHLEEN KELLEY-LAINÉ

PART 4
Links rediscovered   113

12 Introduction to Wladimir Granoff's presentation on
    Balint at Lacan's seminar   115
    MARTINE BACHERICH

**13 Presentation on Balint at Lacan's seminar *Freud's papers
on technique*, 26 May 1954**   120
WLADIMIR GRANOFF

**14 Lacan's Balint: Synergies and discords in a
professional friendship**   145
DANY NOBUS

Contributors   *173*
Index   *177*

Series Editor's Foreword

Michael Balint is one of the most important figures in twentieth-century psychoanalysis, who furnishes a direct link between Ferenczi and the "school of Budapest," on the one hand, and Winnicott and the British Independent tradition, on the other. Although Balint cannot be said to have been forgotten, he has been overshadowed, and it is the aim of the editors of this two-part gathering of essays—the first such collective engagement with his life and work—to restore to Balint the share of the limelight that is rightfully his.

As befits as cosmopolitan and multifaceted a figure as Balint, the contributions to this team effort encompass his world as much as his work; his down-to-earth practicality as much as his soaring flights as a theorist; and his relationships with colleagues and interlocutors (above all, his first wife, Alice, and most unexpectedly, Lacan) as much as his individual life. In addition to sponsoring a "Balint revival," the editors have found room in their home for two of the "lost children" of Hungarian psychoanalysis, Tibor Rajka and István Székács-Schönberger. Acts of remembrance are simultaneously festivals of mourning, and those commemorated here include not only such past masters, but also two of the mainstays of our present-day Hungarian family, André Haynal and Ferenc Erős, who did not live to se e the publication of their chapters in this book.

Psychoanalytic time is not linear, and already in this compendium devoted to Bálint Mihály's Budapest years, we can catch glimpses of his reincarnation as Michael Balint in London. But for a more complete staging of Balint's second act, readers will have to await the companion volume in the History of Psychoanalysis series.

Peter L. Rudnytsky
Series Editor
Gainesville, FL

Preface

Michael Balint is a key figure in psychoanalysis. Despite his many original contributions, there are still important steps to take in terms of placing his ideas in historical context and accounting for how they "travelled" from Budapest to London. Until 1938, Bálint Mihály lived in Budapest, where he was one of the central figures working with Sándor Ferenczi. He also collaborated closely with his wife Bálint Aliz (Alice Balint), developing new ideas in psychoanalytic theory and technique. In 1938, his emigration to the UK brought both losses and new beginnings. This is the first of two volumes, *Michael Balint and his World: The Budapest Years* and *Michael Balint and his World: The London Years*, which capture the traumatic dislocations of forced migration—threatening basic trust and primary love—but also the creative opportunities for arriving at novel paths in psychoanalysis. Both volumes offer original insights into the clinical and theoretical vocabulary of Balint, and into his contributions to object relations theories.

Aiming at a "Balint revival", this publication and its intended companion volume bring together the work of psychoanalysts, social thinkers, historians, literary scholars, artists, and medical doctors who draw on Michael Balint's work in a variety of ways and who tell the story of his contribution from various perspectives. A "Balint revival" necessarily involves tracing Balint's creative disagreements as well as his collaborations, both in Hungary and the UK, setting these exchanges in the climate of scientific, social, and cultural developments of the time. *Michael Balint and his World* traces the development of psychoanalytic thinking as it happens in a network of living relationships, including the story of several "lost children" of the Budapest School, and reconstitutes Balint's important early contributions on primary love.

The last section of this volume concerns Balint's relationship with Lacan, and the extended discussion of Balint's work in Lacan's first public seminar in Paris in 1954. Balint had left Hungary by then, but attention was still directed to the ideas of the Budapest school, in both theory and technique. This section includes an unpublished presentation about Balint's work at Lacan's seminar, by the eminent psychoanalyst Wladimir Granoff, and an introduction by his wife, psychoanalyst Martine Bacherich, giving rare insight into the context in which the paper was delivered.

Readers concerned with the story of psychoanalysis and the development of psychoanalytic theory will find much to engage and surprise them in this volume. Likewise those interested in clinical practice or the applications of psychoanalysis to the cultural sphere. The broken arc of Balint's life marks a rupture within the field of psychoanalysis, but could stand as a symbol for the many professionals who are forced to leave their country during dark times and start a new life in another country, with revived hopes about a less traumatic future. Balint's work and history resonates today.

About the Editors

Judit Szekacs-Weisz, PhD, is a bilingual psychoanalyst and psychotherapist. Born and educated (mostly) in Budapest, Hungary, she has taken in the way of thinking and ideas of Ferenczi, the Balints, Hermann, and Rajka as an integral part of a "professional mother tongue". The experience of living and working in a totalitarian regime and the transformatory years leading to the fall of the Berlin Wall sensitised her to the social and individual aspects of trauma, identity formation and strategies of survival. In 1990, she moved to London, where, with a small group of psychoanalysts, therapists, artists and social scientists, she founded Imago East-West to create a space where diverse experiences of living and changing context and language in different cultures can be explored and creative solutions found. She has written extensively about body-and-mind, trauma, emigration, changing context and social dreaming. Publications include *Lost Childhood and the Language of Exile* (Imago East West & Freud Museum, 2004 and Phoenix 2022) She is the co-editor of *Ferenczi and his World* (Karnac, 2012), *Sandor Ferenczi for Our Time* (Karnac, 2012) and *Sandor Ferenczi-Ernest Jones Letters 1911-1933* (Karnac, 2013).

Raluca Soreanu is Professor of Psychoanalytic Studies at the Department of Psychosocial and Psychoanalytic Studies, University of Essex, UK, and psychoanalyst, member of the Círculo Psicanalítico do Rio de Janeiro, Brazil. She is the author of *Working-through Collective Wounds: Trauma, Denial, Recognition in the Brazilian Uprising* (Palgrave, 2018) and the co-author, with Jakob Staberg and Jenny Willner, of *Ferenczi Dialogues: On Trauma and Catastrophe* (Leuven University Press, 2023). Between 2015 and 2019 she studied the archive of psychoanalyst Michael Balint, held by the British Psychoanalytical Society, with the support of a Wellcome Trust grant. Since 2022, she is leading a five-year interdisciplinary research project *FREEPSY: Free Clinics and a Psychoanalysis for the People: Progressive Histories, Collective Practices, Implications for Our Times* (UKRI Frontier Research Grant), aiming to produce a new global figuration of psychoanalysis as a progressive discourse and practice. She is Academic Associate of the Freud Museum, Editor of the *Journal of the Balint Society* and Editor of the *Studies in the Psychosocial* series at Routledge.

Ivan Ward is Head of Learning Emeritus at the Freud Museum London and former manager of the museum's conference programme. A mixed-race father of two girls, he is the author of a number of books and papers on psychoanalytic theory and the application of psychoanalysis to social and cultural issues. Recent publications include 'Everyday Racism: Psychological Effects' in *The Trauma of Racism: Lessons from the Therapeutic Encounter* edited by Michael Slevin and Beverly Stoute (Routledge, 2022). He is an Honorary Research Fellow at UCL Psychoanalysis Unit.

Acknowledgements

This volume is the fruit of the international conference "The Balints and their World: Object Relations and Beyond" organised by Judit Szekacs-Weisz, Raluca Soreanu and Ivan Ward at The Freud Museum London, in December 2018. The editors would like to thank the director, Carol Seigel, and everyone at the museum who contributed to the success of the conference. Series editor, Peter L. Rudnytsky, supported the project from the beginning and was a continual source of expertise and advice. Tom Keve worked with us on the Hungarian chapters and made a substantial contribution to the project as a whole. A special thanks should go to him. The editors are also grateful to James Darley for his meticulous editorial attention, and to the Routledge editorial team for their steadfast engagement with the volume.

Contributor Affiliations

Martine Bacherich is a psychoanalyst in private practice in Paris, and member of the Société de Psychanalyse Freudienne, France.

Antal Bókay is at the University of Pécs, Hungary.

Anna Borgos is at the Institute of Cognitive Neuroscience and Psychology of the Hungarian Academy of Sciences.

Antonella Bussanich is a visual artist, France and Italy.

Ferenc Erős (1946–2020) is in the Department of Social Psychology, Faculty of Humanities of the University of Pécs, Hungary.

Gábor Flaskay is a psychoanalyst at Hungarian Psychoanalytical Society.

Wladimir Granoff (1924–2000) is at Société Française de Psychanalyse and Association Psychanalytique de France.

André Haynal (1930–2019) is at Swiss Psychoanalytical Society and University of Geneva.

Kathleen Kelley-Lainé is at Societé Psychanalytique de Paris and Honorary Member of the Hungarian Psychoanalytical Society.

Zoltan Kőváry is a clinical psychologist, Budapest.

Zsuzsa Mérei is a clinical psychologist, Paris and Budapest.

Dany Nobus is at Brunel University, London, UK.

Raluca Soreanu is in the Department of Psychosocial and Psychoanalytic Studies, University of Essex, UK, and Círculo Psicanalítico do Rio de Janeiro, Brazil.

Judit Szekacs-Weisz is at British Psychoanalytical Society and Hungarian Psychoanalytical Society.

Julianna Vamos is at Société Psychanalytique de Paris and Bluets Maternity Hospital, Paris.

Ivan Ward is Head of Learning Emeritus, Freud Museum London.

Editors' Note

In putting together this volume, we faced the issue of the multiple uses of Hungarian names. This is not just an editorial issue, but it is an important reflection of diverse aspects of emigration and dislocation. By way of clarification, we offer below a bilingual list of the names that are most frequently used in the pages of this book. We also note that Hungarian names usually list the surname first, followed by the given name.

English usage	Hungarian original
Sandor Ferenczi	Ferenczi Sándor
Alice Balint	Bálint-Székely-Kovács Alíz
Michael Balint	Bálint Mihály
Istvan Hollos	Hollós István
Vilma Kovacs	Kovács Vilma
Frederic Kovacs	Kovács Frigyes
Edith Ludowyk-Gyomroi	Ludowyk-Gyömrői Edit
Sandor Rado	Radó Sándor
Geza Roheim	Róheim Géza
Istvan Szekacs-Schonberger	Székács-Schönberger István
Imre Hermann	Hermann Imre
Margaret Mahler	Schönberger Margit
Judith Dupont	Dormándi Judit
André Haynal	Hajnal András
Ferenc Eros	Erős Ferenc
Judit Szekacs-Weisz	Székács Judit

Chronology of Michael Bálint's Life

1896	Born on 3 December, Mihály Móric Bálint (Bergsmann), son of Dr Ignác Bergsmann.
1910–1914	During his high school days, he reads *The Interpretation of Dreams* and *The Psychopathology of Everyday Life* but is not convinced.
1914	Commences medical studies.
1915–1917	Serves on the Russian, later the Italian front, is wounded and discharged.
1918	Falls in love with Alice Kovács, daughter of psychoanalyst Vilma Kovács, and lends her *Totem and Taboo.*
1919	Hears Ferenczi's university lectures but is not impressed with them.
1920	Moves to Germany with Alice and works as a chemist and bacteriologist.
1921	He and Alice start their first training analysis with Hanns Sachs.
1923	Enters the University of Berlin and is awarded a doctorate of philosophy.
1924	The couple return to Budapest. Bálint commences a two year long, second training analysis with Ferenczi.
1926	Member of the Hungarian Union of Psychoanalysis.
1927	Conducts seminars for general practitioners in training.
1931	Assists in organising the Budapest Psychoanalytic Clinic and becomes its assistant director.
1935	Promoted to director of the Clinic.
1936	Specialist in internal medicine and psychiatric medicine.
1939	Emigrates to the UK with Alice and their son János. Becomes consultant psychiatrist in Manchester. Alice Bálint suffers a stroke and dies.
1944	Marries Edna Oakshott. They separate in 1947 and divorce in 1952.
1945	Moves to London. He is informed of his parents' suicide following the Nazi occupation.
1947	Becomes a British subject.
1947	Joins the Tavistock Clinic in a senior position.
1951–1953	Scientific secretary of the British Psychoanalytical Society.

1953	Marries Enid Eichholz.
1955	Head of the Medical Department of the British Psychoanalytical Society. He has his first heart attack.
1957	Visiting professor in Cincinnati, Ohio.
1961	Retires, but continues to work in University College Hospital until 1968.
1968	President of the British Psychoanalytical Society.
1970	Suffers a heart attack and, after two weeks in hospital, he dies on 31st December.

Part 1

Budapest trails

Chapter 1

A brief introduction to the Balints and their world

Object relations and beyond

Judit Szekacs-Weisz

Michael Bálint was a most important figure in the history of contemporary psychoanalysis.

Looking at the Bálint story sometimes from Budapest and other times from London, it often seemed to me that *two* Bálints exist:

The first one is *Bálint Mihály*, a young doctor from pre-war Budapest searching for his professional and personal place in a profoundly changing world. The second is the middle-aged, more mature figure of *Michael Balint* in England where he became one of the leading figures of the Tavistock Clinic and president of the British Psychoanalytical Society.

Looking into the kaleidoscope of history we first see him as a central figure of the younger generation around Sándor Ferenczi in pre-war Budapest working together with his wife Székely-Kovács Alíz (daughter of Vilma Kovács, a most influential "foremother" of Hungarian psychoanalysis).

> Alice and I read, studied, lived and worked together. All our ideas – no matter in whose mind they had first arisen – were enjoyed and then tested, probed and criticised in our endless discussions. Quite often it was just chance that decided which of us should publish a particular idea.
>
> Apart from psychoanalysis, Alice's main interest was anthropology and education, mine biology and medicine and usually this factor decided who should write about the idea. We published only one paper jointly, though almost all of them could have been printed under our joint names.
>
> (Balint, 1952)

A formidable model for creative couples who live, work, think, and write together!

We'll try to follow them in the climate of scientific, social, and cultural developments of the time, and in the network of their living relationships, while observing stages in the development of their psychoanalytic thinking.

The venue is Budapest: this beautiful, seductive city with its climate and culture which has been fundamentally maimed by wars, emigration, and a totally new social system by the second half of the last century

DOI: 10.4324/9781003309826-2

To conjure up the atmosphere of the place and time let us first turn to Tom Keve, our knowledgeable colleague researching the historical mood of contemporary Budapest – that multicoloured backdrop to Central European narratives of psychoanalysis.

The Budapest of the twentieth century was very much a *fin de siècle* creation. In 1896, Budapest, and indeed the whole of the Kingdom of Hungary, celebrated the one thousandth anniversary of the Magyar tribes' conquest of the Pannonia basin. The extensive and resplendent festivities attended by the Imperial family and dignitaries from overseas were not only intended to mark the Magyar Millennium, they also proclaimed to the world Hungary's arrival as a full fledged, modern European nation and celebrated the emergence of Budapest as a metropolis on the West-European, but especially Parisian model.

(Keve, 2018)

André Haynal invites the reader to enter the cultural sites of the city:

… A town of merchants, small craftsmen, the university and broad boulevards with those famous cafes where ideas and influences were exchanged between intellectuals, journalists, poets and novelists – circles in which Ferenczi, too, moved. The intelligentsia... consisted largely of émigrés from the different lands of the monarchy. The prevailing mixture of languages and cultures was typically Central European. The philosopher Georg Lukacs, later to become a Marxist, and Bela Balazs, the librettist of two of Bartok's most famous works (*The Wooden Prince* and *Bluebeard's Castle*), are good examples: Lukacs wrote most of his works in German, whereas for Balazs the language was now German, now Hungarian. Sándor Ferenczi set down his clinical Diary in German!... [T]he cosmopolitan culture of the major cities of Central Europe was to impress its stamp deeply on twentieth-century culture in general through its expatriate geniuses and talents.

(2002)

It would be tempting to spend some more time getting acquainted with the place, familiar yet basically different from the spirit and scenes of their later lives, so as to add a sociocultural dimension to their perception and vision of the external and psychic world. Looking at their early professional days and accompanying them on their journey we see the young couple – future psychoanalysts with pioneering concepts – commuting between Budapest and Berlin.

Working at the Charité Hospital in Berlin, Bálint is one of the first doctors – as early as the 1920s – to treat psychosomatic patients with analytic methods. The early 1930s will see him back in Budapest organising groups for doctors to explore the possibilities of psychotherapeutic treatments in general practice. These will be recurring topics. Exploring new areas of scientific research and clinical study will stay with him for decades to come.

By the second half of the 1930s fascism is marching into Central Europe; alarming changes are more and more palpable. Mihály, Aliz, and their little son John are able to leave Hungary on the brink of WWII and immigrate to the UK in 1939 where they are welcomed first in Manchester. Aliz tragically dies of a ruptured aneurism a few months after they settle.

The broken arc of Bálint's life could stand as a symbol for many professionals who were forced to leave their country during dark times and start a new one with renewed hopes about a less traumatic future.

Tragedies, losses, and new beginnings...

Bálint's themes and writings, I believe, bear witness to human drama in the face of traumatisation and to social-individual experiences threatening basic trust and primary love.

Splits and broken linkages... the remains of a forced emigration, obstruct the creative potentials of new beginnings. A migrant's lifework often remains in "pieces" and will be accessible only in its fragments for both contemporary and following generations.

Will it be possible to put the images of the *Hungarian* and the *English* Bálint together? Can one fit the pieces of his manifold theoretical and empirical ideas together so they add up to present one authentic, coherent oeuvre?

The initial years in the new country are strenuous. Wartime Manchester is a most difficult and challenging experience. Bálint takes diverse opportunities – also symbolically – to help him arrive in this country. He obtains his British medical qualifications, and is appointed consultant psychiatrist and director of child guidance clinics.

True to the spirit of the pioneers' generation he believes in the value of research. His interest in biology fertilised by analytical thinking produces extraordinary results. The best example of this is his postgraduate master of science thesis in psychology at Manchester, "Individual Differences in Infancy", systematic study of the feeding rhythm of babies. He even develops an instrument to record his observations.

By the time Ernest Jones and his psychoanalytical colleagues warm up to the idea of paving his way to the capital in 1945, after five years of hard work and research, Michael is eventually able to move.

Both professional and private domains open up in London. He finds an inspiring community of analytical thinkers at the Tavistock Clinic – but not only that. The miracle happens again: he finds a partner who completes his life in all its multiple aspects. He meets Enid Eichholz, later Bálint; the "other" in the creative dyad of his English life.

Groundbreaking theoretical ideas based on his experiences in the world of the consulting room are published during the subsequent years. These become widely known and discussed in professional communities. In *The Basic Fault* (1968), he introduces his "three areas of the mind", enabling him to describe basic aspects of "one, two and three body" object-relational dynamics.

His views on malignant and benign regression in psychoanalytic theory and practice will also come to be seen as essential building blocks of the British Independent Group's thinking. It is less well known that Bálint was instrumental in working out contemporary methods for "case seminars" at the Tavistock Clinic – originally based on his training experiences at the Budapest Psychoanalytic Polyclinic.

> Candidates in the early1930s in Budapest were to present a clinical case to their *technical seminar group* to discuss and reflect upon together with senior members of the clinic who participated. Special attention was paid to difficulties and problems they encountered while treating their patients. Transference and countertransference dynamics were in the focus of their attention: they demonstrated how important it was not to leave candidates alone with their countertransference issues.
> (Székács-Schönberger, 1993)

Bálint's theories and views often seem rather unusual in his contemporary London environment. In the British Society they revive a nearly forgotten voice: the voice of the pioneers, including Ferenczi and the Budapest School.

The first generations learned from experience that psychoanalysis is a territory which is not only multilingual but multidimensional: defined and shaped by history, politics, economy, and sociocultural transformations. They were also aware that if the analyst is not focusing entirely on the internal stage s/he has a better chance to capture something meaningful on the *border* of the external and internal in order to understand the nature of dynamic processes in the analytical encounter and the world one lives in. Bálint's thinking not only revived but also elaborated on Ferenczi's ideas outlined in the latter's ultimate writings, such as the *Clinical Diary*.

It is the heroic Bálint who rescues Ferenczi's priceless manuscripts (the Ferenczi-Freud correspondence among them), fights for their publication, and later enables a devoted circle of colleagues around Judith Dupont to make them available for present and future generations all over the world.

His technical and applied analytical innovations are also remarkable: *focal therapies* are branded by his name. The *Bálint groups* conquer the medical field worldwide after the 1950s, opening eyes and minds to the importance of an analytical understanding in the field of the doctor, his patients, and the illness.

His biographer, Harold Stewart, tried to put the mosaics of his professional life together.

In *Michael Balint: Object Relations Pure and Applied* (1996) he attempts to expand the biography and make the organic links between his theoretical, clinical, and applied psychoanalytical ideas visible, opening up their intrinsic logics and dynamics.

Searching for an appropriate place for Bálint's work, Stewart gives an illuminating and passionate critical study of Bálint's legacy, placing it among those of Winnicott, Klein, Fairbairn, and Bion.

> Michael Balint was kind, generous, understanding and averse to authoritarianism. He could be provocative, high handed, scornful and authoritarian. He could be loved or hated but it was difficult to be indifferent to him. He greatly valued

independence of thought, together with strong argument, and, to use his own terminology, he had much of the "philobat" in him... Such people are essential if psychoanalysis is to continue to develop.

(Stewart, 1996)

Bálint's ideas of the "ocnophilic" and "phylobatic" character types were developed to explain different reactions to "empty space". The ocnophil clings to the familiar, whereas the phylobat relishes the challenge of the unfamiliar "horrid empty spaces", which he embraces instead as "friendly expanses". In Bálint's words: "whereas the ocnophilic world is structured by physical proximity and touch, the phylobatic world is structured by safe distance and sight". They are both "secondary stages, developing out of the archaic phase of primary love as reactions to the traumatic discovery of the separate existence of objects" (Balint, 1968/1979).

Bálint, the outstanding theoretician of object relations, the ambassador of the "Budapest School in England", is to be thanked for keeping Sándor Ferenczi's theories and teachings alive – as an organic aspect of the independent mind, he concludes.

Themes he started to elaborate on in the 1930s – such as primary love, new beginning, psychotherapeutic aspects of regression in clinical practice, the role of the doctor in curative encounters, and the elementary function of the group in supporting this task – reoccur. His understanding and insights keep growing, maturing, and expanding over the years.

Looking at the arc of Bálint's career bending over five decades of his active professional life, one comes to realise that the observable developmental lines reveal a *spiral nature.*

Bálint returns to interpreting them each time on *a higher level.*

Unquestionably, the specific areas of Bálint's analytical explorations do not fit together seamlessly. We have the task to try to weave together the tangible threads into one organic texture.

Our volumes strive to revive the memory and work of the Bálints – together with the main protagonists in their world, both in Hungary and in the UK.

Aiming at a "Bálint revival", as Raluca Soreanu put it, our collections bring together an interdisciplinary network of psychoanalysts, social thinkers, historians, literary scholars, artists, and medical doctors who turn to Michael Bálint's work in a complex way. We also aim to bring back to living memory forgotten figures of the Budapest School of Psychoanalysis, such as Alice Bálint, Istvan Székács–Schönberger, and Tibor Rajka.

Bibliography

Balint, M. (1952). *Primary Love and Psycho-Analytical Technique.* London: Maresfield Library, 1985.

Balint, M. (1968/1979). *The Basic Fault.* London: Tavistock/Routledge.

Haynal, A. (2002). *Disappearing and Reviving: Sándor Ferenczi in the History of Psychoanalysis.* London: Karnac.

Keve, T. (2018). Ferenczi's Budapest. In: A. Dimitrijević, G. Cassullo, & J. Frankel (Eds.), *Ferenczi's Influence on Contemporary Psychoanalytic Traditions: Lines of Development – Evolution of Theory and Practice Over the Decades* (pp. 12–17). Abingdon: Routledge.

Stewart, H. (1996). *Michael Balint: Object Relations Pure and Applied*. London: Routledge.

Székács-Schönberger, I. (1993). Chapter 3. In: V. Kovacs (Ed.), *Fortunatus Öröksége* [Legacy of Fortunatus] (pp. 45–48). Budapest: Párbeszéd Könyvek.

Chapter 2

Michael Bálint, his world and his Oeuvre

André Haynal

Michael Bálint is a person whom I love very much. He contributed tremendously to the renewal of psychoanalysis; he allowed us to think differently about it, without diluting or denaturing it, without cheapening it.

Now, let's take a moment of silence so that our own memories of him may emerge (in Plato's view anyhow, thinking is searching for remembrance). In so doing, we will yet be in the presence of his calmness, of his acceptance, his tolerance, his goodwill, his enduring and benevolent smile, his humour, his ability not to take things too seriously, to be quiet, and yet cheeky, peaceful, and serene.

Michael Bálint is, without any doubt, one of the greatest figures of the post-Freudian generation and among the British innovators of psychoanalysis after the Second World War, including Wilfred Bion and Donald Winnicott, among others. Additionally, he expanded the field of psychoanalytic thinking beyond its original domain.

This chapter will be divided into two sections:

I   Bálint, the man, the human being in his culture.
II Bálint in the history of psychoanalytic thought.

Bálint, the man, the human being in his culture

The details of his biography are complex, but nevertheless decisive. Moreover, as he was growing up, so did the city of Budapest, which became a metropolis at the turn of the twentieth century. Let us examine the different cultural influences which helped give birth to this complex personality.

His cultural and psychoanalytic backgrounds do not have definitive borders. To define him simply as a Hungarian-British individual cannot possibly take into account the complexity of his roots or the experiences punctuating his development. To explore his cultural origins, let us recall the history of Budapest: Buda and its residential hills; Pest, with the university and commerce; and Obuda, an ancient town with origins dating back to the Roman era. These three cities underwent a remarkable transformation in the middle of the nineteenth century, along with the capital of the Habsburg Empire in Central Europe, Vienna, besides other important

DOI: 10.4324/9781003309826-3

regional centres, like Prague. At that time, there began an extraordinary blossom-
ing of commerce, industry, and culture, which is still celebrated to this day.

A brief global perspective of Budapest will be helpful. After two or three cen-
turies of shared existence with Austria, the Czech Lands and other territories,
Budapest became a city, typical of central Europe; a city, 70 per cent of whose
population was reported as German-speaking even as late as 1875. Thus it was
just as far removed from the Hungarian Puszta, the Carpathian Mountains, and
Transylvania as Paris's Rive Gauche is from the hills of southern France. This city,
Budapest, founded as late as 1873, henceforth bore an extraordinarily cosmopoli-
tan culture; the lingua franca was German more so than Hungarian. As for Hungarian, it had been necessary to resuscitate it with some difficulties – the "*nyelvujtás*"
("Language learning") movement at the turn of the nineteenth century envisioned
such a transformation – just as it was later necessary to revive Arabic in North
Africa and Hebrew in Israel.

Isn't it peculiar that the Bálint family was originally called Bergsmann?

He addresses this fact, much later, in a letter to Jones about the story of the Emperor Joseph II who, at the time of the French Revolution (1789–1794) or some
years before, ordained equality in his Empire. The Jews, who often did not carry a
family name, were thus compelled to choose one. The emperor also ordained that
the civil registers would be kept by the state and not by religious communities.
These decrees practically liberated the Jews from the former restrictions that had
discriminated against them. The people living under Austrian rule in the peripheral
regions of the Empire, a little north of the Carpathian Mountains, in present-day
Poland and the Czech Republic, took German surnames at that time. Hence the
name Bergsmann.

Michael's father lived and practised medicine in the district of Pest commonly
called Josefstadt (Józsefváros), a working-class neighbourhood of artisans and
tradesmen. As was often the case at the time, he held his medical practice in his
home. Thus, Michael was raised in a medical environment, that of his father. It
would have been said – and these are the type of wild interpretations that psychoanalysts are inclined to make – that he would have been motivated by his wish to
show his father (and also himself) how to practise *good* medicine.

To give an idea of the cosmopolitanism and multilingualism that characterised
this city, let us mention that Bálint's grandmother did not speak Hungarian, but
rather German; in contrast, his grandfather knew Hungarian quite well. Practising
in Josefstadt, a prevalently German-speaking district, his father only used Hungarian occasionally. It was Michael, in the following generation, who was the first to
complete his studies in Pest and spoke predominantly Hungarian.

Such was this family's background, who, like many others in Budapest, settled
gradually into the shifting and stimulating culture of Pest.

As for the local German-speakers in Pest, besides Jewish immigrants from the
eastern provinces of the Empire, like Galicia, Bukovina, and Lodomeria, there were
also other German-speaking populations from other Habsburg territories (such as
Schwaben, or Swabia).

The culture of Pest was a surprising-enough blend of different influences, where at the turn of the nineteenth century the immigrant Jewish intelligentsia played an important role. According to the statistics at the time, two-thirds of doctors, more than 67 per cent, were Jewish immigrants. What this Judaeo-Hungarian (Cartledge, 2006; Marton, 2006) social stratum brought to the country at this particular moment in terms of culture, as well as an array of scientific disciplines and medical specialisations, should never be underestimated. This group includes a considerable number of well-known individuals: authors like Arthur Koestler, philosophers such as Georg Lukács, mathematicians such as John von Neumann, physicists such as Edward Teller, Leo Szilard, and others, filmmakers such as Alexander Korda, many musicians, and of course Sándor Ferenczi, who, as well as being a direct student and friend of Freud's, brought psychoanalysis to Hungary. Sándor Ferenczi established an atmosphere in Pest that hardly resembled that of other schools of psychoanalysis (perhaps unintentionally, since, under the influence of his temperament and his diverse training background, he preferred not to proceed within a formal academic framework).

Ferenczi, who remained single for a very long time, lived in a hotel on a boulevard of Pest. The Hotel Royal was nothing like the usual bourgeois home. After delivering his informal teaching in his hotel room, he received his colleagues at the café in the evening. It was in this atmosphere that Bálint received his "psychoanalytic education" over snacks at a café table. They spoke about Sándor's "great experiment", which is how Michael referred to Ferenczi's encounters with his patient R.N. (Elizabeth Severn) and the difficulties with this analysis.

Bálint in the history of psychoanalytic thought

The repercussions of the First World War significantly changed this world in which Bálint grew up. Born in 1896, he was a young man when war broke out. Having completed his medical studies, he found himself on the front in Russia, then in Italy, and finally on the southern front of what would after the war become Yugoslavia. Bálint was wounded on his finger – a wound which makes one wonder: was it the consequence of actions in battle or the result of self-harm motivated by his pacifist convictions? This question was never cleared up.

The end of this war brought about a total collapse of the political and social order of Hungary and Austria, the end of the Austro-Hungarian Empire.

An encounter with a young woman, Aliz Székély-Kovacs, who later became his wife, introduced Bálint to the reading of Freud's *Totem and Taboo* (1912–1913). By the way, she also happened to be Judith Dupont's aunt. Subsequently, Aliz and Michael moved to Berlin together in 1921, where the Institute of Psychoanalysis opened at that time, and they continued their training there. At the same time, Michael worked in internal medicine at the institute of Zondek, a well-known endocrinologist, where he had his first contact with the psychosomatically ill, and in the biochemical laboratory of Otto Heinrich Warburg who in 1931 became a Nobel laureate.

Of Berlin, he didn't only hold happy memories. He found the Institute of Psychoanalysis very "Prussian", that is, hierarchical. Once Michael's analysis with Hanns Sachs ended, the Bálints returned to Budapest, where psychoanalysis was discussed as much in cafés as in schools. He continued his training with Ferenczi and there he forged the fundamental bonds that would link them for the rest of his life. So much so that Bálint eventually became the executor of Ferenczi's literary estate. It would be too simple to reduce this to just a master–pupil relationship. It was more. Michael exclaimed once, jokingly, in the middle of a speech that "it is my unresolved transference"! It was a profound and complex relationship indeed...

After returning to Budapest, he practised for several years in that city, working concurrently at the university clinic for internal medicine, in a small room which was normally used for radiography, and so was without a window and rather dark. It was in this dark room that he attempted to understand the internal life of some of the patients for whom he was caring.

It was also at this time, between the two wars, in Budapest, that he made his first attempt at coming together with other practising physicians, in a sort of *Urform,* an original form of the groups later known as "Balint groups". For political reasons, this label is no longer used in the country of his origin. Nevertheless, several doctors and friends met at the Institute of Psychoanalysis under his guidance to discuss their cases. At that time, under Horthy's semi-dictatorial and anti-Semitic regime, gatherings of more than three people at a time had to be reported – "announced", they said – and were recorded by the police.[1] A detective would come to take notes, and everyone ignored exactly *what kind* of notes were being taken. Over time, the situation became increasingly untenable, in part due to the regular violation of medical confidentiality. Eventually a double solution was found: on the one hand, discontinuing the group in Budapest, and on the other, taking care of the detective, at his request, as he realised that he needed as much care himself as the patients about whom they were speaking! We might call this a "Budapest solution".

In 1938, the year of the Anschluss, the German occupation of Austria, Hungary felt itself increasingly threatened by the Wehrmacht, the German army. A new wave of Jewish emigration was set in motion: the Bálints and their son John, with the help of Ernest Jones and John Rickman, were able to obtain a visa for England.

Later events, notably the fate of his parents, who took their own lives at the very last minute to escape arrest and deportation, illustrates the tragic times that awaited this family, and so many others, in their country.

For Michael, emigration opened up a period of life in a dramatically new British environment – first in Manchester, where he retook all of his exams and, in order to pursue a PhD, initiated a very original research study on babies. The Budapest school contributed greatly to infant observation, which was then in its own early stages (Spitz, Mahler, Hermann, etc.). (By the way, Bowlby considered himself a bit of a student of Hermann.) In this study, Bálint addressed the suckling rhythms of babies, observing that each baby has a unique pattern of suckling, which is influenced by her state of emotion but based on an individually distinct fundamental rhythm. It was pioneering research of great importance, for what is known today as the foundations of our mental apparatus, and also for understanding environmental influences, notably affective influences of the mother–child relationship. Bálint thus made a significant contribution to the biopsychological foundations of the life of newborns, even though this theme did not become the primary focus of his later research.

It was also in Manchester in 1939, just one year after their arrival, that Michael lost his wife, Alice, prematurely, to a ruptured aneurism.

After the war, following several years of "exile" in Manchester, he spent the last phase of his life in London, essentially at the Tavistock Clinic. It was there, in 1953, that he met Enid Eichholz, a social worker who treated patients with marital problems. Michael and she found themselves as co-therapists and this professional relationship resulted in marriage. Enid, also an immensely creative psychoanalyst, accompanied him as his wife and collaborator until his death in 1970 and faithfully kept a portion of his notes and correspondence, which she entrusted to the University of Geneva for safe keeping under my care. She was his companion in a relationship marked by exemplary harmonious collaboration and closeness. When asked for his opinion as to whether a long-standing relationship can stay harmonious, Michael, never short of a joke, answered that you can try it even more than once!

It was within this setting in London that his life and professional activities found their place. He was one of those who contributed immensely to the renewal of psychoanalysis at the time, along with eminent members of the British Independents and other friends like Joseph and Anne-Marie Sandler ...

For Bálint, it wasn't only a question of refreshing certain parts of the theory (such as that of narcissism), but also of extending the influence of analysis through the understanding of human behaviour in fields as far from the analytic couch as the Swiss ski slopes (from his personal memories, as he mentioned in *Thrills and Regressions*, 1959)! He was deeply interested in problems linked to medical practice. Based on his years in Budapest, he reflected on the doctor/patient relationship and investigated it through exchanges in groups of doctors, as already mentioned (*The Doctor, His Patient and the Illness*, 1957).

The idea of the "Balint group" already appeared in Ferenczi's work. Bálint took strong interest in it as an important potential application of psychoanalytic thought. He was also dissatisfied with the limited number of patients that he was able to care for over the course of his life and wished to broaden the number of people benefiting from his care.

Psychoanalysis cannot be passed on by instruction or by hierarchy, but always by an authentic message set against a backdrop of experimentation, discovery, *Ein-fälle* (literal translation: "dropping or falling in of ideas"), which happen by surprise in a spirit of creativity. His idea of "training cum research", as he called it, approached training as a transformation of personality through experience and "research", and at the same time highlighted his eternal curiosity which motivated him so forcefully and provided the path to enlightenment and discovery.

For me, one of Bálint's most significant messages is not to be scared of regression, but to work with it as a partner, which may lead to a new beginning. Jumping into the sea (evoking Ferenczi's *Thalassa*), crossing the waters and always staying confident in them, is an important aspect of the psychoanalytic cure. Not getting hung up on the structures of ego psychology but exploring the unconscious in the company of the analyst, in a deep transference, on a journey which is also a renewal of life. All of this takes courage, and Bálint had quite a lot.

So, he taught us always to remain close to life's events, as semantically expressed in all verbal or non-verbal forms of communications by the analysand, thus attracting and guiding the underlying overture of meaning. He softened theory by always attaching it to clinical practice. To demonstrate Michael's independence of mind, let me add an anecdote: while he was a visiting professor in Cincinnati, during a supervision, he put his hand gently on a presenter's folder thus suppressing dependence on the pre-existing text and opening the space to association, *to freedom*. This should remain an indelible symbolic gesture in psychoanalytic history. It recalls a model of supervision conceived by his mentor Sándor Ferenczi as a pursuit of personal analysis with the same training analyst, *on the couch*.

I entitled my work on Ferenczi, *A Psychoanalyst Unlike Any Other* (2001), but this statement can also be applied to Bálint. In fact, in many ways, he also was unlike any other. Primarily, but not only, by his lineage within psychoanalysis, notably through the Budapest school to the British Independents, groups characterised among other things by their informality, which Bálint considered as *proof of freedom*, especially in the most important domain of training. *Free*dom and *free* association echo each other: without freedom, there is no analytic process. Bálint, a psychoanalyst, was so "unlike any other", in his focus on granting freedom, and in welcoming the unexpected, the surprising.

His clinical acumen, which could already be appreciated in his early contributions, continued to prove its influence through to the end of his work. Let us also mention that his hitherto unpublished papers, stored in the private archives of Judith Dupont, are now in the London Freud Museum, and the ones formerly at the University of Geneva under my supervision are now relocated to the British Psychoanalytical Society archives in London.

Freud, the neurologist, an extraordinarily cultured man, gave the world in the twentieth century a new perspective of mankind determined by his unconscious, by his sexuality, by his desires, comprehended through his language, his lapses, his regressions. This was Freud's gift to his century and an attempt at answering the question, which was also that of Wittgenstein and of the Viennese philosophical circle: when we speak, what are we truly saying? An issue to which Freud added, in his response, the dimension of the unconscious, incorporating the obscured, the hidden side of the implicit.

Bálint's work is a brilliant continuation of this line of new theoretical insights recorded in the three great principal works of the master of Budapest and London: *Primary Love and Psycho-analytic Technique* (1952a), *Thrills and Regressions* (1959) and *The Basic Fault* (1968).

We sense beyond Vienna, beyond Freud, the infusion of Budapest and London which inspired Bálint, momentum and mélange in the *freedom* of life. And this, always, in the atmosphere of informality acquired in the Café Royal or the Café Emke on the boulevards of Pest. He felt that he was free to innovate within the Freudian intellectual framework.

To conclude, let us stress his theory based on experimentation, on freedom and against every inclination to solidify psychoanalytic theory into an ideology. Free, experimental, responsible for his own life, respectful of others, iconoclastic from time to time, always innovative and creative, Bálint lives on with us and does not cease to inspire us. My own personal experiences, my respect and affection for Michael have marked my life.

Note

1 In Lyon, under German occupation, gatherings of more than *one* person were forbidden.

Bibliography

Balint, M. (1952a). *Primary Love and Psycho-Analytic Technique*. London: Tavistock.
Balint, M. (1952b). New beginning and the paranoid and the depressive syndromes. *International Journal of Psycho-Analysis, 33*: 214–224.
Balint, M. (1956). *Problems of Human Pleasure and Behaviour*. New York: Liveright.
Balint, M. (1957). *The Doctor, His Patient and the Illness*. London: Pitman Medical.
Balint, M. (1959). *Thrills and Regressions*. London: Hogarth.
Balint, M. (1968). *The Basic Fault: Therapeutic Aspects of Regression*. London: Tavistock.
Cartledge, B. (2006). *The Will to Survive: A History of Hungary*. London: Timewell.
Dupont, J. (2015). *Au Fil du Temps ... Un Itinéraire Analytique*. Paris: Campagne Première.
Freud, S. (1912–1913). *Totem and Taboo*. S. E., 13: vii–162. London: Hogarth.
Haynal, A. (1988). *The Technique at Issue. Controversies in Psychoanalysis from Freud and Ferenczi to Michael Balint*. London: Karnac.
Haynal, A. (2001). *Un Psychanalyste pas Comme un Autre. La Renaissance de Sándor Ferenczi*. Paris: Delachaux et Niestlé.
Marton, K. (2006). *The Great Escape: Nine Jews Who Fled Hitler and Changed the World*. New York: Simon & Schuster Paperbacks.

Remembering André Haynal (1930–2019)

Judit Szekacs-Weisz

Figure 2a.1 One of André Haynal's last photos, taken at the conference 'The Balints and Their World: Object Relations and Beyond' Freud Museum, 2018

André Haynal – the eminent psychoanalyst, psychiatrist, scholar, author, and teacher – passed away on 7 November 2019, at the age of 89 (Figure 2a.1). He understood Balint's ideas; his clinical suggestions, his language, and also his background.

In 2014, he donated the whole Balint Archive, previously under his care, to the British Psychoanalytical Society. In a letter to the Society, recalling the extraordinary moment of receiving the Archive, he wrote:

DOI: 10.4324/9781003309826-4

In 1984, Enid Balint (herself an important psychoanalyst) entrusted me with many documents of Michael, Enid and Alice Balint, called by us the Balint Archives.

In fact, these Archives are a real treasure for psychoanalytical research. During their stay at the Geneva University, they were appreciated by frequent visits of scholars from the entire world. London taking over this precious material now can continue making it accessible to the researchers on a broad basis. Michael Balint having been one of the presidents of the British Psychoanalytic Society, it seems convenient that in that historical centre which is London, an important part of his oeuvre should survive.

All these documents, together with the ones now housed in London's Freud Museum may allow researchers to throw light on a whole line of evolution in psychoanalytic thinking.

(Haynal, June 28th, 2014)

The combination of the Ferenczi–Balint archives in close proximity to one another, in London, is a profound tool for researching early psychoanalytic history, as well as the close relationship between Freud and Ferenczi.

André Haynal was born in Budapest. He grew up in Hungary during dark times, experiencing fundamental social-political changes, war, persecution, individual and collective traumatisation, and diverse unsettled conditions of history in space and time.

In 1956, the young medical student had to leave the country searching for a place where he could finish his training and hopefully settle down. Switzerland was to become his new home.

André's ideas on psychoanalytic theory and clinical practice, his understanding of change and development in the psychoanalytical world and beyond, and his authentic personality made him a trusted central figure of the Ferenczi Renaissance. He regarded sincerity and freedom as basic factors of being and watched over the next generations with an unlimited capacity of care. He lectured, ran seminars, and supervised practically all over the world, with a special focus on Europe and America. His generosity in supporting young analysts (and also the more "mature" ones), keeping up the spirit even in difficult and tense situations, with courage and tact, while relentlessly standing his ground, commanded respect.

André also had a tremendous sense of humour and playfulness. He was never too busy to share a few words of encouragement and hope accompanied by that famous smile with twinkles in his eyes looking at you: holding you, nurturing your belief in the meaning of relationships, and in the power of genuine feelings and thinking.

He left us in 2019, but for the circle of professional friends, his family, and the wide international community of Ferenczi children and grandchildren, he left a rich legacy of lasting professional and human value.

Judit Szekacs-Weisz
2022 London

Chapter 3

The problems of education and society in the Budapest School of Psychoanalysis

Ferenc Erős

Sándor Ferenczi and Mihály Bálint are certainly the leading figures of Hungarian psychoanalysis. Due to historical circumstances, a major part of their legacies are now in England, where Bálint and his wife immigrated in 1939. The Ferenczi Archives in the London Freud Museum, the Bálint Archives at the British Psychoanalytical Society, also in London, together with the Ferenczi's House Archives in Budapest, and other collections in Europe and in the United States, are now part of an international network of living archives, a "work in progress", which has already achieved important results. As the French philosopher Jacques Derrida explained in his essay on "Archive Fever" (*Le mal d'archive*): the archive itself is part of the archive, therefore, an archive is never finished, but is always open ended. Or, as Judit Székács-Weisz formulated in her introduction to the "Living Archives Project":

> Documents, like people, have their own stories. They speak to us of the past: they are fragments of cultural history, records of their age. They not only report facts and knowledge, but offer us insight into relationships and emotional reactions that bring new life to events, even if they are already known.
>
> (Székács-Weisz, 2015)

In this chapter, I will review some of the activities of the Hungarian Psychoanalytic Association in which both Alice and Michael Bálint played a leading role. The facts are mostly known, but I want to focus on a specific feature of the Association's activities: a growing emphasis on infancy, childhood, child rearing, and pedagogy. Additionally, I will speak about a new archival source, a diary documenting the daily life of a children's home in provincial Hungary, written by Erzsébet Farkas, a disciple of Kata Lévy.

Kata Lévy joined the Association in 1928, while her husband, Dr Lajos Lévy, was one of the five members who founded the Association in 1913. She was the sister of Anton von Freund, a philanthropist and industrialist, the chief benefactor of the psychoanalytic movement in 1918. The Lévy couple hosted Sigmund Freud and his wife in the Freund family villa. Kata Lévy evoked her memories of the Freuds in an interview with Kurt Eissler in the 1950s (Lévy-Freund, 1990). She

DOI: 10.4324/9781003309826-5

was trained as a teacher in special needs education for handicapped children and worked extensively in the field of pedagogy and social work.

The prevalence of pedagogical topics goes back to Ferenczi's fundamental 1908 paper on "Psychoanalysis and education". In this, his first psychoanalytic publication, he was already critical of the dominant social relations and the authoritarian educational practices of the age, "the prohibiting and deterring commands of moral education based on the repression of thoughts", adding that "nowadays, mankind is educated into introspective blindness" (Ferenczi, 1999, p. 27). Ferenczi's early recognition of the social consequences of instinctual repression had been further developed in his later socio-critical papers, as well as in his two classic works, "On introjection and transference", and "Stages in the development of the sense of reality". These contributions present a theoretical basis for understanding the process by which "introspective blindness" emerges, and how grown-ups relate "their own unfilled and repressed wishes" to their children through fairy tales (1999, p. 81). Ferenczi's ideas were further developed by his "analysand, pupil, friend, and successor" (Dupont, 1993), Michael Bálint, through his own theoretical and clinical insights into topics such as the very beginning of the subject's life, namely the infant–mother relationship, the "basic fault", the significance of object relations, and primary love as opposed to primary narcissism. Michael Bálint first met Ferenczi in 1919, when he attended the latter's university lectures. After returning from Berlin, Bálint was in analysis with Ferenczi, as was his wife, Alice. She, together with Anna Freud, Hermine Hug-Hellmuth, and Melanie Klein, was one of the pioneers of child analysis and of the application of psychoanalysis to the broad field of education. Her 1931 book, *The Psycho-Analysis of the Nursery*, and her later papers, written in collaboration with her husband, represent a systematic attempt to apply Ferenczi's ideas on primary object relations to child rearing practices. As Ferenczi wrote in his preface to Alice's book: "She threw heavy stones into the long stagnating water of the psychology of education" (1931b, p. 11).

The concentration on childhood and education by the Budapest school did not arise simply from clinical experience of a small number of psychoanalysts, or from an internal development of theoretical concepts, but was also part and parcel of a much broader trend. This aimed to open the frontiers of psychoanalysis towards the understanding of larger social problems, to apply this understanding to mental health issues, and to enlighten and help the masses suffering from poverty, neurotic illnesses, and sexual misery. The roots of this trend lead us back to the Vth International Congress of Psychoanalysis, held in Budapest in the autumn of 1918. The main topic of the congress was, as is well known, war neurosis. Ferenczi, equipped with four years of experience in treating neurotic war casualties and victims of extreme violence, pointed out in his keynote speech:

The mass experiment of the war caused many kinds of grave neuroses, among them such conditions that were certainly not caused by mechanical effects. Thus, neurologists are due to acknowledge that something was missing from their calculations, namely, the psyche.

(1921, p. 6)

Freud, in his lecture on the "Lines of advance in psycho-analytic therapy", fore-saw a future in which "the conscience of society will awake", and will compel it to take responsibility for its psychological as well as material well-being. He also proposed the creation of outpatient clinics staffed by psychoanalytic clinicians, where "treatments will be free". At such clinics, analysts would "be faced by the task of adapting our [psychoanalytic] technique to the new conditions" (Freud, 1919, p. 167). To realise Freud's vision, Kata Lévy's brother, the Hungarian indus-trialist Anton von Freund, offered a significant sum to support psychoanalysis – specifically, for establishing a publishing house and library in Budapest, as well as an outpatient clinic that would provide analysis free of charge (Danto, 2005, p. 31).

Responding to the Freudian manifesto, psychoanalytic clinics (Ambulatoria), were opened in Berlin, Vienna, London, and Budapest. The historical details of the foundation of these pioneering outpatient clinics have been described by Eliza-beth Danto (2005). It is important to emphasise that the primary concerns of these early clinics were the treatment of children and adolescents, and the provision of guidance and counselling for young people, as well as for educators and parents. I should add that an outstanding role in such activities was also played by others, especially Melanie Klein, Ernst Simmel, and Siegfried Bernfeld in Berlin, as well as Wilhelm Reich and Otto Fenichel in Vienna. It is likely that the segment of the population most adversely affected and traumatised by the war and the post-war political and economic crises was that of children and adolescents. This was a "fatherless generation in which the "war in the souls" continued in a "society without the father" (Federn, 1990). As the British historian Michael Roper (2016) has shown, the "anxious child" in Klein's case studies was prefigured by the shell-shocked soldier, and the figure of the traumatised veteran reappeared in the figure of the post-war child.

In opposition to "Red Vienna" led by Social Democrats, and to the cosmopoli-tan, libertarian Berlin of the Weimar period, two capital cities which welcomed and generally supported psychoanalytic clinics, the situation in Budapest was quite dif-ferent. After the failure of the Councils' Republic in August 1919, Hungary came under the rule of the counter-revolutionary, authoritarian regime of Admiral Hor-thy. A "numerus clausus" law was introduced by the government which radically limited the number of Jewish students admissible to universities, and in practice women were denied entry into higher education. In general, the education sys-tem remained rather conservative and authoritarian, under the dominance of the Catholic Church and other religious organisations. The cause of child welfare and protection, which was mostly in the hands of private and ecclesiastical charitable associations, and depended on volunteers and benefactors, was unable to cope with the problems arising from poverty, hunger, and growing up without one or both parents. Neglect and abuse were commonplace in homes, schools, and other in-stitutions. In my opinion, the main motivation for turning the focus of Hungarian psychoanalysts towards the child was the perception of this misery, and a specific social sensitivity stemming from the ethos of Ferenczi's early works (reinforced in his *Clinical Diary*). Another motive could be an attempt to break out from the relative isolation and marginalisation in which the Hungarian psychoanalytic group found itself after the war and the subsequent, failed revolutions. "The child" (*das Kind*), though it could have been seen as an apolitical, or even a "neutral" theme, could be an important channel for opening up towards larger segments of society. There had been two particular strata where psychoanalytic ideas about children and education might have fallen upon fertile soil. First of all, in the circle of enlightened middle class urban women, mothers, teachers, and other professionals who were attracted to psychoanalysis, since it promised a more empathic understanding of social conflicts, as well as their own life crises, of "feminine" problems concerning sexuality, of their relationship with their children and pupils, and of their conflicts between motherhood and professional life. (See Anna Borgos's book [2018] about women in the Budapest School.) The seminars and courses announced by the Psychoanalytic Association, which were held mostly by women, established a system of further education. They offered a means for encountering and assimilating exciting, new, modern, progressive ideas. They provided a kind of alternative university system, operating independently and outside the walls of official universities from which the attendees of these seminars had been excluded, by law or by their lack of financial means.

An additional audience came from the socialist workers' movements, workers' academies, and other fora of socialist self-education, organised by the Social Democratic Party. In this context I must mention Béla Székely, a friend of the Freudo-Marxist poet Attila József, and follower of Wilhelm Reich, who held lectures at meetings of the Association of Socialist Physicians, and who also worked as a therapist treating sexual problems of young people in outpatient clinics established by workers' organisations. He was editor of the periodical *Emberismeret* ('Human Knowledge'), a review dealing with Freudian and Adlerian psychology and their relation to Marxism. Székely's book, reflecting on Alice Bálint's *The Psycho-Analysis of the Nursery*, was published in 1934 under title *Your Child – Handbook of Modern Education* (reviewed by Edit Gyömrői). (See Balint [1953] for the English edition.) There were strong ties between psychoanalysts and the political Left, namely the Socialist and Communist movements. These connections made analysts suspect in the eyes of the authorities. In his interview with Bluma Swerdloff (2002), Michael Bálint noted that the clients of the outpatient clinic of the Hungarian Psychoanalytic Association were under constant police surveillance (Figure 3.1).

In spite of this repressive atmosphere, the Hungarian Psychoanalytic Association became increasingly involved in training psychoanalysts, disseminating psychoanalytic ideas to a larger audience, and opening its therapeutic facilities to the public. The training institute of the Association was established in 1926. From its beginning, Alice Bálint held courses of lectures there on analytical child psychology, which lay people could also attend. The foundation of the training institute was followed by the establishment of outpatient clinics. The first psychoanalytic

Figure 3.1 Excursion to Csillebérc, 1931. From the left: Ferenc Pákozdy, László
Gereblyés, Gyula Illyés, Imre Szántó, Attila József, and Béla Székely.
Photo: Tibor Arató (?) With permission of the Petőfi Literary Museum,
Hungary

outpatient clinic of the Association was established in 1930 "under the direction of
Frau Dr. M. Dubovitz, under the auspices of the Hungarian League for the Protection of Children" (Hermann, 1930, p. 354). The opening of the Clinic was publi-
cised by the Hungarian News Agency. In his correspondence with Freud, Ferenczi
relates that they "asked me to organise a psychoanalytic consultancy for children
together with their parents". He remarks that the "blemish in this invitation is that
the Adlerians may also set up office hours there" (Ferenczi, 1930). Dubovitz's
clinic already had a precedent, a consultancy for psychopathic children at the Graf
Apponyi Poliklinik, a newly established modern hospital in Budapest (on Szövet-
ség utcai kórház). In the framework of this consultancy children with learning,
personality, and behavioural disorders were treated. It handled approximately 160
cases yearly. There was also a daytime home where analytically trained doctors
took care of children with behavioural disorders or those living in poor material
conditions, and some cases were referred for psychoanalytic treatment (*ZPP*, 1934)

Margit Dubovitz's clinic was, however, soon dissolved (for financial reasons).
The next step was the establishment of the Association's own outpatient clinic
in 1931. It was first announced in the Association's bulletin in 1929, in the following words: "The Hungarian Psycho-Analytical Society is arranging a Psycho-
Analytical Out-Patient Clinic at Dr. Ferenczi's private consulting-rooms. The Clinic
will open this autumn and will complete the scheme for the Training Institute" (Hermann, 1929, p. 538). In 1931 the bulletin published the following item of news:

After a long struggle with the official authorities, permission has been granted for the institution of a Polyclinic to be called *Allgemeines Ambulatorium für Nerven und Gemütskranke*. The clinic has already begun its work in suitable premises (I. Meszaros-u. 12). The Society asked Dr. Ferenczi to assume the direction of the Polyclinic, with Dr. M. Bálint as deputy. In addition, the following attend for consultation: Dr. Hermann, Dr. Hollos, Dr. Pfeifer and Dr. Révész. Dr. Almásy devotes the greater part of his time to the Institute as Assistant.

(Hermann, 1931, pp. 520–521)

Ferenczi wrote to Freud in 1931:

Here at home things are going along very lively in the Society. The young people, mostly women physicians, are eager for work; the laymen and laywomen are occupying themselves mostly with the analysis of children. A young [female] colleague became a psychoanalyst for a workers' organization (child protection). Another child protection society, in which Frau Dr. Dubovitz was keeping hours, dissolved, unfortunately (financial difficulties). In place of this I can this time officially give you the unexpectedly pleasant information that, *thanks to the efforts of Dr. Bálint, Frau Kovács, and one of her patients, despite vehement opposition from the State Health Council, permission to establish the polyclinic was finally granted us by the Ministry of Public Welfare. We have, totally from our own means, rented a five-room apartment and will set it up in a few weeks,* so that I will already be able to report to the Congress the beginning of the therapeutic and instructional activity there. As you see, we are completely dependent on the help of the members, while Berlin, Vienna, and London have munificent helpers.

(1931a, my emphasis)

We can also reconstruct the history of the foundation of the Clinic from Bálint's interview:

We were very squeezed in the University, under the Horthy regime and all the anti-Semitism, and analysis was considered a very left thing. We had all sorts of troubles. The other members of the Society all tried to accept things: "This is what it is and we have to live with it." I said: "Nonsense. Times are changing, we have to do something." So, first I got through the revision of our statutes – because of a government action at that time – then I got all sorts of things moving. I got some money, and gained permission – it had to be a special permission by the government to open a clinic. Generally, the people accepted that they were beaten. I never accepted that. Never accept that you have to put up with it, the opposite, you ought to do something, was my attitude. So, I got the permission, after a very long struggle with the authorities. *Everyone was against it, of course – the medical profession, the university, the General Medical Council. Eventually we got the permission and we opened, and we had a very nice institute, with quite a good load of work.*

(Swerdloff, 2002, pp. 390–391, my emphasis)

It is difficult to reconstruct the manifold activities of the Institute. Here I am only able to cite a few facts which might be of interest. For example, we know from a 1937 statistical yearbook of Budapest that the number of appointments at the Clinic that year was "8429, and the cost of its maintenance was 3747 Pengős" (Schuler, 1937, p. 251).

Edward Glover (1937) writes in his report to the Fourteenth International Psycho-Analytical Congress held in Marienbad:

> In Hungary, in addition to the regular active work of the Society, there are three special features of interest. One is the extension of interest from Budapest to other towns. In one of these, Békés-Csaba, the interest in analysis is so lively that an informal group, in contact with the main Society, has been constituted. *Secondly, there has been great activity in the direction of child analysis and analytical pedagogy.* Thirdly, we note that the Hungarian Society is making determined and successful efforts to emerge from its relative isolation and, by means of exchange lectures and in other ways, to forge contacts with analysts elsewhere.
>
> (Glover, 1937, p. 96, my emphasis)

Erzsébet Farkas, as I mentioned before, was a participant in the educational seminars of the Psychoanalytic Association. The programme, which was directed by Kata Lévy, was particularly rich. In addition to Kata Lévy, regular speakers included Alice Bálint, Edith Gyömrői, Margit Dubovitz, Klára G. Lázár, Alice Hermann, István Hollós, Lillian Rotter, and others. There was a large audience who regularly attended the meetings: mothers, teachers, doctors, and university students among them. These workshops or seminars were also a meeting point for a network of young progressive intellectuals. Several of those who were instructors, or who had trained there, played an important role in the modernisation and reorganisation of the Hungarian educational system *after* the Second World War – Alice Hermann, Emmi Pikler, and others (Eva Hoffer's interview, 1987) (Figure 3.2).

"Where Are You, My Sons?" is the title of the edited version of the diary I mentioned at the beginning of this chapter. Its author, Erzsébet Farkas, was born in 1917 to a lower middle class Jewish family in Budapest. Her ambition was to be a teacher, but she was not admitted to the teachers' training college. After graduating from high school, she worked as a clerk and bookkeeper at various companies. She also studied English and was very much interested in psychology. When she lost her job, she worked as a babysitter and private house tutor for families. Between 1936 and 1938 she regularly attended the seminars of the Psychoanalytic Association for educators and parents. As I already noted, her main instructor was Kata Lévy. It was there that she became acquainted with the teachings, theories, and conceptual framework of modern psychology, and how to apply them. In the autumn of 1938, Erzsébet moved with her five-year-old son Matyi to the Hungarian town of Békés, where she undertook the task of running a children's home. The owner of the premises and also the founder and managing director of the home was

Figure 3.2 Seminar for pedagogues at the Budapest Polyclinic in the 1930s, with social worker Emmy Gaál (third from right), nursery school pedagogue Éva Sára Vajna (second from left) and Edit Gyömrői sitting at the end of the table, with dark top. With permission of Janos Hoffer

local pharmacist Lajos Goldberger (1888–1944). The home was established by the Hungarian Israelite Patronage Association, a charity organisation for child protection, which maintained several children's homes, consulting offices, as well as professional guidance and training centres. One of the directors of the Association was baroness Elisabeth Weiss, the wife of Alfonz Weiss, son of the rich industrialist Manfréd Weiss, a benefactor in several social, cultural, and health issues. Elisabeth Weiss studied medicine, and was also a psychoanalytic candidate. In the preceding years she was involved in social work, child protection, and had organised summer camps for destitute children under psychoanalytic direction. Especially difficult cases were selected and referred to the psychoanalytic clinic (*ZPP*, 1934, p. 404).

The home, which started up with ten six- to eight-year-old Jewish boys, was designed to give the children a respectable religious upbringing, providing them with a safe, predictable, and affectionate life, educating them and ensuring that they had a proper trade by the age of 18. The children had been abandoned by their parents, or they were orphans, or the parents were unable to support their children because of the deep poverty they lived in. Most of the children were profoundly traumatised; they had been neglected by foster parents and institutes. They had been taken out of the system of Christian foster care or orphanages by the Patronage Association as a reaction to the anti-Jewish laws, implemented in Hungary from 1938 on. Originally, the aim was to save these children for the Jewish community and to save them from persecutions to be expected at other, non-Jewish homes and institutions.

Erzsébet Farkas started to work under extraordinary difficult circumstances: in poverty and isolation, far from the capital, in the shadow of the Holocaust, threatened by the increasing anti-Semitic atmosphere and discrimination. In her isolation she decided to write a diary which survived for more than 70 years, hidden on the bottom shelf of a three-door wardrobe in her Budapest apartment. Erzsébet died in 1991, but she never spoke about her years in Békés. The manuscript, containing almost 500 closely typed pages, was discovered in 2011 by her granddaughter Mária Hódos. A photo album and correspondence amounting to some 200 pages concerning the children's home at Békés also survived. Mária immediately recognised the significance of the diary, and she started to edit and transcribe the text. She also searched archival sources in order to reconstruct the whole story. It took her seven years to find a publisher, but finally the edited diary has been published in book form, with an introduction and notes by Mária Hódos, for whom the discovery of her grandmother's hidden diary also led to the discovery of fragments of her *own* repressed past (Hódos & Farkas, 2019). But that is another story.

Erzsébet's intention of writing regular, almost daily entries in her diary was not only to report events and experiences to Kata Lévy, but also to collect psychological observations about the children as material for eventual discussion at the seminars. The book includes the correspondence between Kata Lévy and Erzsébet Farkas. The letters and the diary reflect the near absurdity of the situation: how to be a mother of ten boys, including her own, instead of being their foster parent? How to correct the basic fault, to recreate primary love for these children who were abandoned by their mothers at a young age, to be put into foster care, only to be removed again, this time from their foster environment? There was an enormous gulf between the world of the nurseries of middle class families in Budapest and the world of the Békés children's home which in the beginning was filled with aggressive, wild boys, who found themselves in an even more hostile environment than previously. In this hopeless situation, described in the diary and letters, Erzsébet, who was not a trained psychoanalyst, tried to implement psychoanalytic insights and principles in her work with the traumatised children. It was, of course, very difficult: for example, in the beginning she had to rely on physical force – beatings – which, naturally, was disapproved of by Kata Lévy. However, gradually, she started to cope with the problems, realising spontaneously the importance of love and autonomy. Hungry for love, these young boys struggled with their past and with each other. They searched for their roles in the new community, sought an understanding and acceptance of their Jewish identity, and competed for the exclusive attention and love of Erzsébet Farkas. Kata Lévy's advice, which extended even to minor details, was very helpful for Erzsébet, but naturally supervision at a distance had serious limits. Nevertheless, the continuous contact with Kata Lévy was extremely important, not so much for practical advice, but rather as psychological support for Erzsébet's survival. However, as time passed, during the more than three years of the existence of the home, Erzsébet eventually succeeded in creating an atmosphere of a "new beginning", and in forming a "republic", a genuine community, of children, emotionally bound together and sharing a common identity and common goals. To achieve this state, Erzsébet had to make heroic efforts, and to fulfil – in her own words – an "apostolic mission".

It was a tragic absurdity of the whole story that when this phase was reached, the "pedagogical experiment" had to be stopped. The final entry in the diary was made in February 1942. The home was shut down by the local authorities, and Erzsébet Farkas moved to Budapest with all the children. As it turned out later, for many of them this was a life-saving journey. All the Jews from the town of Békés, like all provincial Jews in Hungary, were deported, mostly to Auschwitz, during 1944. Erzsébet Farkas and a few of her boys brought up in Békés, including her own son Matyi, the father of Mária Hódos, survived the Holocaust, but several children from the home were murdered. The survivors left Hungary, and again found a "new beginning" in other parts of the world. Mária Hódos succeeded in tracing some them, and even met some survivors or their descendants. But this too, is another story. Kata Lévy and Erzsébet Farkas never met again. During and after the war, Kata Lévy worked for the Patronage Association and the Jewish community helping to organise and supervise children's homes. She emigrated to England in 1954, with her husband Lajos, and died in 1969. Erzsébet Farkas abandoned pedagogy, and worked as a public employee until her retirement. She died in 1991.

The "pedagogical experiment" of Erzsébet Farkas raises a lot of questions about the application of psychoanalysis, about collective nursing and education, and about the residential treatment of children and young people with personality and behavioural disorders. Bálint and the object relations theory have certainly much to say about these experiments which were rather different in their theoretical and methodological foundation. It is worth mentioning a few other experiments conducted in the twentieth century. There was Laura Polányi's pedagogical experiment in Budapest in 1912, Vera Schmidt's psychoanalytic kindergarten in Moscow in the 1920s, Lilly Hajdú's Frim Institute in Budapest, Anna Freud's Matchbook school in Vienna, August Aichhorn's residential homes for "wayward youth", also in Vienna, Siegfried Bernfeld's Baumgarten school in Berlin, Susan Isaac's Malting House School in Cambridge, A. S. Neill's Summerhill school in Suffolk, England, Anna Freud's Hampstead War Nurseries in London, Emmi Pikler's much-debated "Lóczy" nursery home in Budapest after the Second World War, and so on. The Békés children's home was unique in that it was completely isolated, and completely forgotten, and also in that it required not only professional devotion but also sacrifice and personal heroism from its head. Only with Janusz Korczak's work with the children of the Warsaw Ghetto can valid comparison be drawn.

Bibliography

Balint, A. (1953). *The Psycho-Analysis of the Nursery*. London: Routledge, 2017.

Borgos, A. (2018). *Holnaplányok: Nők a Pszichoanalízis Budapesti Iskolájában* [Tomorrow's Girls: Women in the Budapest School of Psychoanalysis]. Budapest: Noran Libro.

Danto, E. A. (2005). *Freud's Free Clinics. Psychoanalysis and Social Justice, 1918–1938*. New York: Columbia University Press.

Dupont, J. (1993). Michael Balint: Analysand, pupil, friend, and successor to Sándor Ferenczi. In: L. Aron & A. Harris (Eds.), *The Legacy of Sándor Ferenczi* (pp. 145–157). Hillsdale, NJ: Analytic Press.

Federn, E. (1990). *Witnessing Psychoanalysis: From Vienna Back to Vienna via Buchenwald and the USA.* London: Routledge, 2018.

Ferenczi, S. (1921). Psychoanalysis and the War neurosis, first symposium. (Held at the Fifth International Psycho-Analytical Congress, Budapest, September 1918.) In: S. Ferenczi, K. Abraham, E. Simmel, & E. Jones (Eds.), *Psychoanalysis and the War Neuroses* (pp. 5–21). The International Psycho-Analytical Library, No. 2. London: International Psycho-Analytic Press.

Ferenczi, S. (1930). Letter from Sándor Ferenczi to Sigmund Freud, February 14. In: E. Falzeder & E. Brabant (Eds.), with the collaboration of Patrizia Giampieri-Deutsch. Translated by Peter T. Hoffer, *The Correspondence of Sigmund Freud and Sándor Ferenczi, Volume 3, 1920–1933* (pp. 387–389). Cambridge, MA: Harvard University Press, 2000.

Ferenczi, S. (1931a). Letter from Sándor Ferenczi to Sigmund Freud, May 31. In: E. Falzeder & E. Brabant (Eds.), with the collaboration of Patrizia Giampieri-Deutsch. Translated by Peter T. Hoffer, *The Correspondence of Sigmund Freud and Sándor Ferenczi, Volume 3, 1920–1933* (pp. 410–413). Cambridge, MA: Harvard University Press, 2000.

Ferenczi, S. (1931b). Előszó. In: A. Bálint (Ed.), *A Gyermekszoba Pszichológiája* (pp. 11–12). Budapest: Kossuth, 1990. [Preface to the Hungarian edition of Alice Bálint's book *The Psychology of the Children's Room* (*The Psycho-Analysis of the Nursery*).]

Ferenczi, S. (1999). *Sándor Ferenczi: Selected Writings.* J. Borossa (Ed.). London: Routledge.

Freud, S. (1919). *Lines of Advance in Psycho-Analytic Therapy.* S. E., 17: 157–168. London: Hogarth.

Glover, E. (1937). Report of the fourteenth international psycho-analytical congress. *Bulletin of the International Psycho-Analytic Association, 18*: 72–107.

Hermann, I. (1929). Hungarian psycho-analytical society (report of first quarter, 1929). *Bulletin of the International Psycho-Analytic Association, 10*: 536–539.

Hermann, I. (1930). Hungarian psycho-analytical society (report of first quarter, 1930). *Bulletin of the International Psycho-Analytic Association, 11*: 353–354.

Hermann, I. (1931). Hungarian psycho-analytical society (report of second quarter, 1931). *Bulletin of the International Psycho-Analytic Association, 12*: 520–521.

Hódos, M. & Farkas, E. (2019). *Fiaim Hol Vagytok?* (Napló az 1938–1942 közötti évekből) [My Sons, Where Are You? (Diary from the years 1938–1942).] Budapest: Tinta Könyvkiadó.

Hoffer, É. (1987). An interview with Éva Hoffer (Budapest, December 15, 1987) by F. Erős & Zs. Vajda. Manuscript.

Lévy-Freund, K. (1990). Dernières vacances des Freud avant la fin du monde [Freud's last vacation before the end of the world]. *Le Coq-Héron,* Un peu d'histoire: Freud, Ferenczi, et les autres [A little history: Freud, Ferenczi, and the others], *117* (juillet): 39–44. In German: Erinnerungen an den Sommer 1918. *Luzifer-Amor,* 2012, *25*(50): 52–61. [Original document undated: Library of Congress Archives, Washington, Sigmund Freud Papers, Interviews and Recollections, Set A, Box 124, Folder 56. https://loc.gov/resource/mss39990.12456/?st=gallery].

Roper, M. (2016). From the shell-shocked soldier to the nervous child: Psychoanalysis in the aftermath of the First World War. *Psychoanalysis and History*, *18*(1): 39–69.

Schuler, D. (1937). Hatósági és társadalmi embervédelem budapesten. 2. kötet [Official and social human protection in Budapest. Volume 2]. *Budapesti Statisztikai Közlemények* [Budapest Statistical Bulletins], *90*(1).

Swerdloff, B. (2002). An interview with Michael Balint [1965]. *American Journal of Psychoanalysis*, *62*(4): 383–413.

Székács-Weisz, J. (2015). *Living Archives Project*. Unpublished project proposal.

ZPP. (1934). Berichte. Psychoanalytische pädagogik im jahre 1934 [Reports. Psychoanalytic pedagogy in 1934]. *Zeitschrift für Psychoanalytische Pädagogik*, *8*(11–12): 403–407.

Chapter 3a

Remembering Ferenc Erős (1946–2020)

Judit Szekacs-Weisz

Figure 3a.1 Ferenc Erős with Buda Castle in the background, 2018

We are mourning the death of one of our closest colleagues and friends (Figure 3a.1).

Ferenc Erős, eminent social psychologist, doctor of the Hungarian Academy of Sciences, was a founding member of the Sándor Ferenczi Society and remained a pillar of the Ferenczi movement both internationally and in Hungary. He was a member of Imago International in London and the president of Imago in Budapest.

He lived and worked in Budapest but was active in research, teaching, and education abroad. He was able to open up a multigenerational scientific and human stream, welcoming creative minds of diverse cultural and social backgrounds from

DOI: 10.4324/9781003309826-6

distant lands. Erős researched and wrote extensively not only regarding the work and life of Sándor Ferenczi but of trauma theory, transgenerational effects of the Holocaust, authoritarianism, the psychoanalytic and social contexts of gender and the body – just to mention a few areas of his interest.

He was the chief editor of *Thalassa* and Imago Budapest for over 20 years, creating a multidisciplinary platform to review and discuss relevant issues of our prefession. In addition to his scholarly work, he also published poetry (*The Tales of Goffman*) and a Central/East European intellectual picaresque (*The Miracles of Szagundelli*) with paradigmatic stories of awesome historical accuracy embedded in human experience and life-enhancing humour.

An excellent lecturer and revered teacher, he initiated the Theoretical Psychoanalysis programme of the Doctoral School of Pécs University which acquired a legendary status among generations of students in Hungary and abroad. This is what his students had to say about "Feri":

He was an integrative, organising, school creating, and charismatic person of his profession, reflecting critically not only on the history of psychoanalysis but also on contemporary social phenomena and their consequences.

He set an example for how a professor and a student, a senior researcher and a graduate student can work together as partners.

He represented democracy, solidarity, and love.

Without him our team will never be complete again...

Judit Szekacs-Weisz
2020

Chapter 4

"I look into a room through a round gap". Alice Bálint's life, work and diaries

Anna Borgos

A short biography[1]

During her short life (she was only 41 at her death) Hungarian psychoanalyst Alice Bálint inspired and was inspired by many of her contemporaries, and carried out a rich programme of theoretical, therapeutic, and educational activities. Her interests were genuinely interdisciplinary; besides psychoanalysis she was engaged in the equally new sciences of ethnology and cultural anthropology, which she successfully integrated in her analytic thought. Her application of psychoanalysis to child-rearing and pedagogy was also influential. Her new approach to the mother-child relationship – which she, like her husband, Michael Bálint, considered as an active love relationship, a "primary object-love", from its beginning – made her one of the forerunners of object relations theory. This chapter aims to reconstruct Alice Bálint's life and oeuvre and introduce her recently discovered diaries, with a special focus on her notes taken while in analysis with Sándor Ferenczi (Figure 4.1).[2]

Alice Bálint (née Székely-Kovács) was born in 1898 in Budapest to a middle class Jewish family. She was the daughter of Vilma Kovács, one of the very first Hungarian female analysts and the creator of the "Hungarian system" of training analysis (Kovács, 1936). Vilma Kovács divorced her first husband, Zsigmond Székely after a few years and married Frigyes Kovács, a wealthy architect who financially supported psychoanalysis. The three children from the first marriage stayed with the father until Alice, at the age of 12, escaped with her siblings to join the new family. She was a high school classmate of Emmi Bergsmann (the sister of Mihály[3] Bálint) and Margit Schönberger (later Margaret Mahler). She pursued her university studies in several different places and disciplines. She completed six terms in mathematics at the Faculty of Philosophy of Budapest University (1916–1919), by which time she had already acquired an interest in anthropology, economy, and psychoanalysis.[4] In 1920 she completed two terms at the Faculty of Law (Political Sciences Department) at the University of Vienna.

She already knew Mihály Bálint (1896–1970) from high school, but they got into closer contact only in 1918, and this proved to be a lifelong, mutually influential relationship both emotionally and intellectually. Mihály Bálint recalls the time and significance of their encounter as such:

DOI: 10.4324/9781003309826-7

Figure 4.1 Alice Bálint, passport picture, 1927 (with permission of Judith Dupont)

Then, in 1918 – that is very important – I fell in love with my wife. We were both students. She studied mathematics. Both of us were interested in analysis, too, although she didn't come to Ferenczi's lectures. I really do not know why not. She gave me, lent me *Totem and Taboo*. [...] Her real field was anthropology, and *Totem and Taboo* was one of the fundamental books in it. [...] She was this kind of human being, like me, interested in everything, she studied mathematics as well.

(Swerdloff, 2002, pp. 386–387)

After their wedding in 1921, they moved to Berlin,[5] where they could pursue professional training as well as flee the anti-Semitic atmosphere in Hungary.[6] Alice Bálint attended the Political Sciences Department of Friedrich-Wilhelm University (1921–1923), studied ethnology, and worked at the Museum für Völkerkunde (Ethnographic Museum). In 1922, the couple started an analysis with Hanns Sachs but they were unsatisfied with his overly theoretical sessions. Alice Bálint became an external member of the Berlin Psychoanalytic Society,[7] where she gave a few lectures on female psychosexual development, the Mexican War hieroglyphs,[8] and South Californian and Indian myths.

In 1924, the couple returned to Budapest and finished their analysis with Ferenczi. In 1925, Alice enrolled in Ferencz József University in Szeged where she studied geography for one term, having already submitted a thesis in October 1924 based on her work in the Berlin Ethnographic Museum.[9] In 1925, their son János was born. Alice wrote extensively on his development in her diary (including photographs) between 1925 and 1936 and probably integrated these observations into her theory of the early mother-infant relationship. She became an active member of the Hungarian Psychoanalytic Society in 1926, was elected into the training committee, worked in the Polyclinic,[10] and also maintained a private practice. She held courses in psychoanalytic child psychology for teachers and parents, presented at seminars and congresses (see Giefer, 2007), and published regularly.

In 1939, the political situation forced the couple to emigrate from Hungary. They managed to find refuge in Manchester in January with the help of Ernest Jones, John Rickman, and probably Michael Polányi, who had already fled there from Berlin in 1933 (Mészáros, 2014). The letters of Alice to her brother-in-law (László Dormándi) in Paris suggest that they started to settle down in their new environment, and in July 1939 Alice became a member of the British Psychoanalytical Society. However, they struggled financially, and the war preparations infiltrated their daily life.

> The country is very much preparing here. […] People are constantly called on to store enough food for one week and stuff like that. In the meantime, under the influence of the optimistic English disposition, of course sometimes we completely forget about it all and settle for eternal peace. We are still satisfied with the English. We have a little money now, but it's not yet possible to *live* on that, just to get along. Now we are focusing on receiving guests in the first place. Emmi[11] will be the first, then, I hope, Olgi,[12] Juci,[13] and my parents.[14]

Another letter also reports on their financial situation and the number of their analytic hours. Alice still hoped to be able to bring her mother to England. The last sentences indicate their common experiences regarding the loneliness and alienation of immigrants.

> The lack of money, in less exciting forms, is prevalent here, too. Nevertheless, it seems that we can get away without major loans or perhaps with no loan at all, which we can be satisfied with. Unfortunately I have only one hour daily, Misi has four; three of them are paying. […] Currently I'm terribly agitated about the visa for Mum. [...] I'm haunted by the nightmare that the outrage will break out before they could leave. What you write about your loneliness I can understand well. Although M[anchester] is not so big and strangers are more respected than in Paris.[15]

Manchester became the scene of loss. On 29 Augus 1939, only some months after the immigration and three days before the outbreak of World War II, and 25 days before Freud's death, Alice Bálint died of a ruptured aneurysm, at the age of 41. Next year, her mother, Vilma Kovács, died in Budapest, and after the Nazi occupation Mihály Bálint's parents committed suicide. In 1945 Mihály Bálint moved to London, where he joined the Tavistock Clinic in 1948.

Official obituaries emphasise Alice Bálint's ability to connect and organise, her professional networking activities, as well as her attractive personality among the Central European child analysts.

She was especially well-known and appreciated in the countries of Central Europe. The close contact of the Budapest group with those in Prague and Vienna would have been hardly conceivable without her initiative and activity. She was one of the organisers of the intellectual exchanges of child analysts between Vienna and Budapest.

(Hoffer, 1940, pp. 102–103)

"Her colleagues in the country of her adoption had begun to embrace the charm and liveliness of her personality and were looking forward to a future in which she would make many valuable contributions to their common work" (Balint, M., 1940, p. 116).

Oeuvre and reception

Alice Bálint's intellectual development was firstly and primarily grounded by her family background, principally her mother and the cultural milieu that surrounded the family. Her diary reveals how diverse and up-to-date her fields of interest were. Her psychoanalytic thinking was continually shaped by her anthropological and pedagogical connections. Among the analytical mentors, the most direct influences came from Freud, Ferenczi, Imre Hermann, Géza Róheim, and Anna Freud.[16]

Ferenczi's influence, apart from the concrete knowledge he spread, manifested itself in her freedom of thought and experimentation. As Alice Bálint wrote regarding his professional attitude affecting both men and women:

He was an individualist and his teaching manifested itself mostly in communicating his often changing ideas and experiments to us – albeit in his own suggestive manner – and leaving us to use as much as we could and wanted. [...] The freedom Ferenczi left to his disciples and the courage with which he kept encouraging them to see the things of daily practice with ever fresh, naive eyes is surely one of the best we could get from him apart from the content of his thoughts.

(Bálint, 1936a, p. 47)

Obviously, her husband, Mihály Bálint, cannot be left out of the influences, although this relationship was more of a mutual interaction, a human and intellectual co-operation, the traces of which can be found in the works of both of them. As Zsuzsanna Vajda wrote in 1995, "Mihály Bálint interpreted the same observation from the point of view of self-development and theory, while Alice Bálint specifically from the questions of parent-child relationship and practical education" (p. 47) (Figure 4.2).

Figure 4.2 János Bálint, Mihály Bálint and Alice Bálint, 14th International Psycho-analytic Congress, Marienbad, 1936 (with permission of Jane Balint)

Alice Bálint's only book published in her lifetime, *A gyermekszoba pszichológiája* (*The Psychology of the Nursery*) was soon translated into four languages: German, French, Spanish, and English – the last translated and introduced by Michael Bálint, with a foreword to the American edition by Anna Freud.[17] It was reviewed in *Child Study*[18] and even in *The New York Times*.[19] Her theoretical and educational articles published in international psychoanalytic periodicals (*Internationale Zeitschrift für Psychoanalyse, Imago, Zeitschrift für Psychoanalytische Pädagogik*) and progressive Hungarian pedagogical journals (*Gyermeknevelés, A Jövő Útjain*) were collected in 1941 in the volume *Anya és gyermek* (*Mother and Child*, Bálint, 1941), including her two last papers[20] presented at the Manchester psychoanalytic seminar. The manuscript of another paper presented in March 1939 in London ("Altruism, Aggression, and Reality Sense") can be found in the Archives of the British Psychoanalytical Society,[21] together with a critical, unfortunately anonymous response.

In her writings she contradicts the Freudian views on early attachment at certain (significant) points. The debate on Freud's primary narcissism was already beginning with Ferenczi and Hermann's theory of clinging. Alice (and Mihály) Bálint connect to this by considering the mother-child relationship a dual union and then as a primary subject relationship, in which the baby is actively involved from the beginning, and the relationship, beyond the instinctual endowment, is also of a social nature. Its form, after the earliest period of passive love of the object, manifests itself as an active object love whose primary love object is the mother. The baby's particular fear of being dropped, as pointed out in a study by Alice Bálint, is a sign of the fear of loss of security and, connecting to that, of love (Bálint, 1933b). Applying the withdrawal of love as an educational tool can cause lasting injuries in adapting to reality – the child believes it is enough to obey in order to be protected from all dangers. According to Judith Dupont (2012), the first steps towards the idea of ocnophil and philobatic regression developed by Michael Bálint (1968) are already found in this study.

The role of the mother is not only central in its "primary" sense; the development of the infant's subsequent cognitive abilities is also linked to the quality of their relationship. She gives herself to the baby, but also has to be "struggled for", and by managing this task she helps the infant in developing a sense of reality and also in separating self and object. The primary object relationship is inherent in the function of the id; the sense of reality and love are closely linked (Bálint, 1939).

So to love – in the social sense – means on the one hand the acknowledgement of the fact that the object of our love is not identical with ourselves, and on the other the ability to maintain our friendly feelings even when satisfaction is suspended. Both conditions require a certain degree of maturity of the sense of reality.

(Bálint, 1933a, p. 36; emphases in the original)

The following excerpt of her diary, describing the behaviour of her one-year-old son, demonstrates a very personal and expressive episode of the process of developing the "sense of reality" and learning to delay the fulfilment of needs, which is based on a primary love relationship and trust. He seems to relieve his tension through "transitory objects".

He knows the more serious side of life now too. Sometimes he bears troubles with great patience, at other times he starts crying desperately just for the faint chance of me e.g. leaving the room. Today I was reading while he was getting about in the playpen. There was complete silence and I didn't pay attention. When I looked up, there the little tot was standing, with his thumb in his mouth, the blanket in his other hand and sucking his thumb, wide open eyes. When I looked at him, he started to laugh and jump immediately. The little man must have very much been waiting for me. When I took him into my lap, after a brief joydance he fell asleep right away and did not wake up to any noise.[22]

(At the end of 1925)

She points out the relationship between the infants' bodily development and their emotional environment: neglect may cause physical symptoms too (1931a). Mother's love, according to Alice Bálint, is an "archaic love" based on mutual and complementary needs. She points out the psychological effects of modern civilisation's prolonged childhood through anthropological examples, parallels, and contrasts. Her ethnological-anthropological knowledge is manifested in a few international studies (1923, 1926, 1935a), as well as in a comprehensive article on totemism (1927a), and reviews of the works of Géza Róheim (1927b, 1928, 1933c, 1935b), German ethnographer Josef Winthuis (1929, 1931b), and Lithuanian-born South African psychoanalyst Wulf Sachs's book, *Black Hamlet* (1939b).

Her anthropological readings also persuaded her that there was no universal or "natural" form of child-rearing.[23] At the same time, she did not consider repression an unnatural and necessarily painful process, provided that the inevitable renunciation and adaptation happen "at the lowest price" (1931a, p. 23), that is, the parents support it by preparing the child for reality not through their authority but through authenticity and sincerity. Parents have to dare to enter the regressive world of the nursery; at the same time, children have to learn to respect their parents' needs. The capacity for adaptation and for tolerating stress is inevitable for functioning in life, but flexibility in giving up instinctual satisfactions and enjoying freely embraced desires without a sense of guilt are skills at least as important (see Bálint, 1932, 1936b).

Alice Bálint's activities as an educational consultant were also remarkable; in her articles and answers to parents' questions, she wrote very openly about various taboo issues, including onanism and sex education, from a psychoanalytic viewpoint but in a clear and intelligible language.[24] This is what Sándor Ferenczi emphasises too in his foreword to the Hungarian edition of *The Psycho-Analysis of the Nursery*:

> She threw a heavy stone into the long stagnating waters of psychoanalysis and child education. [...] But psychoanalysis itself dared to touch the sensitive issue of childrearing only in the last decade. [...] The author of this book, with her outspokenness and openness that alone is worthy of science, in her approach perfectly illustrates the group of those who besides all their conservatism do not reject new and sometimes bold ideas.
>
> (Ferenczi in Bálint, 1931a, p. 11)

The contemporary reception of Alice Bálint was relatively lively. Her female psychoanalytic colleagues, Alice Hermann and Lilly Hajdu, have both written a review of *The Psychology of the Nursery* (Hajdu, 1931; Hermann, 1931). The review of writer and critic Endre Illés in the literary journal *Nyugat* (West) – which was otherwise open to psychoanalysis and published a few studies of Ferenczi too – while at the beginning acknowledges and analyses the findings of Freudianism, reflects the lay reservations towards psychoanalysis as reducing interpretations to sexuality and failing to go beyond the individual.

> Alice Bálint writes of the evolution of this deepest geological layer. She shows the longitudinal section of development. [...] The chapters interpret this process within an orthodox and somewhat too rigid Freudian dogmatics [...] and her work finally reduces merely to the erotica of the nursery. [...] This book demonstrates the general mistakes of Freudism: its excessive sexual onesidedness

and extreme individualism, besides recognising the crucial foundations laid by Freud, induce the desire for the revision of Freudism and for turning it to another, more collective direction.

(Illés, 1931, pp. 670–673)

Anna Freud's supportive foreword to the 1954 American edition of *The Psycho-Analysis of the Nursery* (published under the title *The Early Years of Life*) also shows Alice Bálint's acknowledgement and international embeddedness. Together with Michael Bálint, she influenced the object relations theories in the first place, but Jacques Lacan also referred to her in his seminars suggesting that she underlay her husband's theory on regression.[25] Jonathan Sklar explores the work of Michael Bálint in the context of Alice and Enid Balint and gets to this conclusion:

I would suggest that Michael Balint's work on regression can be seen as being buttressed by Alice Bálint's essential paper 'Love for mother and mother love' (1939) at one end of his thinking, and half a century later by Enid Balint's 1989 paper on 'Creative life' at the other, both of which add a key dimension to his work.

(Sklar, 2012, p. 1025)

The diaries

Anna Freud proposed that I entrust her with the letters of Prof. [Freud] to the Doctor [Ferenczi] – under seal – in order to put them in a safe place in case of bombing. I thought of also including the diaries of Alice, and those written in her girlhood. [...] I took them out, fell into reading them and I was done for. How much love, intelligence, kindness, desire to live; freshness and I don't know what else there is in them. The whole world went down again, I relived the Tatras, the October revolution, the Hungarian Commune, Alice's stay in Szeged, all the adventures of our love. How rich I was that all this belonged to me, she was entirely mine, she loved me with all her heart. After that I became very calm. [...] I decided not to part from Alice's writings, there will certainly be difficult times when I will need their help.[26]

The above quotation from a letter by Michael Bálint to his brother-in-law one year after the death of his wife, Alice Bálint, gives us an impression of both her personality and the nature of their relationship.

Alice Bálint's diaries[27] cover the years between 1917 and 1929, and the last notebook includes some entries from the period between 1931 and 1936. The years 1922, 1924, and 1928 are missing; she either did not keep a diary then or these parts did not survive. After 1925, the entries (illustrated by photos) follow her son's development. It is an especially rich and interesting document in many respects, written in an original style, revealing her thoughts on herself and the events around her with remarkable maturity and sincerity, touching upon politics, love, womanhood, professional life, and her future plans. The diary, for the most part, is rather abstract, "inductive", at least in the sense that it rarely reports on her daily activities for their own sake. It mostly deals with general questions regarding her personality, different philosophical, social, and political issues, women's roles, scholarly interests, and occasionally with her family, especially her mother, Vilma Kovács, and later (in 1923) with Sándor Ferenczi. From the autumn of 1918 she writes extensively about the evolution of her love and relationship with Mihály Bálint – more through her reflections, comments, dilemmas, enthusiasms, and doubts than through the "events" themselves.

A question remains over who the "implied reader" of this diary could be. It is clear that she regularly showed it to Mihály Bálint who also had a chequered booklet that Alice may have read in return.

> I would like to write about a lot of other things, but it bothers me to know that you will read it. I decide in vain not to show you, I know I can't manage it; and still there are things I'm not sure if it's right, necessary or nice to tell about.
>
> (20 January, 1921)

Being aware of this, one can presume a certain selectivity, stylisation, control, and construction in the writing; however, such selectivity is inevitable even if we are the only readers of our writing, because of the reconstructive nature of narration, and even autobiographical narration.

The most turbulent part of the diary is the period between 1918 and 1921, in obvious relation to political events of the time (the proclamation of the Hungarian republic, then the short-lived Hungarian Republic of Councils,[28] and the subsequent counter-revolution and White Terror), which were followed and commented on by the author with notable political awareness. These years involved intense personal, social, and political changes and movements that concerned her as a young adult amidst emotional and career choices, as an "emancipated" woman, a converted Jew, and as a member of an upper middle class family with socialist inclinations.

Alice Bálint in analysis

The notebook for 1923 consists almost exclusively of analytic notes, dreams, free associations, and interpretations. She refers to her analysis with Ferenczi, which she perhaps pursued that spring and summer, visiting home from Berlin, then continued (together with her husband) after returning to Budapest in 1924. Feeling that the therapy was incomplete, she practises a kind of self-analysis through writing, touching upon some significant personal and professional problems, routinely using psychoanalytic terminology. The entries analyse her dilemmas regarding her female and scholarly roles on the one hand and her attachments to her most significant objects on the other – her analyst, her husband, and her mother. These texts demonstrate how her conflicts with sexuality, motherhood, and professional life relate to her attitude to the analysis, and to Ferenczi himself.

Hungarian female analysts had powerful master-disciple relationships with Sándor Ferenczi, which seem to have been a bit less hierarchical compared with those in the Viennese scientific community.[29] Ferenczi's openness and affirmative attitude definitely inspired women to enter the profession. One of his letters to Max Eitingon on 31 May 1931 indicates a female "wave" within the younger generation of analysts: "Here at home things are very lively in the Society. The young people, mostly women physicians, are eager to work; the laymen and laywomen are occupying themselves mostly with the analysis of children" (Cited in Freud & Ferenczi, 2000, p. 411). Ferenczi's "motherly" intersubjectivity was fruitful and progressive both in therapy and theory, although his experiments sometimes led to transgressive and problematic situations, as in the case of Elma Pálos (Forrester, 1997), or to controversial results, as in his mutual analyses.[30]

In her notes made during the analysis, Alice Bálint repeatedly reflects on the typically "female" dilemma of work vs. motherhood which appears as a question of choice. (Her son will be born two years later.) The question is raised in connection with Ferenczi's discouraging attitude towards scientific activity compared to childbirth, which contradicts his above-mentioned openness towards women's professional participation in psychoanalysis. "Constant fluctuations between work, science and motherhood; as for science I feel as if F[erenczi] forbade it, as for kids as if he wanted it, so both are in Übertr[*agung*] [transference]" (14 July 1923). She has a definite scholarly ambition, together with a fear of "getting stupid" if she becomes a mother.

> Did not he [Ferenczi] suggest to me the desire for a child instead of science? Why doesn't he want me to work? [...] What will happen if I have a child? I will get completely stupid; I won't be able to read. If I get pregnant now, I won't be able to analyse, and before I have the time again, I will forget everything. I want to compile a lecture again quickly, that is very good, I like presenting a lot. Where is that proof-sheet? I want to enjoy my work.
>
> (14 July, 1923)

Her later field of research, the study of the mother-child relationship, can be conceived as a kind of resolution for this internal and external conflict, and through this subject she could also connect to one of the major fields of the Budapest school, the early mother-infant relationship.

One of her dreams gives a rather direct account of her anxieties regarding her "fitness" to become a psychoanalyst. She indicates that it is her persistent transference and inability to detach herself from her analyst that makes her incompetent in conducting analysis herself.

> At Ferenczi's, in a rather spacious room in a large house with wide steps and *Bogengänge* [arches]. I tell him I came because I feel my analysis is not completed; we start the session and I want to talk in a way to make F. offer to continue the therapy; F. almost agrees but I mess it up again, jump up, pacing up and down

and start accusations rather intensely, telling him how I'm converting, that I have constant *Unterleib* [belly] complaints; F. takes it very morosely and declares that if I insist on choosing this solution, then it's not possible to help me. A great fear and anxiety captures me and I ask him whether I can still analyse. F. says not really, and I especially cannot teach analysis. [...] F. says that one who was not able to transform herself completely cannot be an analyst. I'm becoming more and more scared, I start clutching F.'s hand, clinging to his arms, crying terribly and begging him to help me. By then F. is a woman, rather tall and dignified and relentless; I: "then I'll commit suicide", F. doubts it.

(6 October, 1923)

Her strong (also sexual) transference and ambivalence towards Ferenczi is a returning motif of the entries, but as far as it can be judged, on Ferenczi's part it was kept within the limits of the analyst-analysand relationship. (Later, they became close colleagues and friends.) This difficult relationship influences and is influenced by other significant and conflicted themes in the entries as well – most notably her relationships to sexuality, femininity, and the profession. Ferenczi appears as an idealised father, a mentor, and a desired friend (like that of her mother).

I want that too, a father, as a crutch, a father who loves me and is proud of me. If I work, will he be proud of me, or rather get angry because I'm not doing what he considers right. But he did not want to give me directives. I still feel he [...] opposes my becoming an analyst. I would like to keep a little bit of *Fixierung* [fixation] reciprocated with friendship, like Mum.

(14 July, 1923)

It indicates a strong trust that she showed her (probably earlier) diaries to Ferenczi, as a December 1939 letter from Alice's sister, Olga, to their mother suggests: "She had an old chequered diary that she loved a lot, left from her girlhood; I don't know if it has been found, I know that she gave it to the doctor for reading, then it was somehow misplaced".[31]

Psychoanalysis (both in the role of the patient and the professional) empowers and even "obliges" her to speak openly about taboo issues, her sexuality in the first place. She is explicit that the transference also constitutes an obstacle for joyful sexuality with her husband. The therapy did not make her capable of detaching herself from the therapist:

F. is in me. – In the morning I deuted[32] the dream like I want a child but I want it from Ferenczi; that is, I want him to be in me. – M[isi] found it out, too; he threatened me with trouble if the child resembles Ferenczi. I love M. But this ugly F. is between us, I want to forget him and I'm angry that he shows up just in the moment of determination, threatening me by saying the cure was useless since I cannot bear separation.

(14 July, 1923)

I accuse F., he did not cure me. Last week insensitivity and great inner resistance against C[oitus], I feel fright or a complete emptiness.

(7 August, 1923)

In a fantasy letter to Ferenczi she admits the failure of her therapy, especially regarding her relation to sexuality. It seems that by the 1920s a healthy woman psychoanalyst was supposed to enjoy sex without any complexes. The fact that it was not so easy even for an emancipated and individually empowered person suggests that the influence of restrictive social/gender norms was still prevailing.

The difficulty of detachment ("*Loslösung*") is related to her basic need for a father figure and a father-daughter attachment. It influences her relationship with her husband as well, with whom she tries to create this relation by infantilising herself, which results in an asexual condition and a general joyless and closed state of mind.

The analysis is finished as far as I consider the clarity of my own psychic structure for me, but the "Loslösung" has not happened, and I'm starting to sink – can I do it on my own? During the whole therapy very cowardly emotions have been revealed and I just realise now that it was completely different, a real adoration, I adore him, love him and long for him, I cannot give up a father even if he is unattainable and does not love me; I can't transfer this feeling to someone else. I keep trying to turn Misi into a father, but it does not succeed, I get more and more infantile so that I make him an adult this way. – I am very miserable, the c[oitus] libido has sunk deep again, I can't scrape it out in any way, I have no, no real pleasure, unfolding, devotion, or abandon in life. I keep looking for substitutions and I always feel that it is a substitution.

(10 August, 1923)

Her ambivalence towards her mother appears in the diary, as well. Her mother is a multiple role model: as one of the very first female analysts, as a close friend of Ferenczi, and also as a mother (Figure 4.3). Alice Bálint feels a strong attachment and respect, but also a great deal of envy and aggression towards her.

I still don't feel equal with M[um]. It's perhaps because I don't have a child. Besides, sometimes I feel that M[um] is infantile now, with her new scholarly ambitions. This is also a regression to an earlier stage, although in the form of sublimation. [...] Rivalry with Mum, defiance of Ferenczi.

(7 August, 1923)

It seems that her envy is primarily directed to her mother's unproblematic friendship with Ferenczi.

An earlier dream in which I relate to M[um] my Übertr[agung] desires; she smiles sardonically, saying that she has accomplished her will and kissed F. As

Figure 4.3 Alice Bálint with Mihály Bálint, Austria, around 1935 (with permission of Judith Dupont)

if a light rose in me. Of course, Mum was brave. It's just a question of courage. And a firm determination emerges in me to travel to Budapest for the kiss immediately.

(14 July, 1923)

This great anger is all for F.; I'm struggling so much with whether I'm healthy or not, although I still love F[erenczi]. And M[um] is simply on good terms with him and she can deny all sensual *Fixierung* without any problem, so I take revenge in my dream and report to F. that she is not alright.

(6 October, 1923)

Her complex feelings and repressed passions towards her mother are interconnected with her relationship with Mihály Bálint as well: "I've never criticised Fricke more than M[um] allowed; I would like her to do the same and let me forget Misi's faults if I feel like it. Or perhaps I project my hostile feelings against M[isi] on M[um]" (13 August 1923). "Fricke" is the nickname of Frigyes Kovács, the second husband of her mother, Vilma.

Finally, I would like to cite a longer excerpt from the diary: a description and interpretation of a dream, which documents the complex interrelations of the different topics, persons, and problems of her life and also the process of their deciphering through a serious (both associative and conscious) self-analysis. The dream is mostly built around the body and sexuality, featuring Ferenczi, Bálint, and her mother.

I'm looking into a room through a round gap (keyhole?), I see F[erenczi], I'm watching him; he notices me, takes his hat angrily and is about to leave. […] I'm sitting with my back towards F. and pretend nothing was moving in me. F. takes my shoulder, happy amazement, I don't move, he caresses my face, still a motionless happiness. F. tells me to just tell him about my feelings, not be so passive. I fling myself around his neck and cry, asking him not to be angry with me for still thinking about him, I'm healthy though. I'll do everything, I'll have a kid too, but this little *Fixierung* [fixation] seems to remain, and he shouldn't hate me for taking analysis with him. He laughs, saying he doesn't hate me at all, on the contrary.

[…] Round gap: vagina, I've been looking at it a lot recently, perhaps for the first time with such a thoroughness since my childhood, I've been watching it long, it has impressed me in a special way, but it was not repulsive like [illegible]. Misi has also checked it for treatment. – I feel I am a room, F. is sitting in that, I'm looking in through the vagina and F. is sitting there. – In a lake[?] there is a movie image where one can see all kinds of things through a keyhole. – I'd like to see a coitus. Talking with M[isi] about "*unordentliche Bilder*" [improper pictures]. I'd like to know how things are going on between Mum and F., or between F. and other patients, whether he treats them like me. Fear of the return of *Underwert* [probably *Unterbewertung* is meant – underestimation] ideas, it comforts me that he also sent Mum away relentlessly on 24th, but he contacts her now. The present situation is an exile, I'm in the hallway, like in the dream. – I mostly get only to the hallway at C[oitus] too, the tension is increasing, but the *Entladung* [discharge] is still very insufficient. It gets stuck in me. […] I've seen M's p[enis], it was nice, it was not so terrible as I'd imagined. […] It must be strange if sy [somebody] sees this beastly body part a lot, I almost never see mine.

[...] *He took his hat angrily.* I'm afraid that he is angry if I don't get cured and then I can never face him again. I want to see him only when I'm healthy. But I'm angry, too.

[...] To the gap. – F. was talking about the *Beherbergungslust* [approx: the desire for nesting], I'm pondering about it a lot, yesterday during c[oitus] I enjoyed it very much that I hold sy between my legs and he feels so good there.

[...] *As if nothing was moving in me*: It is a child that moves in a woman. What does it mean that I pretend as if it doesn't? I don't know; I pretend that I don't want it, while I do? At c[oitus] I still pretend, although I know that there is something that wants to move. I still don't release myself completely because I can't forgive that the complete release at the last session failed, I had to leave. I'd like to believe that he loves me in some way, because I'm afraid that my confidence is in danger if he doesn't appreciate me, either.

[...] The dream was good, it was great to cling to his neck and also to cry, and that he assured me that he loved me – although like his child.

(14 July, 1923; emphases in the original)

The dream represents "*Fixierung*" [fixation] again, the intense attachment, clinging to Ferenczi (which for her indicates the failure of the therapy) and also Ferenczi's desired approval of her devotion. Associations to the therapy and sexuality are expressed in relation to, and as symbolising each other. She interprets movement and release concerning the therapy and coitus at the same time. The image of the reception – the "absorption" – of Ferenczi, is almost cinematic. ("I feel I am a room, F. is sitting in that, I'm looking in through the vagina and F. is sitting there".) The dream represents another key issue, the difficulty of sexual liberation and satisfaction. She interprets the desire for peeping at a coitus ("primal scene") in a wider, object-relational framework, as a need to see into the relationship of Vilma Kovács and Ferenczi, as well as Ferenczi and his patients.

Her thoughts on the invisibility of female genitals are reflected later in Kleinian theory. The negative fantasies about the male genital (soothed by reality), and her reflections on the visual presence of the "animal" instinct organ are remarkable, as well. She is remarkably open in recording her thoughts on sexuality, especially if we assume that she shared this with her husband. It is a question how much this is due to the nature of analysis itself and to the "good patient" who feels that she eventually has to associate everything with "that" as an ultimate origin and explanation of all other phenomena and symptoms.

Conclusions

Alice Bálint's diaries may serve as a rich primary resource for reconstructing her personal and professional development and dilemmas and the history of her most significant relationships. Their more general "yield" is that they provide a valuable insight into the social and political circumstances of early twentieth-century

Hungary and its opportunities and limitations for a (middle class, Jewish) woman with diverse talents, intellectual ambitions, and self-reflection.

Her joint work with Michael Bálint was rooted in and founded on an emotionally rich, equal, and consciously maintained good partnership and on the sharing of their thoughts about themselves and the outside world.

> She was interested in all sorts of things. We gradually parceled out analysis between us two, but it was not a formal thing. She was more interested in children and mother-child relationships, education and anthropology – that was her specialty – and my field was biology and psychosomatic medicine. But all the other interests of ours were joint.
>
> (Swerdloff, 2002, p. 390)

This is confirmed by the words of Michael Bálint in the introduction to his book *Primary Love and Psychoanalytic Technique*, where he emphasises that all of their work before 1939 grew out of joint thoughts:

> Starting with our shared enthusiasm for *Totem and Taboo* till her death in 1939, Alice and I read, studied, lived and worked together. All our ideas […] were enjoyed and then tested, probed and criticized in our endless discussions. Quite often it was just chance that decided which of us should publish a particular idea. Apart from psycho-analysis, Alice's main interests were anthropology and education, mine biology and medicine, and usually this factor decided who should write about the idea. We published only one paper jointly, although almost all of them could have been printed under our joint names.
>
> (M. Balint, 1952, p. 6)

It is questionable, though, whether and how Alice's contribution actually appears in these joint accomplishments. Especially since (according to her sister's observation) in this mutually fruitful collaboration it was often Alice who helped her husband organise and clarify his developing thoughts and their expression: "How important it always was that with her clear mind, Alice cleaned Misi's rambling thoughts and especially that she forced him to express himself in a direct, unambiguous and clear way".[33] As one may tend to search for the traces of Michael Bálint in Alice Bálint's works, it would also be worth rereading Michael Bálint through Alice.

Notes

1 For a more detailed biography, see Dupont, 1993, 2002a, 2002b, 2012, 2015; Harmat, 1994; Borgos, 2018.
2 In 1984 Michael Bálint's widow, Enid Bálint, bequeathed the biographical and professional documents of Michael, Alice, and Enid Bálint to psychoanalyst André Haynal. These documents were available in the Geneva medical university until 2014. André

Haynal's book (1988) largely relies on these materials. In 2014, the documents were transported to London, to the Archives of the British Psychoanalytical Society. The 13 notebooks, written in Hungarian from 1917 to 1929 (including a recipe booklet) are part of the (not very extensive) materials from or about Alice Bálint. For the information about the archive in Geneva I would like to thank Ágnes Földházi. I also thank the staff of the Archives of the British Psychoanalytical Society for their help in accessing the diaries. The English translations from the diaries and letters quoted in this paper are my own.

3   When talking about their joint pre-war lives, I will keep the original Hungarian first name, Mihály.

4   The brief biographies also mention anthropological studies, but I have not found any trace of those.

5   On the traces of the Balint couple during the Berlin period, see Vogelsänger, 2010.

6   The direct threat is indicated by Imre Hermann's recollections of the times after the fall of the Republic of Councils: "Bálint was forced to seek refuge at the university apartment of one of the professors from the atrocities of the Awakening Hungarians' commandos" (Hermann, 1982).

7   The list of lectures is found in a detailed Alice Bálint bibliography (possibly compiled by Michael Bálint). British Psychoanalytical Society Archives, London (Alice and Michael Bálint's bequest).

8   For its published version see Bálint, 1923.

9   Its title is "Az északamerikai Prärie törzsek társadalmi szervezete" [The social organisation of North-American Prairie tribes]. The thesis is in the possession of Jane Balint, whom I thank for sharing this information.

10 This was the public and free ambulatory psychotherapeutic clinic for adults and children, which was opened in 1931 and headed by Ferenczi and after his death by Mihály Bálint. On similar "free clinics" in Europe, see Danto, 2005.

11 Emmi: Emilia Bergmann, Mihály Bálint's sister.

12 Olgi: Olga Székely-Kovács, Alice's sister.

13 Juci: Judit Dormándi, the niece of Alice Bálint.

14 Letter from Alice Bálint to László Dormándi, 19 July, 1939. Freud Museum Archives, London, Sándor Ferenczi's bequest. (Emphasis in the original.)

15 Letter from Alice Bálint to László Dormándi, 11 August, 1939. Freud Museum Archives, London, Sándor Ferenczi's bequest.

16 She also wrote a review on Anna Freud's book (Bálint, 1930), while Anna Freud wrote a foreword to the American edition of The Psycho-Analysis of the Nursery (1954).

17 In German: Alice Bálint, Die Psychologie des Kinderzimmers. Zeitschrift für Psychoanalytische Pädagogik, 1932, 6: 49–130. In French: La vie intime de l'enfant, Gallimard, Paris, 1937. In Spanish: La vida intima del niño. Orientacion Integral Humana, Buenos Aires, 1939. In English: The Psycho-Analysis of the Nursery. Routledge & Kegan Paul, London, 1953; The Early Years of Life. Basic Books, New York, 1954. The German edition was republished in 1966, with the foreword of Michael Balint. Alice Bálint, Psychoanalyse der frühen Lebensjahre. Ernst Reinhardt Verlag, Munich, 1966.

18 Helene S. Arnstein, The early years of life. A psychoanalytic study. Child Study, 1954/ Winter: 35.

19 Joost A. M. Meerloo, A miracle re-enacted: The early years of life: A psychoanalytic study. By Alice Bálint, with a preface by Anna Freud. New York Times, 1954, November 14.

20 Az elfojtásról [On repression]; A felettesénről [On the superego] (1939).

21 Alice Bálint, Altruism, Aggression, and Reality Sense. Manuscript, BPS Archives. London, Alice and Michael Bálint's bequest, 1939.

22 BPS Archives, London, Alice and Michael Bálint's bequest.

23 Otto Fenichel, responding in a 1935 "Rundbrief" to a manuscript sent to him by Michael Bálint, criticises him and the neo-Freudian analysts over 15 pages for placing culture

beyond the instincts. He also reprehends Alice Bálint for her "one-sided culturalism". See Danto, 2005.

24 These papers were collected in a posthumous volume (Bálint, 1941).

25 For Lacan, Alice Balint heroically demonstrates "that maternal need displays exactly the same limits as any vital need, namely that when one no longer has anything to give, well one takes ... [in primitive society] when there is nothing left to eat you eat your child" (Lacan, 1988, p. 210) – a reading that pays tribute to Alice Balint for recognising the negative component of this relation. Using this as his template while remaining perhaps more conventionally within its terms, Michael Balint bases his account of primary love on the mother-infant relationship in terms of the satisfaction of a need to which the maternal object corresponds (Sklar, 2012, p. 1019).

26 Letter from Michael Bálint to László Dormándi, 5 June 1940 (in Dupont, 2002b, p. 363).

27 The notebooks are kept at the British Psychoanalytical Society Archives, London (Alice and Michael Bálint's bequest).

28 The Republic of Councils in Hungary was a short-lived (133 days) independent communist republic established in Hungary between March and August 1919.

29 Ferenczi's progressive views on women's issues and sexuality are represented, e.g. in his papers "Szexuális átmeneti fokozatokról" [On transitional stages of sexuality], *Gyógyászat*, 1906, *46*(19): 310–314; and "Az ejaculatio praecox jelentőségéről" [On the significance of ejaculatio praecox], In: Ferenczi: Lélekelemzés. Értekezések a pszichoanalízis köréből [Essays in psychoanalysis] (pp. 86–89). Budapest: Dick Manó, 1910.

30 On Ferenczi's mutual analysis with Elisabeth Severn (RN) see Ferenczi, 1995; Brennan, 2015; Rudnytsky, 2017.

31 Letter from Olga Székely-Kovács to Vilma Kovács, 4 December, 1939 (Judith Dupont's property).

32 In the original: "deutoltam" (= I interpreted), putting a Hungarian ending to the German verb.

33 Letter from Olga Székely-Kovács to Vilma Kovács, 7 February, 1940.

Bibliography

Bálint, A. (1923). Die mexikanische Kriegshieroglyphe atl-tlachinolli. *Imago*, *4*: 401–436.

Bálint, A. (1926). Der familienvater. *Imago*, *12*: 292–304.

Bálint, A. (1927a). A totemizmus [Totemism]. *Századunk*, *2*: 43–55.

Bálint, A. (1927b). Géza Róheim: Australian totemism. *Imago*, *13*: 541.

Bálint, A. (1928). Róheim Géza: Magyar néphit és népszokások [Hungarian folk beliefs and folk customes]. *Századunk*, *3*: 181–183.

Bálint, A. (1929). Őstársadalmi kutatások [Researches on ancient societies]. *Századunk*, *4*: 589–590.

Bálint, A. (1930). Anna Freud: Psychoanalyse für Pädagogen. *Századunk*, *5*: 174.

Bálint, A. (1931a). *A Gyermekszoba Pszichológiája* [*The Psychology of the Nursery*]. Budapest: Pantheon. New edition: Budapest: Kossuth, 1990. In English: *The Psycho-Analysis of the Nursery*. London: Routledge & Kegan Paul, 1953; *The Early Years of Life*. New York: Basic Books, 1954.

Bálint, A. (1931b). Tudós hittérítők harca [The struggle of scholar missionaries]. *Századunk*, *6*: 221–222.

Bálint, A. (1932). Tiltás és megengedés a nevelésben [Prohibition and permission in child-rearing]. In German: Versagen und Gewähren in der Erziehung. *Zeitschrift für Psychoanalytische Pädagogik*, 1936, *10*: 75–83.

Bálint, A. (1933a). A szeretet fejlődése és a valóságérzék [Development of the feeling of love and of the sense of reality]. In: S. Freud et al. (Eds.), *Lélekelemzési Tanulmányok* [*Studies in Psychoanalysis*] (pp. 30–40). Budapest: Párbeszéd & T-Twins, 1993.

Bálint, A. (1933b). Über eine besondere Form der infantilen Angst. *Zeitschrift für Psychoanalytische Pädagogik, 7*: 414–417.

Bálint, A. (1933c). Géza Róheim: A csurunga népe [The people of Csurunga]. *Imago, 19*: 564.

Bálint, A. (1935a). Die bedeutung des märches für das seelenleben des kindes. *Zeitschrift für Psychoanalytische Pädagogik, 9*(2): 113–116.

Bálint, A. (1935b). Géza Róheim: The riddle of the Sphinx: or, human origins. *Imago, 21*: 505.

Bálint, A. (1936a). Handhabung der übertragung auf grund der ferenczischen versuche. *Internationale Zeitschrift für Psychoanalyse, 22*: 47.

Bálint, A. (1936b). Szabad – nem szabad. Általános irányelvek [Allowed – not allowed. General guidelines]. In: Bálint (Eds.), *Anya és gyermek* [*Mother and Child*] (pp. 103–108).] Budapest: Párbeszéd, 1990.

Bálint, A. (1937). Die grundlagen unseres erziehungssystems. *Zeitschrift für Psychoanalytische Pädagogik, 11*: 98–101.

Bálint, A. (1939a). Liebe zur mutter und mutterliebe. *Internationale Zeitschrift für Psychoanalyse, 24*: 33–48. In English: Love for the mother and mother-love. *International Journal of Psycho-Analysis*, 1949, *30*: 251–259. In: Bálint, M. (1952). *Primary Love and Psychoanalytic Technique* (pp. 109–127). New York: da Capo Press, 1986.

Bálint, A. (1939b). Wulf Sachs: Black sun. *British Journal of Medical Psychology, 9*(2): 273.

Bálint, A. (1941). *Anya és Gyermek* [*Mother and Child*]. Budapest: Pantheon. New edition: Budapest: Párbeszéd, 1990.

Bálint, A., & Bálint, M. (1939). On transference and counter-transference. *International Journal of Psycho-Analysis, 20*: 223–230. Republished in Balint, M. (1952). *Primary Love and Psychoanalytic Technique* (pp. 213–220). New York: da Capo Press, 1986.

Balint, M. (1940). Alice Bálint. *The International Journal of Psycho-Analysis, 21*(1): 116.

Balint, M. (1952). *Primary Love and Psychoanalytic Technique*. New York: da Capo Press, 1986.

Balint, M. (1968). *The Basic Fault. Therapeutic Aspects of Regression*. London: Tavistock.

Borgos, A. (2019). Alice Bálint and her diaries: … This little fixation seems to remain... *Psychoanalysis and History, 21*(1): 23–52.

Borgos, A. (2021). *Women in the Budapest School of Psychoanalysis: Girls of Tomorrow*. Abingdon & New York: Routledge.

Brennan, B. W. (2015). Decoding Ferenczi's clinical diary: Biographical notes. *American Journal of Psychoanalysis, 75*(1): 5–18.

Danto, E. A. (2005). *Freud's Free Clinics. Psychoanalysis and Social Justice, 1918–1938.* New York: Columbia University Press.

Dupont, J. (1993). A Kovács–Bálint dinasztia [The Kovács–Bálint dynasty]. In: V. Kovács (Ed.), *Fortunatus Öröksége* [*The Heritage of Fortunatus*] (pp. 7–12). Budapest: Párbeszéd Könyvek.

Dupont, J. (2002a). L'exil avant l'exil. Michael et Alice Bálint. *Topique, 80*(3): 95–101.

Dupont, J. (2002b). Excerpts of the correspondence of Michael and Alice Balint with Olga, Ladislas, and Judith Dormandi. *American Journal of Psychoanalysis, 62*(4): 359–381.

Dupont, J. (2012). Alice Bálint, a short but productive life. In: J. Szekacs-Weisz & T. Keve (Eds.), *Ferenczi for Our Time* (pp. 69–75). London: Karnac.

Dupont, J. (2015). *Au Fil du Temps ... Un Itinéraire Analytique*. Paris: Campagne/Première.

Ferenczi, S. (1995). *The Clinical Diary of Sándor Ferenczi*. J. Dupont (Ed.). Cambridge, MA: Harvard University Press.

Forrester, J. (1997). Casualties of truth. In: J. Forrester (Ed.), *Dispatches from the Freud Wars. Psychoanalysis and Its Passions* (pp. 47–106). Cambridge, MA: Harvard University Press.

Freud, S., & Ferenczi, S. (2000). *The Correspondence of Sigmund Freud and Sándor Ferenczi, Volume 3, 1920–1933*. E. Falzeder, E. Brabant, & P. Giampieri-Deutsch (Eds.). Cambridge, MA: Belknap Press, Harvard University Press.

Giefer, M. (Ed.) (2007). *Korrespondenzblatt der Internationalen Psychoanalytischen Vereinigung 1910–1941*. Available from: http://luzifer-amor.de/fileadmin/bilder/Downloads/korrespondenzblatt_1910-1941.pdf

Hajdu, L. (1931). Bálint Alice: A gyermekszoba pszichológiája [The psychology of the nursery]. *Magyar Psychologiai Szemle, 4*(3–4): 95–96.

Harmat, P. (1994). *Freud, Ferenczi és a Magyarországi Pszichoanalízis [Freud, Ferenczi, and the Hungarian Psychoanalysis]*. Budapest: Bethlen Gábor Könyvkiadó.

Haynal, A. (1988). *The Technique at Issue. Controversies in Psychoanalysis from Freud and Ferenczi to Michael Balint*. London: Karnac.

Hermann, A. (1931). Bálint Alice: A gyermekszoba pszichológiája [The psychology of the nursery]. *Századunk, 5*: 457–458.

Hermann, I. (1982). Souvenirs de Michael Balint (1896–1971). *Le Coq-Héron, 85*: 45–49.

Hoffer, W. (1940). Alice Bálint. *Internationale Zeitschrift für Psychoanalyse und Imago, 25*(1): 102–103.

Illés, E. (1931). Egy pszichoanalitikai tanulmány. Bálint Alice: A gyermekszoba pszichológiája [A psychoanalytical study. Alice Bálint: The psychology of the nursery]. *Nyugat, 24*(24): 670–673.

Kovács, V. (1936). Training and control-analysis. *International Journal of Psycho-Analysis, 17*: 346–354.

Lacan, J. (1988). *The Seminars of Jacques Lacan, book 2* [1954–55]. Cambridge, MA: Cambridge University Press.

Mészáros, J. (2014). *Ferenczi and Beyond: Exile of the Budapest School and Solidarity in the Psychoanalytic Movement during the Nazi Years*. London: Karnac.

Rudnytsky, P. L. (2017). Introduction. The other side of the story: Severn on Ferenczi and mutual analysis. In: E. Severn (Ed.), *Discovery of the Self. A Study in Psychological Cure* (pp. 1–20). London: Routledge.

Sklar, J. (2012). Regression and new beginnings: Michael, Alice and Enid Balint and the circulation of ideas. *International Journal of Psychoanalysis, 93*: 1017–1034.

Swerdloff, B. (2002). An interview with Michael Balint [1965]. *American Journal of Psychoanalysis, 62*(4): 383–413.

Vajda, Z. (1995). Bálint Alice: A gyermekszoba a legtitokzatosabb dolgok egyike [Alice Bálint: Nursery is one of the most mysterious things]. In: J. Vajda (Ed.), *A Pszichoanalízis Budapesti Iskolája és a Nevelés [The Budapest School of Psychoanalysis and Education]* (pp. 47–62). Budapest: Sík Kiadó.

Vogelsänger, P. (2010). Alice und Michael Bálint in Berlin (1921–1924). *Luzifer-Amor, 23*(45): 169–178.

Part 2

Creativity and primary love

Chapter 5

Therapy, object relations and primary narcissism

Metapsychology in the early works of Michael Bálint

Antal Bókay

Michael Bálint has regularly been mentioned in the company of Winnicott and Fairbairn as one of the founders and developers of object relations theory. Such theories "may be defined as those that place the internalization, structuralization, and clinical reactivation (in the transference and countertransference) of the earliest dyadic object relations at the center of their motivational (structural, clinical, and genetic and developmental) formulations" (Kernberg, 2005, p. 1175). Bálint, following the Ferenczi tradition, worked in this frame and developed a coherent theoretical background that unfortunately has not been followed (or barely mentioned) by later researchers. Bálint has also been surrounded by silence concerning the metapsychological position that was developed in his first book, *Primary Love and Psycho-Analytic Technique*. A telling fact is that Kernberg in his excellent encyclopaedia entry quoted above did not mention Bálint's name at all when presenting object relations theory. Bálint did not fare better with his contemporary fellow psychoanalysts, as very few references can be found to Bálint's work in the publications of the like-minded leading analysts of the period. Indeed, there is no sign of Bálint's influence in Fairbairn and there is only one short reference on him in the works of Melanie Klein. With this background, it is surprising that a major French contemporary, Jacques Lacan, paid considerable attention to Bálint's 1953 book in three sessions of his 1953–1954 seminar (1975, pp. 203–233). The title of the chapter in the book published later was "Michael Balint's Blind Alleys", and it offered a fairly detailed, absolutely friendly but also critical interpretation of Bálint's psychoanalytic position. Lacan was interested in British psychoanalysis and travelled to Britain to meet some key figures. Lacan's discussion of Bálint, however, may help in elaborating the special character of Bálint's metapsychology.

The Lacan seminar starts with a presentation by Wladimir Granoff, a student of Lacan,[1] the full text of which can be found in this volume. Following this, Lacan presents his related comments. Lacan sensed something congruent with his intentions in Bálint's work: "I wanted to seek the support of someone who is, in lots of ways, close, even congenial to us", he said (1975, p. 203). He rightly places Bálint in the "Hungarian tradition which blossomed around the questions raised by the relation of analysand and analyst, conceived of as an interhuman situation involving persons and, as a consequence, implying certain reciprocity" (p. 209). A resolute definition that refers to

DOI: 10.4324/9781003309826-9

the idea of the primacy of the therapeutic position was an important starting point to explain the background of Bálint's theoretical and metapsychological thinking. Concerning this "Hungarian tradition", Lacan notes that "Around about 1930,[2] the personal influence of Ferenczi came to an end. From then on, it is that of his pupils which makes itself felt" (p. 209). It seems quite consistent for the present reader of Lacan's seminar that while he develops his position and suggests certain crucial parallels with Bálint's ideas he fails to take Ferenczi into serious consideration. Lacan does mention Ferenczi, but he would not detail Ferenczi's deep and more complicated position, or the general psychoanalytic attitude that was central to the circle that Bálint came from. Bálint was the most important follower of Ferenczi but it is also clear that he, in a sense, "civilised" the Ferenczi tradition by making these ideas become more acceptable in his context (the context of Ernest Jones, Anna Freud, Melanie Klein, and so on).

In any case, Lacan and Granoff, who presented Bálint's book[3] at the seminar session, offered a proper summary of Bálint's general psychoanalytic position. The most important connected features of Lacan's concerns are the following:

- Relationality, and a therapy-oriented, object relational foundation.
- The idea of "two-body psychoanalysis" (intersubjectivity) instead of the "one-body analysis" of the earlier period.
- The concept of love.
- The concept of character as a constructive and limiting ego-structure.
- The idea of a difference between passive and active object love and the criticism of primary narcissism.
- The idea of pregenital and genital love.

Therapy-based theory of psychoanalysis

Bálint's central thesis, from which his whole theoretical approach was born, was the idea that psychoanalytic theory and therapy had been separated. The theory had not developed, while therapy and the technique itself opened up completely new avenues in recent psychoanalysis. This was not a new position, and its source was also be traced back to Budapest. As early as 1922, in a book written together with Otto Rank (*Entwicklungsziele der Psychoanalyse*), Ferenczi (1924) emphasised the urgent need for change in psychoanalytic thinking towards a therapy-oriented attitude, where theory would be derived from therapy, and not vice versa. The understanding of therapy as an existential foundation of psychoanalysis was crucial in the writings of the late Ferenczi. The 1933 "Confusion of tongues" paper was an important example of this, while the most radical writing representing the theme was the unpublished (at the time) *Clinical Diary*.[4]

Although Bálint mentioned Ferenczi in his book, he tried to elaborate a new, "Budapest" approach based more on his ideas and the contemporary work of Alice Bálint and Imre Hermann. In his sketch of psychoanalytic history, he mentioned several phases of therapy/theory relation starting from the Breuer-Freud hysteria book, up to contemporary methods concentrating on the analysis of transference.

In the Twenties, following Freud's new publications two approaches were present. The first was a metapsychologically "dynamic" one that "laid more emphasis on 'content', was more concerned with the 'repressed' and the 'unconscious', which meant roughly the inhibited, repressed sexual gratifications, and was aiming at achieving a breakthrough of such repressed instincts" (Bálint, 1953, p. 223). This was the classical "Viennese" position. The other one, the so-called topic (or today, topographical) approach, "laid more emphasis on the study of the habitual defensive mechanisms, which roughly meant the developmental faults in the mental structure, especially the relative strengths of the ego and the super-ego" (p. 223). This was the approach of American ego-psychology. Both the dynamic and the topical approaches, however, were "concerned only with the individual" (p. 223).

A third approach, the one Bálint wanted to follow, was aimed "first and foremost, at understanding and interpreting every detail of the patient's transference *in terms of object-relations*" (p. 225). The most important factor of this was the patient's transference "expressing both general – lasting – sentiments towards the world, and his present – passing – attitudes towards a particular object – his analyst". Transference is "regarded as phenomena of some kind of object-relation – often of a primitive type – which has been revived in (or perhaps by) the psycho-analytical situation" (pp. 224–225). With this, the whole of the therapeutic process was recreated in terms of object relations. According to Bálint, "Our technique was invented and has been mainly developed when working with pathological forms such as hysteria, sexual disorders, character neurosis, all of which have strongly cathected objectrelations" while the theory had been "mainly based on the study of pathological forms which use internalization extensively and have only weakly cathected object-relations" (p. 227).

The core of analytic therapy was the process of transference, a process that brought in repeated narratives and memories of the past: most importantly, the past of the childhood of the patient. In his 1949 paper "Changing Therapeutical Aims and Techniques in Psychoanalysis" Bálint (1951) addresses a Ferenczi-oriented problem, the role of the psychoanalyst's countertransference: "The most important field of investigation for this coming theory must be the *analyst's behaviour in the psychoanalytic situation*, or, as I prefer to phrase it, the analyst's contribution to the creating and maintaining of the psycho-analytic situation" (p. 231). The essentially therapy-oriented (and transference/countertransference) approach was, of course, clearly present in Ferenczi's psychoanalytic position as an important difference from the classical Freudian understanding of therapy and its metapsychological consequences, as well as its theory. It is interesting, however, that Bálint's reference was not Ferenczi, but the transference problem of the Dora case, adding to it the fact that

The *analyst's relation to his patient is libidinous in the same way*; even if we call it 'counter-transference', or 'correct analytical behaviour', or 'proper handling of the transference situation', or 'detached friendly understanding and well-timed interpreting'; this relation, too, *is* libidinous.

(p. 231)

The libidinous transferential and countertransferential therapeutic relation can find its theoretical, developmental parallel in the description of the mother–child relationship in Alice Bálint's papers.

It is also true, however, that important differences could be seen between the positions of Bálint and that of his master, Ferenczi. Bálint believed that the outcome of object relational therapy could result in a fundamental reshaping of the transference, a return to the earliest object relational processes, and through this, a kind of healing could be achieved. This return was cited by Bálint as a "new beginning":

> I have been able regularly to observe that in the final phase of the treatment patients begin to give expression to long-forgotten, infantile, instinctual wishes, and to demand their gratification from their environment (…) I have called this phenomenon the 'New Beginning'.
>
> (pp. 191–192)

The "new beginning" refers to the possibility of reaching back, through transference repetitions in the therapy, to the early childhood memories, the so-called period of pregenital love. By repeating these stories of love or hate relations with the analyst, a new, healthier beginning in the patient's life could be achieved. Such a strongly desired return did not seem possible for Ferenczi, who in his later papers emphasised the countertransferential component of the therapeutical process. He realised that in this process, instead of repressed memories more direct traumatic traces were lurking in the background of the patient's mind. Ferenczi did not talk about "new beginning" but talked – in a much more radical way – about "professional hypocrisy", not as an accidental failure but as an unavoidable, problematic position of the analyst, as an obstacle that cannot be overcome. The essential relationality of the therapy that was called "two-body psychoanalysis" by Bálint was, in Ferenczi's case, the otherwise impossible "mutual analysis". Bálint also allowed some freedom for the patient to require small, childish favours, love gestures from the analyst, but these were very far from the radical therapeutic relation of Ferenczi's mutual analysis. Lacan did not mention Ferenczi, but his concept of "intersubjectivity", the idea of an imaginary, pregenital introjection of the other's desire, is much closer to Ferenczi than to Bálint. Lacan (1975) said that Bálint

> Is completely lacking the conceptual apparatus necessary for introducing the intersubjective relation, he is led to speak of two-body psychology. He thinks that is the way out of the one-body psychology. But it is clear that the two-body psychology is still a relation of object to object.
>
> (p. 205)

Intersubjectivity was not an object relational idea but referred to a traumatic presence in the patient, a primary narcissistic (imaginary) realisation of the other. Lacan talked about "contrary to Balint's perspective (…) a radical intersubjectivity, with the subject's total acceptance of the other subject" (p. 217). And he admits, "there has to be intersubjectivity at the beginning", there has to be "an original intersubjectivity" that operates through *"Nachträglichkeit"* (p. 217) whereby the "'original' state is determined by later events in the subject's life".

Metapsychology based on love

The other major task that Bálint tried to accomplish was the development of a proper theoretical, metapsychological background, one that could be adequate to the new, object relations-based therapy. The central, essentially relational concept, which, in a general way, covers the whole field, is the fundamental idea of *love*. Lacan was right in stating in his seminar that "Bálint's conception is centred on a theory of love, which is more than just a normative or moralizing feature" (p. 204). This love concept was much more essential and special than the usual idea of love. The central focus on love activity meant a crucial change in the metapsychology; it was the realisation of the relational nature of individual existence, a radical reshaping of the classical aim-oriented drive concept. Again, Lacan's concept of "desire" was in a sense on the same plane, but in parallel. Bálint, of course, referred back to Freud, while modifying the original Freudian emphasis. Bálint also mentioned Freud's 1905 *Three Essays on the Theory of Sexuality*, according to which "the two developments – that of sexual aims and that of sexual object-relations – run parallel to each other" (Bálint, 1951, p. 49). This double aspect, according to Bálint, was not followed later, as the theory of drive and sexuality developed in psychoanalysis concentrated predominantly on the sexual aims, and "the chief stress was laid on the changing instinctual aims and their respective sources, that is to say, on the biological aspect" (p. 49). This attitude resulted in a kind of developmental ladder (presented by Karl Abraham and also accepted by Ferenczi and Freud), with the steps of biologically defined, pre-Oedipal-Oedipal developmental phases,[5] even if "it raises considerable difficulties if one tries to date Abraham's phases according to years of life" (Bálint, 1953 p. 51). Bálint's critical suggestion against this logic was that the two developments, the sexual aims and the sexual objects, should be elaborated equally. Bálint himself, however, went one step further, developing his theory based primarily on the second, on the "object" aspect of the double development: "One problem, then, is the development of object-relations, i.e. the development of love. (...) The other allegedly parallel problem, the development of sexual aims (...) I should like to deal with on another occasion" (pp. 51–52). In fact, in his theory, Bálint abandoned the earlier developmental logic of changing sexual aims and completely substituted it with a series of object relational structures, as well as developmental constructs of love in the life of the human being. Instead of a long series of oral, anal, phallic, and genital sources and aims in the development of the human being, he suggested and investigated only two essential love structures, the "pregenital" and the "genital organizations" with both of them depending on object relations.

This rather powerful foundational position of love comes from the Budapest school, primarily from Ferenczi. In a non-professional interview given by him to a major Hungarian daily paper in 1928, Ferenczi defined the idea of love as forming a major difference between his and Freud's attitudes. He argued that: "Freud, in his works, dealt with the instinctual processes in the first years of human life. I built this system on when I investigated the act of love as the definitive moment of human life" (1928, p. 53). Ferenczi believed that for Freud, the central components that constituted the human psyche were the repressed representations of instinctual strivings through which the constructs and layers of the unconscious mind were built up and affected the life and actions of the individual. For Freud, in the "Viennese position", the most important function of therapy was recollection, the reconstruction of repressed thoughts, a process through which the ego could take over the place of the id. Ferenczi interpreted the unconscious as the construct of remnants of relational traces, mostly infantile and traumatic events, images, and narratives; structures that were always operative in the present moment of life even if they were repressed, negated, or forgotten. The unconscious was imagined by Ferenczi as a traumatised relational existence, a constant, repressed child hidden in the adult, in the psyche of the often pathological grown-up. In this situation, repetition was much more frequent and active than recollection, and because of the fully relational nature of existence, transference, and countertransference had an equal role.

Love structures: pregenital and genital love

The most important feature and the result of Bálint's (and more importantly, that of Alice Bálint's) psychoanalytic theorisation in the Thirties and Forties was the systematic delineation of the components of this self-creative love relation, the presence of childish, pregenital relationality in the genital adult. Bálint named two sources: one was his own therapeutic experience, the other was the contemporary psychoanalytic understanding of infantile object relations.

As of the therapeutic experiences (connected by Bálint to Freud and Ferenczi), he wrote about "observable, monotonously recurring features of the analytical situation [that] could be traced back to early infantile experiences", where "much of the early infantile mental processes can be inferred from these easily verifiable observations" (Bálint, 1953, p. 96). These experiences all signified a change in the behaviour of the analysands, as they required a change in the behaviour and reactions of their analysts; it was a kind of request for more narcissistic, one-sided love. According to Bálint, these demands were all coming from very early childish experiences, and if they were satisfied by the analyst, they triggered a positive therapeutic change. Bálint talked about "two essential qualities of these wishes": "Firstly *without exception, they are directed towards an object*, and secondly *they never go beyond the level of fore-pleasure*" (p. 98). An important character of these processes was that the patients "brought these ever-recurring forms of reactions from their early infantile stages" (p. 98). Such therapeutic events were the sources of the so-called new beginning, Bálint's major therapeutic idea: "In the end phase of such treatment, which I have called the 'new beginning', the nature of this first object-relation is expressed quite clearly. It is almost entirely passive" (p. 61). This was the first major concept brought in from Ferenczi: "passive object love". And it was understood as the very first object relation too, where "the person in question does not love, but wishes to be loved" (p. 61).

The other source of Bálint's theory was child analysis (or simply the reconstruction of the infantile position from an object relational perspective). Here, Imre Hermann's anthropological studies and, more importantly, Alice Bálint's child analytical and pedagogical research, were additional sources. It is quite telling that Bálint positions his (Budapest based) 1935 theory in opposition to the so-called Londoners (Melanie Klein and her followers) and the classical, ego-psychologically oriented Viennese theory (p. 61), while in the later paper of 1949, he tried to connect (and in a sense, convert) his theory into Melanie Klein's system.

In this, the central ambition of Bálint was to rewrite the classical (more aim-centred) Freudian developmental structure into an object relational conception. The major new direction was the criticism and, in particular, the refusal of primary narcissism as the earliest phase of human life, forming after autoerotism. This was not an easy task, as both Freud and Ferenczi worked with the concept and phenomenon of primary narcissism. Little wonder that Bálint could not give proper definitions of the key terms that he needed in building up his alternative system.

Regarding narcissism, Bálint quotes two different positions from Freud's 1914 "On Narcissism: An Introduction". According to the first one, "only the auto-erotic instincts are primary" and Bálint quotes Freud: "so there must be something added to auto-erotism – some new operation in the mind – so that narcissism may come into being" (p. 64). This position was accepted by Bálint and, according to him, also by Alice Bálint. The important move was that Bálint presumed that this something else that could be found before narcissism had the quality of an object relation,[6] that narcissism itself was secondary, not an original base, and that "libidinal narcissism must develop during life" (p. 64). The infant's primary object relation was to the mother, an object of early infantile love; but unavoidable traumas, lack of the outside world, and repeated absences of the mother pressed the infant to turn back to himself, to self-love. The other route is to turn towards the outside world, to love the world. This act was "active object-love", that is, "We love and gratify our partner, to be loved and gratified by him in return" (p. 66). It seems that Bálint found some essentially ambivalent, heterogeneous nature in early passive object love, in "pregenital love", which was the point where he introduced the concepts of tenderness and passion. Active object love, genital love, however, "originates in passive object love" (p. 66). This meant that the traces of the infant, the remnants of a very early passive object love strategy are left hidden in every human being, even after growing up. Passive object love is expressed in two possible styles, tenderness, and passion. Bálint, surprisingly, built his conception here not on Ferenczi (who could have been the major source of the tenderness/passion problem), but on Freud's essay entitled "On the Universal Tendency to Debasement in the Sphere of Love" (1912), and the tenderness-passion pair became the routes of the general "sense of reality" process, the process where the child met the boundaries of the outside world. The later Ferenczi, first of all in the "Confusion of tongues" paper (1933), defined passion as a traumatic experience, a kind of unreadability of the intrusion of the world. For Ferenczi passion was, in a sense, countertransferential, an attack coming from the outside world, an unreadable expression, confusion of tongue, or (as Laplanche later suggested), an enigmatic signifier. For Bálint "Tenderness is an archaic quality which appears in conjunction with the ancient self-preserving instinct, and has no further aim, but this quiet, not passionate gratification" (1953, p. 131). Passion, on the other hand, developed in the child through a different type of object relation, an active object love, and genital love was finally understood as the mixture of passive and active object love.

Finally, and this was the place where Bálint's position could be debated, he added some other processes that operate in primary, passive object love. These are like projections and introjections, as well as identification.[7] The question was, however, whether the outside world – the object world – became subjective through these processes. Passive object love took place only in the inner world, which, in a sense, can be taken as an objectless object relation, a construct that was similar (to use the term that Bálint refused) to primary narcissism. To summarise, I believe Bálint's psychoanalytic theory, shaped in his first book, was outstanding, but it was not fully understood or adequately received in contemporary psychoanalysis. It seems that only Jacques Lacan sensed its importance. The crucial idea and task that still is left to be developed in our time is the nature of "relation" in the "two-person" therapy and this term's position in psychoanalytic theory.

Notes

1 The existing English publication of the seminar does not contain this, only Lacan's comments, but the full text is published in this volume.
2 This date is clearly too early. Ferenczi maintained his personal influence in Hungarian psychoanalysis and with Bálint too until 1933. Four of Bálint's papers were written in his lifetime.
3 This presentation might have been the cause and beginning of Granoff's connection to the Ferenczi tradition. Later he published books and papers on Ferenczi and the Budapest school, maintained a connection to Bálint, and he even went to him for supervision.
4 It is important to note that Lacan read the "Confusion of the Tongues" paper of Ferenczi, but he did not know the *Clinical Diary*. Michael Bálint and Alice Bálint, however, as the keepers of Ferenczi's manuscripts, knew the *Diary*. Bálint prepared it for publication, delayed for many years.
5 Lacan seriously criticised this same aspect (naming Ferenczi and Abraham) in his seminar. See: Lacan, 1975, p. 127.
6 It is interesting that the same quote serves Julia Kristeva, in her book on love as the major point of primary narcissism itself: *Tales of Love*, 1984, p. 22.
7 Alice Bálint had an excellent paper on idenfication (1943, pp. 97–107).

Bibliography

Bálint, A. (1943). Identification. *International Journal of Psycho-Analysis*, *24*: 97–107.
Bálint, M. (1951). *Primary Love and Psycho-Analytic Technique*. London: Hogarth.

Ferenczi, S. (1928, December 25). A szerelem végső titkai – Beszélgetés dr. Ferenczi Sándorral. *Pesti Napló*, p. 53.

Ferenczi, S. (1932). *The Clinical Diary of Sandor Ferenczi*. J. Dupont (Ed.). Cambridge, MA: Harvard University Press, 1988.

Ferenczi, S. (1933). The confusion of tongues between adults and the child. In: M. Bálint (Ed.), *Final Contributions to the Problems and Methods of Psycho-Analysis* (trans: Mosbacher, E., pp. 156–167). London: Karnac, 1994.

Ferenczi, S., & Rank, O. (1924). *The Development of Psychoanalysis* (trans: Newton, C.). New York: Nervous and Mental Disease Publishing Company.

Freud, S. (1905). *Three Essays on the Theory of Sexuality*. S. E., 7. London: Hogarth.

Freud, S. (1912). *On the Universal Tendency to Debasement in the Sphere of Love*. S. E., 11. London: Hogarth.

Freud, S. (1914). *On Narcissism: An Introduction*. S. E., 14: 77. London: Hogarth.

Kernberg, O. F. (2005). Object relations theory. In: A. de Mijolla (Ed.), *International Dictionary of Psychoanalysis, Vol. II* (p. 1175). Farmington Hills, MI: Thompson Gale.

Kristeva, J. (1984). *Tales of Love*. New York: Columbia University Press.

Lacan, J. (1975). *The Seminar. Book I: Freud's Papers on Technique (1953–1954)*. J.-A. Miller (Ed.) (trans: Forrester, J.). Cambridge, MA: Cambridge University Press, 1988.

Chapter 6

Primary harmony

Baby observation on infantile hopes and quiet states

Julianna Vamos

In the last 30 years, numerous clinical and scientific studies have demonstrated that Michael Balint's sharp observations, descriptions, and analytical reflections were pertinent to psychic reality – especially for very early human development (Eros, Lenard, & Bokay, 2008). The title of this chapter hints at which part of Michael Balint's work inspires me, based on my own clinical experience. I have had the opportunity to work in two clinical environments, each of which was famous for its innovative practices. The first was in a residential nursery in Paris, related to one in Budapest known as the Pikler Loczy Institute. In a recent article (Vamos, 2015) I described the manner in which this institution and its great humanitarian ethos grew out of the Budapest school of psychoanalysis. The second and current institution, where I have practised for almost 20 years, is the maternity clinic, Des Bluets, in Paris, inspired by the methods of F. Lamaze. Both places give us a lot to reflect on: primary encounters, a beneficial environment, and the wellbeing of the family of a new baby. Observation, as a form of listening attentively to the baby, is an organic part of clinical work and it is both central and transformative. For me it is supported by a double model that I have synthesised in my practice: that of the British Esther Bick and her followers Geneviève and Michel Haag in France, and that of the Hungarian paediatrician, Emmi Pikler.

Michael Balint was an empirical, pragmatic man, who primarily observed, then thought and theorised in consequence. He wrote in 1951:

> Our theory values what is noisy as highly important, and considers what is si-lent as unimportant. It is even possible that silent signs remain unnoticed by the theory, moreover it is certain that they are hardly even mentioned which then leads to the distorted picture of a highly greedy infant.

> (p. 143)

Since the 1950s, observation models have changed. Balint noted, "The quiet state is a primary one, and it deserves study in its own" (p. 114), but there is still a lack of follow-up in the literature. In his contribution for the 22nd international psychoanalytic congress in Edinburgh in 1962, "The Theory of the Parent-Infant Relationship – Contributions to Discussion", he proposed, "According to my idea,

DOI: 10.4324/9781003309826-10

the first relationship, which I call the primary relationship, or primary love, is the harmonious relationship to an undifferentiated environment".

It is on these lines of harmony and tranquillity that my friend Antonella Bussanich and I came up with the idea of an artist's residency within the maternity clinic, Des Bluets. We wished to poeticise the everyday experience of the extraordinary: giving birth and being born; first encounters and the creation of the triad.

Infantile hopes

The Maternité Des Bluets, with its 3,000 births per year, was famous from the 1950s onwards for constantly renewing the methods of prenatal preparation. Faithful to its innovative spirit, facing contemporary challenges (such as medically assisted procreation, the accompaniment of same-sex parents, single parents, couples of varying ethnic backgrounds) obstetricians and midwives were very welcoming not only of my prenatal consultations but also of my post-natal propositions, to raise awareness of the importance of this primal time, giving young families support for the first days, weeks, and months.

In the maternity clinic, I make room visits during the first days, and when the family leaves, I hold twice weekly consultations and run two baby-parent groups. One of these groups functions until the end of the first year.

In his 1951 article on "Love and Hate", Balint noted two relevant considerations that I would like to reflect on. One is on the quality of the object, so the baby can take the *object for granted*. The other is more of a contemporary topic: on *co-operation* from the beginning between the baby and adult. In today's challenging times, the construction of co-operation carries huge importance and is vital on many different levels: from the very intimate personal level to the social one and beyond.

So what are the conditions that permit the object to be "taken for granted" in a "harmonious interpenetrating mix up", as Balint put it in *The Basic Fault* (1968)?

Object taken for granted

What are the expectations of a new or a few-weeks-old baby, or as Balint puts it, what are his hopes? Which is the environment and what are the conditions that permit the attunement (Stern, 1985) and primary intersubjective exchange (Trevarthen, 2015) between mother and baby? How do they actively adapt to each other so that the mother can meet the baby's need? At birth, in addition to the mother's psychic receptivity, some basic expectations of external reality also need to be met, so that as the baby changes his ecological environment, the transition to extrauterine life can start in positive conditions. A major effort is made not to separate mother and baby so that the continuity of his intrauterine sensory world can be better preserved. His mother's solicitude is triggered if skin-to-skin proximity with her is possible. As a concept, solicitude implies a strong consideration of the other, of the baby's expression, that what is coming from him (or her) is to be taken seriously:

in other words, this is the welcoming of the baby, helping his wellbeing. Optimally, it is composed of the following: sensory continuity, creating landmarks from the intrauterine sensory universe conditions to the neonatal sensory expectations; *le regard*, the baby's attachment to parents is a primary need, first from the gaze to the nipple, creating an emotional exchange in his eyes; the rhythm, relating to the attunement to the baby's rhythm, exiting out of our fast-moving efficient society to get into a psychic gestational rhythm.

If these elements can be collected then the harmonious "interpenetrating mix up" comes into existence and keeps on being elaborated. In my groups, I observe couples who experience calm, relaxed moments with their baby. Balint in this article talks about reality testing and the importance of protecting the baby from too much frustration. If both protagonists, baby and mother, have enough pleasure and experience the "harmonious fusion", then things can go well, even if life is complex. Then, parents can introduce the reality principle … in the right dosage. But that is an art. If reality hits hard, support needs to be provided.

Here follows a clinical example of a consultation where the mother is unable to receive the baby, and unable to mirror the baby in her eyes, or show care and attention because of tragic circumstances – a case where the "harmonious interpenetrating mix up" after birth has failed.

Constance: a clinical vignette

Mother consults because the baby refuses to look at her.

This is the second consultation with Mrs B and Constance.

A few days before, Mrs B, pale, exhausted, came with her two-week-old baby, who was sleeping in a sling. I learned then that Mrs B's mother had died a week before the birth of Constance. The funeral took place on the very day of the birth of her daughter. She said that she "completely missed the pregnancy", and then the birth was overshadowed by the funeral. She adds: "Everyone acted as if my mother's death didn't exist. How can people forget about my mother's death just because it was also the day of the birth?!" I give Mrs B a new appointment four days later, hoping to find her baby awake when she comes.

The consultation

The mother is a little less inexpressive and numb from pain and tiredness.

Constance, three weeks old, is awake. Her mother unwraps her from the scarf and puts her on her lap facing me. Constance seems relaxed and calm, as if slowly waking up from a nap. Mother says that they are still not connecting much.

I get up from my seat. I approach them and make a first attempt to communicate with the baby: "Constance, Constance", I am whispering, in a very soft tone; I introduce myself to her, but she squints and slowly closes her eyes. She doesn't want to make any contact, just as the mother described how it is with her. She looks up to the sky and turns her head away. I go back to my seat. Mother is telling me about how she tries to reassure Constance that when she is sad, it is not related to her … She breastfeeds a lot and the baby cries relentlessly, which was not at all the case for her first child.

I make a second attempt to capture Constance's attention: I approach and stand in front of her, like the first time. "Constance, Constance! Hello, hello can we talk a little?" Waiting a little, I call her again. Closed eyes again. She ignores me. As soon as I leave her field of vision, she opens her eyes. I feel strongly that her wishes, as far as I can discern them, have to be respected. And as soon as I get back to my seat, Constance opens her eyes widely.

I share my hypothesis with the mother that:

> In effect, Constance modulates the distance with her gaze. It's her way of telling us that it's a little too much for her to be in contact with me when I am so frontal. It is like dealing with the very intense and complex dynamics at home. I find that she is using a very clever language.

I then make a third attempt, but this time I do not place myself in her field of vision: "I would like to have a contact with you, Constance. If you wish, and when you are ready. Can you turn your head towards me and look at me, then?" This is when Constance turns her head slowly towards me and stares at me intensely. The interpenetrating, sharp, and curious eyes, the open and confident look, are moving and amaze me. "Thank you very much for trusting me, Constance, and looking at me. You are safe here with us, in your mother's arms. We will try to figure out how to make things a little lighter". Then Constance lifts her head towards her mother and stares at her tenderly. We read a lot of love in her eyes. "It's the first time she's looked at me like that!" mother says, astonished.

"Yes, she felt the available space here. That you are not alone with mourning". Constance turns again towards me. I talk to her very softly and then I go back to sit down.

Mrs B tells me of some particular moments, like when she was breastfeeding Constance and had the idea to call her mother … "I thought I was going to call Mom..." she says. Mrs B is then overcome by a strong emotion that she tries to contain. This is when Constance looks up at her mother intensely, with questioning eyes. I get closer again and say: "There's something going on for you, you're trying to comfort mummy, is that it? Is it right? You know you can be a baby here, without worry... I take care of mummy", and then I go back to sit down.

From the initial refusal to this intense communication, there needed to be a therapeutic move. Baby and mother got back in touch, felt more relaxed, and were able to open up. From a position of distance and absence in her relationship, the baby was trying to be her mother's therapist. This was not that harmonious start that we and Michael Balint dreamt about. But it was a step towards it. It could become a new beginning at the age of three weeks instead of later. Later, much later.

The partnership

There is one more element that a baby could expect and hope for. It is the respect of his or her primary competences: motor, relational, and nutritional. In the last 30 years, there have been great advances in this field (through Stern, Trevarthen, Brazelton, and others). The Hungarian Emmi Pikler has put a lot of importance on self-initiated free motor development, and babies' activity and active participation. Balint does not formulate this but when he does talk about co-operating partnerships, there is the active presence of the child.

In these first weeks with a new baby, how does co-operation start off? What is the beginning of the construction of co-operation after birth?

Being aware of the baby's initiative, competences, his freedom to move, inviting him to participate in body care, doing with him what concerns him, are all things that start to establish the basis of future mutual satisfaction. Becoming a partner and a co-operative partner makes sense. It is essential to create the material, environmental, and organisational conditions so that this freedom of movement is unimpeded and safe, so that the creation of collaboration can take place. But this is not enough. This works if, and only if, the adult is motivated by an attitude in which the recognition of the baby's competence is integrated into his way of being, and the collaboration with the baby is taken seriously. The adult thus trained becomes attentive to the baby's initiatives (later attentive to his teasing, counter-proposals, etc.), but also to the slightest defensive expression in his behaviour, his body tensions, for instance, which are understood as a defensive language of his physical and/or psychological discomfort. The baby's physical relaxation during bodily care (bath, nappy change, and so on), is the first sign of his collaboration with the adult.

Conclusion

I will conclude by returning to what is both an essential function and an important condition of the mother-child relationship, namely that what is a libidinal satisfaction for one partner is also a libidinal satisfaction for the other. There is also the idea of the importance of *joy* for mental health. Balint is one of the rare analysts who talks about it. Partnership means reciprocity. Being able to see the competence and free activity of a young child, leaving space for it, respecting it, not impinging on it, is recognising the baby's innate personal potentials, and his developmental trajectory, his idiom. If the mother is free and psychically capable of being concerned with the innate potential developmental trajectory of her baby, if she recognises the importance of good-enough attunement to the rhythm of the infant's needs, and the infant's spontaneous gestures can be met on the infant's terms, then the baby can experience his or her active presence as a partner.

Balint's language, like Ferenczi's, is an empathetic, authentic, emotional one: Balint speaks of primary love, of infantile hopes, a language that the poet masters better than the psychoanalyst. Balint and Ferenczi talk from a sensitive vulnerable space, outside the dominant hierarchic position. These are warm concepts.

In the primary harmony, Balint had the intuition to talk about "being a co-operating partner", and thus, what we would say today is that the baby can be an active partner and active actor. If there is room for the recognition of primary autonomy, then there is a psychic space for a mother/baby differentiation process. And it can be initiated by the child! When the experience of symbiosis can open a space for baby's free activity, then dependency is relative. Being dependent is not being helpless. Then, finally, the baby can be taken for granted as a competent partner.

Bibliography

Balint, M. (1951). Love and hate. In: *Primary Love and Psycho-Analytic Technique* (pp. 141–158). London: Maresfield Library.

Balint, M. (1968). *Az Östörés, a Regresszio Therapiàs Vontakozàsai* [*The Basic Fault: Therapeutic Aspect of Regression*]. Budapest: Akadémiai Kiado.

Eros, F., Lenard, K., & Bokay, A. (2008). *Typus Budapestiensis*. Budapest: Thalassa.

Ferenczi, S. (1908). Psychanalyse et pédagogie. In: *L'enfant Dans L'adulte*. Paris: Payot & Rivages, 2006.

Golse, B., & Roussillon, R. (2010). *La Naissance de L'objet*. Paris: Le fil rouge, PUF.

Haag, G. (1990). Identifications intracorporelles et capacités de séparation. *Neuropsychiatrie de L'enfance et de L'adolescence*, *38*(4–5): 245–248.

Konechikes, A., & Vamos, J. (2014). Etre en mouvement. In: Laurent Danon-Boileau & Myriam Boubli (Eds.), *Le Bébé en Psychanalyse, Monographie de la Psychanalyse*. Paris: PUF.

Kristeva, J. (2013). Métamorphoses de la parentalité. *Revue Française de Psychanalyse*, *77*(5): 1650–1657.

Meltzer, D. (1978). A note on introjective processes. In: *Sincerity and Other Works: Collected Papers of Donald Meltzer*. London: Karnac, 1994.

Pikler, E. (1979). Importance du mouvement dans le développement de la personne: Initiative - Competence. *Spirale*, *50*(2): 175–181, 2009.

Prat, R. (2013, December). Naissance des parents: Chaos et clinique du post-trauma, changement de rythme [Paper presentation]. Colloque: Autant de bébés — Au temps du bébé — Rythmes et développement du nourrisson, Issy-les-Moulineaux.

Stern, D. (1985). *The Interpersonal World of the Infant*. New York: Basic Books.

Stern, D. (1990). *Diary of a Baby: What Your Child Sees, Feels, and Experiences*. New York: Basic Books.

Trevarthen, C. (2015). L'intime musicalité des voix avec le bébé. In: H. Bentata, C. Ferron, & M.-C. Laznik (Eds.), Écoute, ô *Bébé, la Voix de ta Mère* (pp. 241–250). Toulouse, France: Éditions Érès.

Vamos, J. (2015). Free to move, free to be. *American Journal of Psychoanalysis*, *75*(1): 65–75.

Winnicott, D. W. (1958). *De la Pédiatrie à la Psychoanalyse*. Paris: Payot.

Filmography

Vamos, J. (2009). "Free to Move, Free to Be". 30 minute video. Association Pikler Loczy: France.

Vamos, J. (2014). "EnToutRond". 15–20 minute film made for the colloquium of the WAIMH (World Association of Infant Mental Health).

Vamos, J. (2016). "Grandir" 15–20 minute film made for the colloquium of the WAIMH (World Association of Infant Mental Health).

"EnToutRond" and "Grandir" can be seen and bought from the Association APLF, with English subtitles.

Chapter 7

Human links

Antonella Bussanich

Introspection, projection, and connections that human beings have with themselves, with their peers and with everything that surrounds them are some of the subjects of reflection in my artistic research. They have inspired my work from the beginning. Between 2008 and 2012, I was particularly interested in exploring private and subtle moments based on silent or calm relationships with strong emotional content (Figure 7.1).

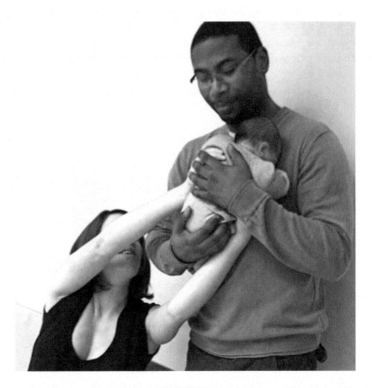

Figure 7.1 Still image from video FAMIGLIE, available on You Tube: Famiglie –
Antonella Bussanich

DOI: 10.4324/9781003309826-11

In 2012, during my artistic residency at the Maternité des Bluets in Paris, working with Julianna Vamos, I made a video work *Famiglie* (Families). The idea was to focus on the symbolic moment where the triad starts. I filmed about 20 young parents in the maternity ward, in a calm and spontaneous atmosphere, a few hours after the birth of their baby. I asked the mother to take some time in silence with the baby in her arms and then, when she felt ready, to hand the baby over to the father (Figure 7.2).

In the video work *Premier regard* (First gaze, 2011), thanks to the collaboration with Boris Guinzbourg – specialist in infantile mobility in water – I was able to film underwater about 40 newborns or very young children between 20 days and four years. This work is normally exposed as a video installation with five big projections (Figure 7.3).

In 2009, in the photographic and video work, *Coppie* (Couples), I filmed 13 couples in their homes. With the camera I explored their spaces, their objects, and their gestures and then asked them to sit in front of each other and look into each other's eyes intensely and for a long time. I asked one of them to hold a small mirror in his or her hand so that I could film their eyes at the same time (Figure 7.4).

When Balint wonders about the evolutionary mechanisms that progressively transform primary love into more mature love and then wonders if these mechanisms are simply "innate" or if they are activated primarily by external stimuli, it is clear that I am sensitive to this type of reflection. Psychoanalysis speaks of the influence of external stimuli in shaping our psyche; epigenetics reveals that external stimuli can modify the functioning of our DNA. The type, the quality of connections between us and others and between us and our environment are fundamental and play a very important role, especially in the first phase of life, making

Figure 7.2 Still image from video PREMIER REGARD, available on You Tube: Premier Regard – Antonella Bussanich

Figure 7.3 Still image from video COPPIE, available on You Tube: Coppie – Antonella Bussanich

Figure 7.4 Still image from video COPPIE – Antonella Bussanich

an imprint that will help us or not to evolve in balance. Understanding which external stimuli are favourable – could this be the key for reducing our anguish and hatred in adult love?

I follow with interest the work of Julianna Vamos, who for years has been observing in particular this first phase of life and who underlines the importance of discerning the environmental influence that helps the newborn find calm, harmony, and freedom.

Chapter 8

Michael Bálint and the Budapest School of Psychoanalysis on the importance of creativity

Zoltan Kőváry

The birth of psychoanalytic creativity research

The first 15 years of psychoanalysis (from 1895 to 1910) can be interpreted as the discovery of the "languages of the unconscious" one after the other, how the unconscious expresses itself in different ways by affecting several psychological phenomena (Kőváry, 2017). In 1895, Freud (and Breuer), studying psychopathology, identified "the language of symptoms", which means that neurotic symptoms have meaning, and they express intrapsychic conflicts. The second important step was the discovery of the "language of dreams" in 1900. Freud realised that the dream contents his patients spontaneously mentioned during psychoanalytic sessions could be understood by using the free association technique. But understanding his patients walked hand in hand with understanding himself, because Freud began to use dream interpretation in his self-analysis at the same time (related to the death of his father), recognising the similarities between symptoms and dreams. As dreams are everyday phenomena, their study allowed Freud to transform psychoanalysis from a clinical method and theory to psychoanalysis as a general, comprehensive "depth psychology" (Freud, 1916–1917). It led to the discovery of "the language of parapraxes" (1901), "the language of jokes" (1905) and "the language of arts" (1907, 1908, 1910). This 15-year process also demonstrated the development of Freud's own scientific creativity, and that the products of the unconscious are all linguistic in nature (Kőváry, 2017).

This process reached its climax in 1910 when Freud published *Leonardo da Vinci and a Memory of His Childhood*. The work is of great importance in the history of psychoanalysis – and psychology. This is the first ever written systematic analysis of eminent artistic creativity and the introduction of a new research method called psychobiography. The idea of psychobiography was formulated as an approach that is different from the medical pathographies that had existed before, written by psychiatrists like Paulus Möbius (Kőváry, 2011). The Leonardo essay also introduced new and important theoretical concepts, for example, narcissism, and it can be considered as a first reference to the significance of early object relations, the mother-infant bond (Blum, 2001). Harold Blum emphasises that this work supported Freud's endeavour to extend the application of the psychoanalytic

DOI: 10.4324/9781003309826-12

method to new territories and also gave him a chance to continue his self-analysis – indirectly. Freud's initiative supported the birth of "applied psychoanalysis", the application of psychoanalysis for the human sciences (Rank & Sachs, 1916).

The role of the Budapest school

In the 1910s to the1930s, the Budapest School of Psychoanalysis played a specific role in the evolution of psychoanalysis as a human science (Harmat, 1994). Psychoanalysis was not welcomed by the medical sciences or official institutes in Hungary – at least partly due to anti-Semitism. Hungarian psychoanalysts, led by Sándor Ferenczi, had to orient themselves towards human sciences and their representatives in order to be recognised. For example, the progressive literary journal *Nyugat* ("West") welcomed the writings of psychoanalysts, and editor-in-chief Hugo Ignotus was one of the first members of the Hungarian Society of Psychoanalysis. So the Budapest school was extremely open towards the questions of human sciences, and this influence was mutual. Hungarian writers like Dezső Kosztolányi, Frigyes Karinthy, and Milán Füst were not only interested in the new science of the human soul and mind, but they were all good friends of Ferenczi's and visited him in his home frequently for some private "theoretical training". Dezső Kosztolányi was a good friend of psychoanalyst István Hollós, who translated *The Interpretation of Dreams* into Hungarian. Due to his linguistic interest Hollós intended to create a psychoanalytic theory about language use. In this work (which remained unfinished but was published in Hungarian a few years ago, see Hollós, 2002), his supervisor was Dezső Kosztolányi, one of the greatest masters of the Hungarian language. During their co-operation they invented the Hungarian versions of several Freudian expressions, and Kosztolányi immortalised Hollós as Dr Moviszter in one of his most significant novels, Édes Anna, one of the greatest pieces of modern Hungarian literature (Harmat, 1994).

It's worth mentioning Dezső Kosztolányi's cousin and friend Géza Csáth (1887–1919), as the complex creativity of Csáth was a specific compound of arts and psychoanalysis (Kőváry, 2013). Dezső Kosztolányi and Csáth (born as József Brenner) grew up together in Szabadka, Hungary, and their outstanding literary talent manifested itself very early. Csáth was a superb painter as well, and his musical giftedness was equally strong, so his nephew called him a "triple artist". Nonetheless, he chose to be a physician, more precisely a psychiatrist, as he became interested in psychoanalysis, which he saw as a mixture of art and science. In his short stories he manifested his diverse and complex creativity, but it was not enough for him: as a young debutant psychiatrist he began to apply his theoretical psychoanalytic knowledge in the case of a woman diagnosed with paranoid schizophrenia, and he formulated his findings in a book called *Az elmebetegségek pszichikus mechanizmusa* (the psychic mechanism of mental illnesses). This book later became part of his literary oeuvre under the title *Egy elmebeteg nő naplója* (Diary of a mad woman) (Szajbély, 1989). Due to his pervasive morphine addiction – which began at that time, and in my opinion, was not independent from the "wild analysis" he conducted with this psychotic patient (Kőváry, 2013) – he was not welcomed in the Budapest school by Ferenczi. The otherwise brilliant Csáth had become peripheral in Hungarian intellectual life, mentally deteriorated, and in the end he murdered his wife and committed suicide.

Michael Bálint on creativity

Although Ferenczi was also interested in the questions of the human sciences, two of his disciples, Michael Bálint (1896–1970) and Imre Hermann (1889–1984), got involved in this subject even more deeply, and they both constructed systematic theories in the field. Bálint published three writings that contain explicit ideas on artistic creativity and also on the wider significance of creative activity. These are "Notes on the Dissolution of Object-Representation in Modern Art" (1952), *Thrills and Regressions* (1959), and *The Basic Fault* (1969). I will focus on the last two, and I start a discussion with the latter, because *Thrills* contains more complex and thorough explorations. According to Bálint (1969), "creation" is the third area of the mind (the other two are "basic fault" and the Oedipus complex), with no object (or at most pre-objects) on the scene. A large number of phenomena can be identified in this area, says Bálint: not only artistic creativity but scientific discoveries, the under- standing of something or somebody, also the outburst of psychological or somatic "illnesses" and the spontaneous recovery from them. Creation itself is not available for psychoanalytic observation due to the lack of object relations, says Bálint; it is manifest only when the final products of the activity emerge as objects. Creation is coming from the area of primary love and basic fault, and reactions like this in these primitive dimensions are probably occurring constantly. The Oedipus complex also originates in the basic fault, and it can facilitate or weaken the creative processes.

In *Thrills and Regressions* (1959) Bálint is more detailed and thorough. Hu- man life, as he supposes, begins with complete harmony called primary love, a union with the (maternal) object. It is followed by the discovery of the object's separateness which leads to two possible reactions, which are not mutually exclu- sive. *Ocnophilia* is an autoplastic reaction, which regains the wishful (re)union by accommodating to the object, while *philobatism* is alloplastic; the philobat is rearranging the environment, the outer world, in order to recreate the harmony differently. Bálint linked creativity to philobatic attitudes, because philobatism re- quires educing skills. These skills are the following: (1) the emotional acceptance of depression (which is related to the separateness of the object), (2) the ability of reality testing and self-criticism, and (3) finding a roundabout way to gratify the original need (bonding to the object). Within the last Bálint distinguishes three pos- sible ways: (a) *love* by conquering an object, which object from the psychoanalytic point of view is replacing the primary object, (b) *narcissism*, and (c) *sublimation*. In his opinion sublimation is a "progression for regression", in order to recreate in reality something of the harmony that existed before the discovery of separate objects. Ocnophilic and philobatic techniques are being internalised, forming an efficient psychological shell against anxiety, but at the same time they also narrow the experience of life. Thrills (enjoyment in amusement parks, for example) and artistic creativity in Bálint's interpretation are (philobatic) rebellions against this efficient shell, benign forms of regression to get in touch with the real self (or in other words, to gain freedom). With this concept Bálint really got close to some existential ideas.

In the Appendix of "Thrills and Regressions", Bálint explicates further valuable ideas on "sublimation and arts". Art, says Bálint, is the externalisation of the subjective, and this process occurs on the boundaries of the internal and external. (It's not hard to recognise how close this concept is to Winnicott's creativity theory based on his "transitional phenomena" idea; see 1971.) For the artist, and also for the consumer of artistic products, the product might become more valuable than reality, but this judgement requires intact reality testing and self-criticism, which Bálint (1959) mentioned before as an important philobatic skill. So it's no surprise that finally Bálint is evincing the similarities of philobatism (the enjoyment of thrills) and the dynamics of the creative process. They both start with the fear of leaving security, facing the empty world/space. Following this the thrill of entering the philobatic world emerges, and finally the void is becoming filled with objects. The feeling of satisfaction is related to this latest phase. These are roundabout ways to get in contact with human objects, while emphasising the importance of the creative process for its own sake by the artist – reducing the significance of object-relational aspects – and might contain elements of self-defence as well.

If we read Bálint's chapters in "Thrills" carefully, we will face a contradiction. The final goal of creation is "getting in touch with the real self", but in the Appendix it is changed to "getting contact with human objects". I think that this contradiction is related to Cartesian traditions in Western thinking: subjective and objective, external and internal, world and self are seen as separate phenomena as the result of the "Cartesian split". In phenomenological-existential approaches (May, 1958) or in the "post-Cartesian psychoanalysis" of Robert Stolorow, George Atwood, and Bernard Brandchaft (1994) – based on phenomenological traditions related to Edmund Husserl and Martin Heidegger – self and other (or the world) are not supposed to be totally separated, as it is famously expressed in Heidegger's concept of "Dasein" (Heidegger, 1927). So getting in touch with the "real self" and with "human objects" in creativity or in philobatic experiences are not different things; they are two sides of the same coin. We find something similar in the concept of "selfobjects" by Heinz Kohut; selfobjects help human beings to develop and sustain the cohesiveness and meaningfulness of self-experience (Kohut, 1980). In my opinion this relatedness is also beyond the Cartesian split, because experiencing an empathic "selfobject" is about experiencing the real (cohesive) self at the same time. The similarities between Bálint's psychoanalysis and Kohutian self-psychology are not accidental, as Bálint was a kind of a "forerunner" of self-psychology (Ornstein, 2002). Kohut's theory can be interpreted as a bridge between psychoanalysis and existential-humanistic psychology (Tobin, 1990), and Kohut in his late years worked with the Heidegger-follower Robert Stolorow, who was deeply influenced by Kohut (Stolorow, Atwood, & Orange, 1999). From the

2000s, Stolorow got himself into Heidegger's philosophy (2011), and his "post-Cartesian psychoanalysis" or "phenomenological contextualism" is very close to existential endeavours.

Imre Hermann on creativity

Imre Hermann (1889–1984) was one of the most prominent representatives of the Budapest school (Harmat, 1994). He was interested in the psychology of cognition, so he began to consider the possible connections between psychoanalysis and experimental/general psychology quite early (Hermann, 2011a). He was also occupied with the "comparative psychology" of the apes that later became ethology. At that time, when psychoanalysis was still operating with the idea of an "oral" partial instinct to understand the nature of the infant's early psychological development, Hermann (1984) formulated the idea of the "clinging instinct".[1] "This happened at about the same time as Harry Harlow began to conduct groundbreaking experiments with monkeys, and long before (the also Hungarian) René Spitz's observations of infants or John Bowlby's 'attachment theory'" (Stern, 1985). According to Hermann (1984), the "clinging instinct" is the common biological heritage of apes and *Homo sapiens* and supports the survival of the babies. The Freudian oral erogenous zone is an important component of this instinctual system, says Hermann, but visual and manual components are equally important to gain satisfaction, so they are also erogenous zones, and they are all parts of the "eye-mouth-hand system" serving the clinging instinct. In humans, clinging is easy to frustrate in the early years, because of the lack of tangible hair on the mother's skin and also because it is common that the baby is separated from the mother's body too early. But later speaking can be a successful tool to bridge the physical/psychological distance between the self and the object, so Hermann believed that disorders of speech, like stuttering, are related to unsuccessful clinging (Klaniczay, 2001). Hermann's theory on the clinging instinct influenced Bálint's ideas on philobatism and ocnophilia (Harmat, 1994).

Hermann was extremely interested in the psychology of creativity. He formulated a theory (1930) on talent, although Freud believed it to be impossible to analyse. During his studies on this subject, Hermann (2011b) contributed (or could have contributed) the development of psychobiographical method and also wrote a book on the psychological relation between perversion and musicality (1999). In his talent model (1930), Hermann distinguished three elements of talent: (1) "talent as a whole" is a bio-psychological potential within the person (nowadays we would call it "giftedness"); (2) there are always "external triggering forces" that support the emergence of this latent "talent as a whole" – these are life historical events and the subjective meaning of them that cause conflicts, traumas, or crises; and (3) while "driving partial roots" are related to the sublimation of archaic partial instincts (oral, anal, phallic) that Freud described. In some cases, as we will see, visual and manual instinctual elements identified by Hermann can be equally important. These instinctual wishes ensure the motivational background of the creative activity.

It is also notable to take a look at Hermann's contribution to the psychobiographical method. Psychobiography was a relatively new method when Imre Hermann began to utilise it in creativity research. In the 1920s, he wrote several psychobiographies, which are the earliest systematic analyses of highly creative persons in the history of Hungarian human sciences using this method (Hermann, 2011b). But the significance of these writings goes beyond that. Hermann's articles challenged the standards of similar psychoanalytic writings of his time as his perspective was mostly beyond the "clinical view". Although Freud emphasised that pathography (a kind of "psychopathological psychobiography") cannot show anything new about the artist (Mack, 1971), several analysts such as Marie Bonaparte, Edmund Bergler, or the Hungarian, Lilla Wagner, used clinical concepts like psychopathological ideas in their art-psychological writings at that time (Kőváry, 2011). Instead of "diagnosing" the artist, Hermann (2011b) considered the role of dynamic aspects like "complexes", pointing out the importance of cognitive process and the role of regression. He does not think that an illness can be a "cause" for any kind of creative activity; illness, as a "pain experience", can be a source of some necessary psychodynamic changes. Also, we can see that Hermann's papers contain epistemological and methodological reflections, which were very rare among psychoanalysts at the time. In these kinds of psychoanalytic explorations, says Hermann, we use historical data, and not analytic material that we get from analytic sessions. It means that we take creative discoveries as fantasies, because fantasies are the products of thinking that are not limited by the reality principle, so the unconscious can affect these psychological contents. We know, says Hermann, that important artistic or scientific ideas never come into existence without the contribution of the unconscious, which is why a psychoanalytic approach to them is justified. What the analyst can do is to try to find some congruencies between the creative product and the psychological material related to life historical experiences.

Hermann's other outstanding contribution was the widening of the focus of psychobiographical research. Until then psychoanalysts had mostly been dealing with questions of artistic creativity. Due to his interest in natural sciences, Hermann (2011b) began to study the psychology of natural scientists like Gustav Theodore Fechner, Charles Darwin, or outstanding Hungarian mathematician János Bólyai and physician Ignác Semmelweis. These scientists, writes Hermann, are exceptionally fine examples of productive thinking. To investigate their products and life history is the best way to study how creative thinking is influenced by personal factors, because it cannot be observed in another way at all. This approach was radically original at the time. Psychoanalysts had been studying mostly artistic creativity formerly, because of art's subjective nature the interrelations between the artist's personality and her/his creative products are more obvious and can be investigated psychologically. But as scientists tend to be objective, are there any detectable interrelations between their personality and their works at all? According to Hermann the answer is yes, and it seems that with this opinion he was decades ahead of his time; the first comprehensive handbook on the "psychology of science" was published only 90 years later in the twenty-first century (Feist & Gorman, 2013).

Applying the ideas of Bálint and Hermann: the case of Tivadar Csontváry-Kosztka

Tivadar Csontváry-Kosztka (1853–1919) is considered to be one of the most significant painters in Hungary's cultural history. During his life he remained unknown
and his works were almost sold for burlap, but decades after his death he was
discovered. It is said that when there was an exhibition of his works in Paris after
World War 2, a visitor called Pablo Picasso asked for permission to investigate the
paintings one evening after closing time. According to witnesses, after his investigation the upset Picasso stated that he had never imagined that there was another
great painter in the twentieth century – other than himself (Szabó, 2014).

Csontváry's talent manifested itself in a very special form. Until the age of 26
he hadn't shown any sign of artistic giftedness. After facing a devastating and traumatic event (a great flood in Szeged, southern Hungary) he experienced a "calling"
from a higher power: a voice told him that he would be the greatest painter of
the "Napút" (greater than Raffael), so Csontváry made a decision that he would
dedicate his whole life to painting. "Napút" was a neologism, meaning "Sun-way"
or "Sun-road", suggested to him by an angel during an acoustic hallucination.
Csontváry became an artist, a person with penetrating religious obsessions, and –
although never hospitalised – showed signs of severe mental disturbance. I mention some examples of his eminent works here so the reader can check them out
on the internet: "A taorminai görög színház romjai" (Ruins of the Greek theatre in
Taormina), "Baalbek", "A jajcei vízesés" (Waterfall at Jajce), "A magányos cédrus"
(Lone cedar tree), "Római híd Mostarnál" (Roman bridge at Mostar), "A nagy Tarpatak a Tátrában" (The great Tarpatak in Tatra), and "Zarándoklás a cédrushoz"
(Pilgrimage to the cedar tree) (Kőváry, 2018).

I believe that one can interpret some features of Csontváry's creativity successfully with the help of Bálint's and Hermann's ideas. The emergence of Csontváry's
creativity is easy to grasp with Hermann's (1930) talent theory. As I mentioned
above, according to Hermann, talent has three components: (1) "talent as a whole",
which is the sum of the person's biological and psychological potentials. Its actualisation depends on (2) "external triggering forces" that can be traumas, crises,
and conflicts, but other kinds of human experiences like peak experiences (Maslow, 1998) can also facilitate actualisation. Abraham Maslow claimed that these
experiences are acute identity experiences as well, supporting the protagonist's
commitment emotionally.

Csontváry's creative potential and attitude hadn't manifested itself before the
age of 26. Experiencing the great flood in Szeged, Csontváry met the dark side of
"Mother Nature". According to his *Autobiography* (1982), he had formerly idealised it in a psychoanalytic sense (as a part of a "manic defence"), in order to keep
the emotional balance of his self, which is harmonising with the opinion of Alice
Miller (1990), who says that the love of nature can be a substitute for the missing
maternal object. I think that this personality organisation could be the basis of a condition that Pertorini (1966) characterised as Csontváry's "premorbid psychopathy"

(I think nowadays we would refer to it as a personality disorder). So in Csontváry's case the experienced psychological conflict between the idealised and the devastating representations of Mother Nature led to the emergence of the Kleinian depressive position (Segal, 1964) in his psychic life. During the crisis – according to the trauma theory of Sandor Ferenczi (1933) – his self had fragmented. A part of it became fixed to the trauma, causing him post-traumatic symptoms like repetition of the trauma in visions (Pertorini, 1966). Another part regressed on the level of the paranoid-schizoid position, causing psychotic symptoms. The third part progressed, forming the creative subsystem of the personality (creative self) (Beres, 1957). His creative self was a result of a restorative process, which was a complex reaction to the experience of the depressive position. According to Melanie Klein, the elaboration of this conflict is related to reparation and creativity; this process includes grief work and symbol formation (Segal, 1964). In the end, the creative self will take the psychological burden of the entire personality (Kőváry, 2018); so we can see that eminent creativity is coming into being not *because of* but *in spite of* psychopathological involvement (Beres, 1957).

The third aspect of talent is what Hermann (1930) calls "driving partial roots". With this factor he refers to Freud's theories on sublimation of infantile partial instincts. These partial instincts from the early phases of libido organisation are the motivational factors to sustain the urge to create. In Freud's theory (1916–1917) these are sexual, aggressive, and narcissistic impulses related to the oral, anal, and phallic phases of psychosexual development. But Hermann's previously mentioned "clinging instinct", the visual and manual components, are also important ingredients in the sublimation process. The erogenous zones of the clinging systems, the eye and the hand, are significant in the psychology of visual arts. The painter "falls in love" with visual impressions, relating to the object with eyes, and executes the creative process with hands (Rank & Sachs, 1916). The "libido cathexis" of these areas (eye and hand) is not accidental, because from a psychoanalytic point of view the sublimation of these instinctual urges is supporting a symbolic reconnection with the mother. This is related to Hans Loewald's (1988) reformulation of sublimation; he interpreted sublimation as "reconciliation" between the subject and the object. We can see that hands might become a central motif in the work of some modern painters like Salvador Dalí (Kőváry, 2009) or Egon Schiele (Resnik, 2000). Csontváry fits into this line: and if we take a look at some paintings of Csontváry ("Önarckép" [Self-portrait], "Az öreg halász" [The old fisherman], "Marokkói tanító" [Spiritual teacher from Morocco]) we can see that hands appear in his paintings frequently, and there is a great emphasis on them. In a psychobiograhical research we would consider "frequency" and "emphasis" as primary indicators of psychological saliency (Alexander, 1990). We will return to the role of these indicators later.

Bálint's ideas (1959, 1969) can be also very useful in analysing the creativity of the Hungarian painter. According to his life history Csontváry was undoubtedly a philobat (Kőváry, 2018). He had been wandering the Mediterranean area and the Near East alone for years in order to find the proper subject matter for his work.

Studying his paintings it appears that he was in a kind of a love relationship with the "friendly expanses" of Mother Nature that Bálint (1959) mentions as a feature of philobats. The paintings of Csontváry often represent huge panoramas of natural landscapes including these "friendly expanses".

According to Bálint's theory, the artist as a philobat unconsciously intends to recreate in reality something of the harmony that existed before the discovery of separate objects, in order to undo separation trauma, the basic fault. In Bálint's view basic fault is the common root of creativity and severe psychopathology (which are both significant in Csontváry's life), so we have to consider its possible role in Csontváry's life history and fate. We have to be very careful, because the reconstruction of early (infantile) psychodynamic moments without evidence might turn analysis to speculation, which is the sign of "bad psychobiography" (Schultz, 2005) as we fall into the pitfall of "originology" (Erikson, 1977).

In 1966 a Hungarian psychiatrist Rezső Pertorini wrote a pathography on the painter's life and work. In this renowned book, he emphasised that the features of Csontváry's art were strongly related to his psychotic illness ("paraphrenia expansiva"). According to the data gained from available documents, there is no sign of early emotional traumas in Csontváry's life, so Pertorini considers this illness to be an "endogenous" one. (This is an old psychiatric expression introduced by Ernst Kretschmer in the late nineteenth century – nowadays we would say that it was constitutional or genetic.) But in modern-day psychobiography, pathography is mostly considered as a sign of "bad psychobiography" because diagnosis is always "reducing the complex whole of personality to static psychopathological categories" (Schultz, 2005, p. 10), and it leaves an impression that it is the illness, and not the person, a "being in the world", which is responsible for the products of outstanding creativity.

If we take a look at some documents of Csontváry's life and his activity, we shall find so-called "indicators of psychological saliency" (Alexander, 1990) that are related to primary love and the basic fault, which Bálint considered to be the sources of both outstanding creativity and severe psychopathological manifestations. (1) In his *Autobiography* (1982) Csontváry forgets to mention (!) that he had a mother (*omission*, as indicator). (2) In the same book he refers to an early emotional trauma in a very strange way. He writes that when he was a boy, he and his father (whom he mentions several times with great respect) travelled to a northern Hungarian town called Eperjes on a horse-drawn carriage. They visited a house, where three young smiling girls greeted them. Csontváry writes that at that moment he realised that something "tricky" had happened to his life as an infant: he had been separated for ever,[2] and following this he mentions immediately that he became a merchant's assistant. This strange formulation (putting the house incident with the girls, the memory of separation, and his future occupation beside each other) is an indicator of psychological saliency that Alexander (1990) calls *isolation*. (3) One can see the emphasis on the love of Mother Nature in Csontváry's *Autobiography* and also in his paintings. (*Emphasis* is also an indicator according to Alexander.) The autobiography is full of admiring descriptions concerning natural phenomena, while the subject of the paintings is often (Mother) nature, the way Csontváry experienced this phenomenon subjectively. According to Bálint (1959) art is the externalisation of the subjective (or in other words, fantasy). The externalisation of the inner fantasy, or "sublimation" (in arts) is aiming to recreate in reality something of the harmony that existed before the discovery of separate objects, which activity is related to philobatic attitudes. Mother Nature might become a significant substitute for the primary (lost) object, so it can serve as an idealised good love object (Dodds, 2011). For the ones who failed to establish a secure attachment with the mother in the early years, the relationship with Mother Nature can be crucial (Miller, 1990). (4) The emotional intensity of experiencing a devastating natural phenomenon, the great flood in Szeged in 1879 is also remarkable. Psychologically it can be seen as the experience of the dark side of Mother Nature, the bad abandoning and harmful object that was formally exiled by splitting, denial, compensative idealisation (of the bright side). This organisation can be related to Kleinian manic defences (Segal, 1964) and might have been the basis for Csontváry's strange personality that Pertorini (1966) characterised as "premorbid psychopathy".

But facing the bad (abandoning, haunting, destructive, anxiety provoking) part of Mother Nature probably crushed this organisation and forced Csontváry to face the depressive position, the necessary integration of good and bad parts of the object. Csontváry's solution for this conflict was unique: one part of his self became fixed to the trauma, one part regressed to the paranoid-schizoid position that led to psychotic manifestations, while a third part became his creative self. The creative part produced reparative fantasies, which were later externalised as paintings. According to Melanie Klein (Segal, 1964), the creative reparation of the ruined and lost object, the elaboration of the depressive position, is psychologically based on mourning, symbolisation, and sublimation. Klein also found that in children's analyses, it often begins with drawing. (5) We can see that there are a lot of mother-infant representations in Csontváry's paintings that were created between 1903 and 1908 ("Hajótörés" [Shipwreck], "Siratófal" [Weeping wall], "Hídon átkelő társaság" [Company crossing the bridge], "Baalbek", "Zarándoklás a ciprushoz" [Pilgrimage to the cypress tree], "Mária kútja Názáretben" [Maria's fountain in Nazareth]). This kind of *frequency* is also an indicator of psychological saliency (Alexander, 1990). On these mother-infant representations, the bonds are so intimate and close (symbiotic) that the body of the mother sometimes cannot even be distinguished from the child's. According to Freud (1908e) the personal psychological source of artistic creativity is unconscious fantasy (also a basis for dreaming and psychopathology), so we can suppose that Csontváry's unconscious mind might have been full of fantasies of harmonic, symbiotic mother–infant dyads (an experience he missed due to the early separation he mentioned). The psychological aim of these fantasies is the reparation of pre-traumatic conditions to gain emotional satisfaction. The externalisation of these subjective contents is called sublimation (Bálint, 1959) – a "reconciliation" between the subject and the object, as Loewald (1988) later formulated it.

Last but not least Bálint (1959) claimed that philobatism is related to male erection and potency. If we examine Csontváry's "Önarckép" (Self-portrait) that shows him during painting, we can discover an interesting element. On the painting his right thumb is going through the hole of the palette, but this part of the painting is ambiguous: the finger can also be seen as a penis at the same time. Seeing one thing also as another at the same time – this is condensation, a primary process of the unconscious, related to the language of dreams and artistic creativity (Kőváry, 2017). Although Csontváry never had a life partner and he lived ascetically, and his art was mostly of a spiritual nature, it seems that he couldn't escape referring to sexuality at least once – and *primacy* is also an indicator of psychological saliency (Alexander, 1990). According to Ferenczi (1924), sexual intercourse at least partly symbolically fulfils a wish to return to the body of the mother.

Conclusion

The representatives of the Budapest School of Psychoanalysis (Ferenczi, Hermann, the Bálints) contributed to the development of psychoanalysis and psychotherapy with several significant innovations. It is less well known that some of them were interested in the topic of artistic creativity, and had original ideas concerning this subject. Michael Bálint related creativity to primary love, basic fault, and philobatism, and he identified it as a "progression for regression", a roundabout way to get in contact with human objects and the real self. Imre Hermann (who influenced Bálint) also significantly contributed to the development of this research area. His talent theory, the accentuation of eye and hand as erogenous zones in the process of sublimation (which are highly important in the case of painters), and his contributions to the development of psychobiography as a method in psychoanalytic creativity research are all remarkable. In this chapter, I have tried to demonstrate that the ideas of Bálint and Hermann can be utilised successfully in psychobiographical research. With the application of Alexander's model of "primary indicators of psychological saliency" I intended to interpret Tivadar Csontváry Kosztka as a philobat who reacted to emotional trauma by developing artistic skills. I also tried to analyse how a triggering external force, a traumatic natural disaster, rearranged his personality structure, which was responsible for the emergence of his creativity, his mental problems, and his spiritual commitment, supporting his existential transformation.

Notes

1 The creator of separation-individuation theory, Margaret Mahler was a disciple of Imre Hermann (Harmat, 1994).
2 He does not specify the nature of the separation, but it is more than likely concerning his mother, whom he does not even mention in his autobiography. It has psychobiographical significance, because mentioning this "separation forever" together with the omission of the mother in the text and frequent mother- infant dyads in his paintings all suggest the 'basic fault'.

Bibliography

Alexander, I. (1990). *Personology. Method and Content in Personality Assessment and Psychobiography*. Durham, NC: Duke University Press.

Bálint, M. (1952). Notes on the dissolution of object-representation in modern art. *Journal of Aesthetics and Art Criticism, 10*(4): 323–327.

Bálint, M. (1959). *Thrills and Regressions*. London: Routledge, 1988.

Bálint, M. (1969). *The Basic Fault: Therapeutic Aspects of Regression*. Evanston, IL: Northwestern University Press.

Beres, D. (1957). Communication in psychoanalysis and in the creative process. *Journal of the American Psychoanalytic Association, 5*: 408–423.

Blum, H. (2001). Psychoanalysis and art, Freud and Leonardo. *Journal of the American Psychoanalytic Association, 49*: 1409–1425.

Csontváry, K. T. (1982). *Önéletrajz (Autobiography)*. Budapest: Magvető Könyvkiadó.

Dodds, J. (2011). *Psychoanalysis and Ecology at the Edge of Chaos*. London: Routledge.

Erikson, E. H. (1977). *Childhood and Society*. London: Paladin Grafton.

Feist, G. J., & Gorman, M. E. (Eds.) (2013). *Handbook of the Psychology of Science*. New York: Springer.

Ferenczi, S. (1924). *Thalassa, a Theory of Genitality*. London: Routledge, 1989.

Ferenczi, S. (1933). A Trauma a pszichoanalízisben [Trauma in Psychoanalysis]. In *(uő): Technikai Írások [Technical Writings]* (pp. 112–118). Budapest: Animula Kiadó, 2006.

Freud, S. (1901). *On Dreams*. S. E., 5. London: Hogarth.

Freud, S. (1905). *Jokes and Their Relation to the Unconscious*. S. E., 8. London: Hogarth.

Freud, S. (1907). *Delusions and Dreams in Jensen's 'Gradiva' and Other Works*. S. E., 9: 141–154. London: Hogarth.

Freud, S. (1908). *Creative Writers and Day-Dreaming*. S. E., 9. London: Hogarth.

Freud, S. (1910). *Leonardo da Vinci and a Memory of His Childhood*. Oxford: W. W. Norton, 1964.

Freud, S. (1916–1917). *Introductory Lectures on Psycho-Analysis (Parts I and II)*. S. E., 15–16. London: Hogarth.

Harmat, P. (1994). *Freud, Ferenczi és a Magyarországi Pszichoanalízis [Freud, Ferenczi and Hungarian Psychoanalysis]*. Budapest: Bethlen Gábor Könyvkiadó.

Heidegger, M. (1927). *Being and Time*. Oxford: Blackwell, 1967.

Hermann, I. (1930). A tehetség pszichoanalízise [Psychoanalysis of Talent]. In: J. Angéla (Ed.) *(uő): Magyar Nyelvű Cikkek és Tanulmányok 1911–1933 [Articles and Studies in Hungarian Language 1911–1933]* (pp. 85–98). Budapest: Animula Kiadó, 2007.

Hermann, I. (1984). *Az ember Ősi Ösztönei [Man's Archaic Instincts]*. Budapest: Magvető Kiadó.

Hermann, I. (1999). *Perverzió és Muzikalitás. Adalékok a Perverzió Dinamikájához [Perversion and Musicality: Contributions to the Dynamics of Perversion]*. Budapest: Animula Kiadó.

Hermann, I. (2011a). *Gondolkodáslélektani Tanulmányok [Studies in the Psychology of Thought]*. Budapest: Animula Kiadó.

Hermann, I. (2011b). *Kreativitás és Alkotás. Pszichoanalitikus Tanulmányok [Creativity and Creation. Psychoanalytic Studies]*. Budapest: Animula Kiadó.

Hollós, I. (2002). Felemelkedés az ösztönnyelvtől az emberi beszédhez [The ascension from instinctual language to human speech]. *Thalassa, 13*: 1–2, 77–117.

Klaniczay, S. (2001). A frusztrált megkapaszkodás szerepe a dadogás etiológiájában [The role of frustrated clinging in the aetiology of stuttering]. In: G. Vikár & A. Vikár (Eds.), *Dinamikus Gyermekpszichiátria* [*Dynamic Child Psychiatry*] (pp. 81–23). Budapest: Medicina Könyvkiadó.

Kohut, H. (1980). *Self Psychology and the Humanities: Reflections on a New Psychoanalytic Approach*. New York: W. W. Norton.

Kőváry, Z. (2009). The enigma of desire. Salvador Dalí and the conquest of the irrational. *PsyArt, 5*: 1.

Kőváry, Z. (2011). Psychobiography as a method. The revival of studying lives: New perspectives in personality and creativity research. *Europe's Journal of Psychology, 7*(4): 739–777.

Kőváry, Z. (2013). Matricide and creativity: The case of two Hungarian cousin-writers from the perspective of contemporary psychobiography. *International Journal of Creativity and Problem Solving, 23*(1): 103–118.

Kőváry, Z. (2017). From sublimation to affect integration: Psychoanalytic approaches to creativity from Freud to self psychology. In: K. Martin & M. Siegward (Eds.), *Psychoanalytic Theory: A Review and Directions for Research* (pp. 65–111). New York: Nova Science.

Kőváry, Z. (2018). De-pathologizing creativity. Psychobiography and creativity research: The case of eminent Hungarian painter Tivadar Csontváry Kosztka. *Journal of Genius and Eminence, 3*: 26–43.

Loewald, H. (1988). *Sublimation*. New Haven, CT: Yale University Press.

Mack, J. E. (1971). Psychoanalysis and historical biography. *Journal of the American Psychoanalytic Association, 19*: 143–179.

Maslow, A. (1998). *Towards the Psychology of Being*. Hoboken, NJ: Wiley & Sons.

May, R. (Ed.) (1958). *Existence. A New Dimension in Psychiatry and Psychology*. New York: Touchstone.

Miller, A. (1990). *The Drama of the Gifted Child: The Search for the True Self*. New York: Basic Books.

Ornstein, P. (2002). Michael Balint then and now: A contemporary appraisal. *American Journal of Psychoanalysis, 62*(1): 25–35.

Pertorini, R. (1966). *Csontváry Patográfiája* [*Csontváry's Pathography*]. Budapest: Akadémiai Kiadó, 1997.

Rank, O., & Sachs, H. (1916). *The Significance of Psychoanalyisis for the Mental Sciences*. New York: Nervous and Mental Disease Publishing.

Resnik, S. (2000). The hands of Egon Schiele. *International Forum of Psychoanalysis, 9*: 113–123.

Schultz, W. T. (2005). Introducing psychobiography. In: W. T. Schultz (Ed.), *The Handbook of Psychobiography* (pp. 3–18). New York: Oxford University Press.

Segal, H. (1964). *Introduction to the Work of Melanie Klein*. London: Hogarth, 1988.

Stern, D. (1985). *The Interpersonal World of the Infant*. New York: Basic Books, 2000.

Stolorow, R. D. (2011). *World, Affectivity, Trauma. Heidegger and Post-Cartesian Psychoanalyis*. New York: Routledge & Taylor and Francis.

Stolorow, R. D., Atwood, G. E., & Brandchaft, B. (1994). *The Intersubjective Perspective*. New York: Jason Aronson.

Stolorow, R. D., Atwood, G. E., & Orange, D. M. (1999). Kohut and contextualism: Toward a post-Cartesian psychoanalytic theory. *Psychoanalytic Psychology, 16*(3): 380–388.

Szabó, L. (2014). *Csontváry Kosztka Tivadar* [*Tivadar Csontváry Kosztka*]. Budapest: Kossuth Könyvkiadó.

Szajbély, M. (1989). *Csáth Géza* [*Géza Csáth*]. Budapest: Gondolat Kiadó.

Tobin, A. (1990). Self psychology as a bridge between existential-humanistic psychology and psychoanalysis. *Journal of Humanistic Psychology, 30*(1): 14–63.

Winnicott, D. W. (1971). *Playing and Reality*. London: Routledge, 2005.

Part 3

Lost children of
psychoanalysis

Lost children of the recent history of psychoanalysis

Tibor Rajka MD, 1901–1980

Judit Szekacs-Weisz[1]

Oblivion has blurred or deleted the memory of colleagues who were important figures in our professional life even a short time ago. This chapter sketches the portrait of an analyst who should not be forgotten; displaying his life and work in different snapshots.

Having been part of the Ferenczi revival from the 1980s, experiencing how his ideas reached and penetrated distant areas of analytical thinking in different parts of the world, my colleagues and I became aware that we have a "cultural mission" to execute: the mission to bring back the lost children of the history of psychoanalysis from oblivion and find for them the place they rightfully deserve in the historical memory of our profession.

The first such person to welcome back to international memory will be Tibor Rajka, a contemporary of Sándor Ferenczi.

Although rarely mentioned, Tibor Rajka – "psychoanalytic doctor of the mind", as he described himself – was a member of the first, pre-war Hungarian Psychoanalytic Association. After its destruction and during the ensuing years of semi-legality and semi-acceptance, he was one of the most important figures in the revival of the Budapest dchool and the creation of the second Psychoanalytic Society.

Rajka was born in the first year of the twentieth century, so he was to witness all that the following 80 years brought about in creativity and destruction in Central Europe. He has always been and has remained a "participant observer" of the world in a true sense; he preserved his capacity to reflect, to think, and to act accordingly throughout all the basic changes he lived through.

He was a son of his century. Anna Arato collected the following biographical data for Rajka. He was born in 1901 in Marosvásárhely, Transylvania, a most progressive, liberal, and highly cultural part of Hungary at the time. Rajka and his birthplace developed hand in hand; by the time he was in his middle teens, the formerly small town had grown into a big city with a vivid and progressive intellectual and spiritual life.

The First World War brought about uncertainty and insecurity to politics and ordinary lives alike. These experiences had a formative effect on his intellectual development and eventually also on his career choice.

DOI: 10.4324/9781003309826-14

The analyst as a young man

Anna Arató writes: At the age of 18 Rajka was a romantic young man fascinated by science and literature. Inspired by a thriving Nietzsche cult in Hungary, he wrote a philosophical summary of *Thus Spake Zarathustra*, which he published in a short-lived cultural gazette for students, edited by himself.

"I came to preach the man. I came to be the doctor of your blindness, I came to be the mirror to show the man in yourselves to you" – says young Rajka's Zarathustra. These prophetic words – though obviously in a much more modest, mature, and realistic way – became his manifesto, expressing the guiding principles of his life.

At the end of World War I, the Austro-Hungarian monarchy disintegrated into separate independent states. Hungary being on the side of the losers was required to give up two-thirds of its territory including Transylvania. In 1918, Marosvásárhely was occupied by the Romanians.

In search of his place in the world young Rajka was ready to move. He went to Prague to study medicine. The sweeping force of intellectual and cultural life in contemporary Prague amazed him; he found a world very close to his heart there. However, he would have to leave his beloved city quite soon. Hoping that he could make a proper living in Hungary, where language difficulties would not stand in his way, he was ready to start packing again. His search for an authentic and autonomous life guided him to Budapest where he was able to complete his medical training.

He was to spend years at the neurological ward of Szent István (Saint Stephen's) Hospital, headed by Professor Sarbó, who did not separate neurology and psychiatry. He also expressed a definite interest in the teachings of Freud. Working there Rajka met his first neurotic patients.

Through Stekelian colleagues – this group was going to play an important part in his professional development – he got in touch with Ferenczi, who recommended László Révész to him as a suitable person for his training analysis.

Anna Arató writes: He had to wait until 1931 though, when with great luck he found a job: he became a GP in one of the slums of Budapest, called the Mária Valéria settlement. Personal hardship and his experiences working in such an environment contributed to his deepening sensitivity towards social matters.

Following the requirements of analytical training of the time he had to see patients at the Psychoanalytical Polyclinic founded by Ferenczi. It is most illuminating to recall that in the pioneering clinics in Europe, this included a formative year of clinical training when candidates were expected to work for free!

Graduating in 1937 he became a member of the international psychoanalytical community.

He would cherish and proudly retain his continuous membership of the IPA all through his life.

History marches into your living room – again and again

By the end of the 1930s another, even more brutal war is on the horizon, and the flow of life was interrupted again.

Psychically, the world has not been able to work through the experience of the great wars of the twentieth century – old and new powers rising and falling, re-drawing the borders of empires and of the confines of ordinary lives, irreparable losses, human tragedies, and broken dreams. World War II left an "impossible" task for successive generations who grapple with this inheritance even today.

Rajka can be considered a survivor of the pre-war, first generation. Not being Jewish, he had to face only the "ordinary" type of attacks on the individual and on society, common in the region.

From the time of his graduation, Rajka took an active part in the work of the Hungarian Psychoanalytic Association until 1948, when it was dissolved as a pre-emptive move to avoid persecutory measures of a strengthening dictatorial establishment.

He kept working in the Hungarian health service, never giving up his analytical practice.

After many years working "semi-underground", Rajka was one of the main pro-tagonists raising his voice in favour of the re-establishment of the Society, in order to create the legal conditions which would enable this small, surviving, "tolerated" professional community to begin the enormous task facing them – elaborating the losses and picking up the thread in analytical thinking which has been cut, rup-tured, and buried alive. This second post-war association provided the basis and framework for taking a second look at the experience and formative effects of liv-ing in a traumatised land and for reclaiming its well-deserved place among the na-tions of the psychoanalytic world, where it belonged since its very creation in 1913.

Owing to their efforts, after the 1960s psychoanalysis became increasingly ac-cepted in Hungary. The revival of the Budapest school could begin. Together with Imre Hermann, Rajka laboured hard to resurrect the spirit of the pre-war associa-tion. With a few analysts of the next generation, they worked relentlessly: teaching, consulting, and exploring possible new ways of promoting psychoanalytic ideas and training.

Looking at Rajka's biography, one realises that psychoanalysts of the Budapest school had to digest what history taught them early on: that one cannot escape the facts and effects of external reality; the outside world is likely to march into one's life and upset the existing order, both external and internal. In all circumstances, one has to face and attempt to make sense of such experiences. One has to explore the diverse layers of meaning of individual and societal change and trauma in one's life and work these through as best as one can, in order to be able to live an authen-tic (and autonomous) life.

He was and remained a *clinician,* wherever he worked

A collection of papers and two "books of notes" on analytical technique and methodology were left behind outlining some of his relevant ideas regarding our place and professional identity in the consulting room. He emphasised aspects useful for the therapeutic couple to achieve "wholeness" in working together in the here and now, in a world in constant development and change.

His credo defining the analytical process as a joint encounter between "whole personalities" – including their body, mind, and soul – puts him among the early representatives of object relations theory, shared by most analysts of the Budapest school, including Bálint.

The idea of a multigenerational model came naturally to him. He paid special attention to ensure the coming to light of unelaborated traumas, anxieties, and fears of the previous generation in their analytical session. He was convinced that a sense of continuity can only be reached by working through splits and fragmentations; this is how the past – and that includes the past of our ancestors – can become an integral part of our psychic reality. His approach influenced many analysts who came after him (Szekacs-Weisz, 2022).

The idea of change and growth was central in his thinking. He always tried to view those onto- and phylogenetic moments which could be seen as definitive in the phenomenology of symptom formation. Thinking along developmental lines this way has also been a very hot issue (remember Ferenczi's *Thalassa*!) among contemporary theorists.

Rajka's technical suggestions have always emerged from and were put in the service of, the analytical situation.

Motor, perceptual, and behavioural manifestations were in the focus of his observations. His 1972 paper on "Exposing Behaviour as a Method in Psychoanalysis" makes him one of the first analysts talking about "enactments" and the importance of tackling them – "exposing them" – in our daily clinical work.

"By behaviour", he wrote,

> I mean postural, motor, mimical phenomena and also actions and chains of action in the analytic situation. These provide direct, non-verbal information about the patient, which sometimes carries those contents fixed on the level of 'emotional memory' that cannot be put into words. Special attention has to be paid to understanding and working through these patterns when they are seen operating in the service of resistance.
>
> (Rajka, 1972)

The technique in itself is a simple confrontation, sometimes in a repetitive manner, reflecting Rajka's negative experience in trying to "interpret" compulsive phenomena. It fosters "working through phenomena disturbing analytic work at the very moment they emerge". The effective mechanism is set to work mainly by the patient seeing himself "not in a mirror, *as one sees in the mirror with their own eyes!*"

but through the perception of a person whose views s/he can accept or at least consider in the analytical space.

Another simple technique he taught us was "dream drawing". The aim was to achieve a more profound and multidimensional image of the patient's dreams and dream-like phantasies. While interpreting a dream, at a relevant moment we would encourage the patient to make a drawing of the dream element in question. While drawing, the patient can sit up. Finishing the drawing, which does not have to be either professional or artistic, s/he is invited to lie back on the couch, take the paper in his or her hand, and freely associate to the picture.

The drawing presents the dream content in *spatial terms*. This new dimension always furthers new material to appear, hidden from consciousness thus far.

At different stages of infantile development, experiences, and phantasies become associated with different units of the living space. Working with these drawings helps us make sense of these "topographic childhood memories". They mobilise infantile material associated with, and in a sense "locked in" with, these scenarios in an extraordinarily plastic and vivid manner.

Looking at these drawings within the context of the analytical process creates a space for "controlled sharing". Putting an aspect of the dream "outside", thus making visual material accessible for the therapeutic couple, expands the area of interpretation. This shared experience facilitates the appearance of creative elements and "legitimises" a sense of playfulness as an integral part of the analytical process. Associations mobilised by this "complex" method of interpretative work foster living and working through past experiences in the analytic present and help us see more closely how they survived in the unconscious.

Looking at dynamic processes along these lines also illuminates a basic technical point in Rajka's teaching – in harmony with the Budapest views – emphasising that transference-countertransference processes form an ever-changing constellation.

Sometimes it is most helpful to shift viewpoint and contemplate life experiences from the patient's perspective. Rajka was always interested in the spatial and sensuous qualities of memories. He wanted to understand how patients used their perception and senses as basic sources of orientation in the world. One of his original ideas in this field was to encourage a comparative study of the importance of the sense of smell as an elementary factor of orientation seemingly lost for the human race in modern civilisation. He believed smell played an archaic role in human relations, a function that should be rediscovered and explored in order to explain normal and pathological phenomena related to this form of tele-reception.

For the pioneer generation of psychoanalysts, research was considered a natural tool in analytical enquiry

While searching for evidence to support their ideas regarding the nature and dynamics of observed psychic functions, the pioneers often turned to experimenting themselves.

Searching for a biological model of anxiety in the early 1930s Rajka worked with rabbits.

He found the model he was looking for in the phenomenon of immobilisation. In a series of publications he summarised his attempts to show analogous forms of behaviour in human pathology (1972). Rajka was convinced that in anxiety he uncovered a "basic phenomenon" of psychic functioning. Psychodynamic aspects of anxiety and obsession were relevant topics for him. He compared primary compulsive phenomena to anxiety. He regarded them both as basic components of general mental activity.

A mental case around the turn of the century

The psychoanalyst – if he is truly interested in dynamic processes and does not focus entirely on the internal stage – has to try to apply binocular vision: a parallel testing of both external and psychic reality, in order to develop a view of the world we live in and make sense of it. That may enable us to look at life through the organic prism of feelings and effects associated with our nurturing or traumatising (re-traumatising) environment.

Julia Gadoros writes: Rajka proved that these are also guiding lines in the domain of mental illness. Among his theoretical writings he left a large-scale manuscript, based on Schreber's famous book – well known from Freud's interpretations – *Memoirs of my Nervous Illness* (*Denkwürdigkeiten eines Nervenkranken*), chronicling the development of his paranoid schizophrenia with real apostolic devotion.

In the introduction to his 1972 work (not published until 2005) Rajka wrote:

It is customary to investigate how books reflect the age in which their authors lived. Schreber was not a professional writer, he was only a psychotic. Therefore the mirror in which the age could be reflected is deformed and fragmented. Still it is worth observing what the glass splinters show us – as the peculiarities in refraction can make visible something one might look for in an intact mirror in vain.

His central idea is that in the system of doxasmas (*idées fixes*) the patient transforms the given social reality in congruence with the rules of his psychosis while projecting his psychotic inner world onto the given social reality of his age.

Testing the social reality compared to the psychotic "opus" may enrich our knowledge both of psychotic mechanisms and the particular epoch.

There are parts of Schreber's *Memoirs* directly connected to intellectual trends of the nineteenth century.

Rajka wrote:

It is quite peculiar how this psychotic mind contains so much of the intellectual and political distortions of the *fin de siecle*, the German crisis that paved the way to outbursts of aggression – eventually leading to an age of destruction. Schreber tries to justify his own experiences by the irrationality of the world outside: the catastrophic end of the world is a projection of a psychotic disintegration.

Rajka demonstrated how a strikingly similar sense of destruction is evident in major works of Schreber's contemporaries: writers, poets, and philosophers in search of explanations. He found substantial linkages between Karl Jaspers's ideas and critical questions formulated in Schreber's premorbid mind.

"Doctors facing mental illness are in a paradoxical situation", he continued.

Frequently they are forced to give up their wish for understanding for a long time; they have to stand the test of long months or even years of non-understanding. Symptoms, syndromes and disease are easy to detect in minutes, but that would certainly not be equal to understanding the patient.

Rajka was not only an understanding and caring doctor but also a charismatic teacher. He gave an authentic and most human model for all younger generations to follow. His figure – increasingly resembling the image of St Paul the Apostle on a Russian icon – became a symbol of professional rigour, authenticity, courage, and care. In the last years of his life, he was very ill. He was aware of the fact that his full life was fading away but in spite of the great pain he was to suffer he worked almost to the last minute. True to himself, facing mortality with profound dignity, he was strong enough to embrace life in its full scope and care about a future he knew he would not share with us.

In 1972, summing up the lessons of his life while looking back at the beginning of his century, Tibor Rajka, always the poet, wrote:

Man already saw where he came from but not where he was going. What he had seen was not reassuring. Belief in evolution became empty and lost its meaning. Feelings of unease were born amidst the technical miracles and economic growth. Art and literature expressed the disconcerting confrontation of modern man with his creations, and his painful struggle to fulfil himself and find his place in the world.

His words echoed in our minds when he sent us "going on our way" in search of our self and the concepts, basic assumptions, and values we live by.

Judit Szekacs-Weisz

Note

1 This chapter uses some details of an article by Anna Arató, Julia Gadoros, Gabor Szonyi, and Judit Szekacs-Weisz, Rajka's students, published as "L'opera di Tibor Rajka" in *Il Piccolo Hans*, in 1984.

Bibliography

Arato, A., Gadoros, J., Szonyi, G., & Szekacs, J. (1984). L'opera di Tibor Rajka. *Il Piccolo Hans*, *43–44*: 46–48.

Rajka, T. (1962). *Prophylactics Regarding the Dysfunctions of the Nervous System*. Budapest: Táncsics.

Rajka, T. (1970a). *A Mental Case around the Turn of the Century*. Unpublished manuscript.

Rajka, T. (1970b). God-system in a pathological personality. *Világosság, 3*: 162–169.

Rajka, T. (1971). A doctor's personality and the development of the pathological process in "Schreber's case". *Orvosi Hetilap, 112*: 1143–1148.

Rajka, T. (1972). Exposing behaviour as a method in psychoanalysis. Hungarian Psychological Society Conference. Published 2005 in *Pszichotherapia, 14*: 572–576.

Rajka, T. (1973). Ferenczi Sándor (1873–1933). *Orvosi Hetilap, 114*(47): 2828–2832.

Rajka, T. (1977). Obsessive phenomena and obsessional disease. *Orvosi Hetilap, 118*: 434–438.

Szekacs-Weisz, J. (2022). How to be a bi-lingual psychoanalyst. In: J. Szekacs-Weisz and W. Ivan (Eds.), *Lost Childhood and the Language of Exile* (pp. 21–28). London: Phoenix Publishing.

Chapter 10

Remembering Dr István Székács-Schönberger

Gábor Flaskay and Zsuzsa Mérei

Figure 10.1 István Székács-Schönberger. Photograph presented to the author by István Székács-Schönberger on his 85th birthday (1992)

As is evident from an overview of his career, Dr István Székács was a serious person, a highly educated physician and biochemical researcher, who considered psychoanalysis as a part of natural science (Figure 10.1). In the interviews conducted with him, he often gave the impression of a somewhat rigid, unbending man. As one of his last patients – and not just because of the distance in time that makes softens memories and enhances the built-in nature of the "good object" – I remember quite a different person: an analyst who could adapt to his patients and, if necessary, was able to transcend the limits of his own intellectual world. Bridging the two generations between us would have been impossible if he had not provided a safe space for regression. My memory flashes illustrate how he worked at the level

DOI: 10.4324/9781003309826-15

of the "basic fault" of Mihály Bálint. He was able to transmit the strict but flexible application of limit-frames, and his disciples introjected the importance of a secure atmosphere to enable the emergence of pre-verbal elements, which is essential for the working through of early trauma. Székács-Schönberger's multi-faceted relationship with the analytical society gave his students the freedom to be creative in different applied analytical fields.

Finally, in this chapter, we demonstrate how the psychodrama method, inspired by both the work of the Budapest School and Dr Székács, can work in parallel at verbal and pre-verbal levels. This heritage allows our psychoanalytic patients to be treated simultaneously in our psychodrama group, too.

The post-WW2 history of psychoanalysis in Hungary is mainly associated with three people. They are Imre Hermann, Tibor Rajka, and István Székács-Schönberger. The order is chronological and does not reflect any kind of ranking.

Dr Székács-Schönberger was a protagonist of the twentieth century. He was born in 1907 and died in 1999. He had a turbulent life: he survived two world wars, several bloody revolutions, and massive political, social, scientific, and cultural changes.

He finished medical school in 1932 and studied physics and chemistry at the University of Budapest. From 1927 to 1935, he worked as a biochemistry research intern in Dr Pál Hári's internationally renowned institute. Professor Hári opened a window of opportunity for Jewish medical students and despite the effective numerus nullus prohibition to Jewish candidates, he made it possible for them to gain an education in advanced scientific research. As a Budapest intellectual, he had already read a fair amount about psychoanalysis by that time. He can't have been more than 21 or 22 when he wrote his first essay in which he made an attempt to integrate psychology and biochemistry.

The paper, which he later called "naïve", did not survive. However, the pursuit of integrating the two distant disciplines remained in the forefront of his thinking until the end of his life. The book of his collected essays on psychoanalysis was published in 1991 under the title *Psychoanalysis and the Natural Sciences*.

There could have been two decisive factors when he chose psychoanalysis as a profession. One might have been the influence of Anni Dénes, who later became his wife. She went to Géza Róheim for therapeutic analysis, and so Dr Székács-Schönberger had an immediate impression of how analysis worked. The other was probably the influence of the physician Lajos Lévy, a good friend of his father. Dr Lévy was also the family doctor of Sándor Ferenczi, the Róheim family, and Dr Székács-Schönberger himself.

When it came to discussing existential dilemmas, the young Székács-Schönberger turned to Lajos Lévy, his fatherly friend. He was the one who initially drew Székács-Schönberger's attention to Dr Hári's scientific work and urged him to study at Dr Hári's institute and take part in the research conducted at his laboratory. Lévy was a founding member of the Hungarian Psychoanalytic Society; he strongly supported the idea of getting acquainted with psychoanalysis. An intensive reading period began, following which Székács-Schönberger applied to the chair of the Society's Training Committee, Imre Hermann, so that he could begin training analysis.

He chose the ethnographer, Géza Róheim, as his analyst. Róheim was one of Ferenczi's eminent disciples. After about one and a half years of analysis, according to the practice of the day, he was assigned his first patient to be treated in a control analysis: his personal analysis continued, but the work with his own patient became part of his analysis. It involved exploring the effects of countertransference and his personal "complexes", and how they affected his work as an analyst. The analysis lasted five years and only ended when Róheim emigrated.

Dr Székács-Schönberger also took part in theoretical seminars conducted by Imre Hermann. These dealt mainly with classical elements. The didactic training, which is today called a technical seminar, was directed by Vilma Kovács, Mihály Bálint's mother-in-law. Dr Székács-Schönberger considered Vilma Kovács to be Ferenczi's "most gifted and most truthful" student. The seminar was often attended by practising analysts (Alice Bálint, Zsigmond Pfeiffer, Endre Almásy). For the rest of his life, Dr Székács-Schönberger was of the opinion that the Budapest model was more efficient and served the purposes of training better than the practice of today, when personal analysis is strictly separated from supervision. Later on, he made sure that he ran his training analyses in the same manner.

His first analytic lecture was delivered in Paris at the 15th Congress of the International Psychoanalytical Association (1938). The title was "A Dream of Descartes", in which Dr Székács-Schönberger explored the unconscious motifs of some scientific discoveries by Descartes. The lecture integrated his scientific interest and education with the psychoanalytic approach.

Dr Székács-Schönberger was very proud that Ernest Jones asked for his paper right away so that it could be published in the *International Journal of Psychoanalysis*. Melanie Klein also warmly congratulated him. Dr Székács-Schönberger held Melanie Klein in high esteem. He had made references to her work in his lecture, and in the paper that was published subsequently. He was 32 and had the status of what we would call a psychoanalytic candidate today.

Soon after – in 1939 – he defended his paper written as a precondition of becoming a member of the Hungarian Psychoanalytic Society. The membership paper was later published.

Dr Székács-Schönberger also held Alice and Mihály Bálint in high esteem and enjoyed their company a lot: they mainly kept in touch through the Society. Székács-Schönberger was of the opinion that Alice opened up a direction in psychoanalysis which drew attention to the qualitative components of the mother-child relationship. As for Mihály, Székács-Schönberger appreciated his professional achievements and also cherished his happy disposition, his optimism, and his ability to create a good atmosphere even in difficult situations. He did not take advantage of Jones's offer to move abroad and start a career as an analyst in another country.

Hungarian psychoanalysis flourished in Budapest in the Thirties. This was the time before the major emigration wave started. According to Székács-Schönberger, there were two important groupings, and they represented a conceptual difference, too. One was the circle of Ferenczi's disciples; the other was the "Viennese" Freudian group. Hermann held a special, separate place on account of his instinct theory. However, there was no hostility or struggle for control on account of the different perspectives, but there were professional debates and discussions, the traces of which we can find in the literature of the time.

The prestige of Sándor Ferenczi, which survived even after his death, had a tempering effect on the tensions running underground. It is interesting that, apart from a short period in the late 1970s and early 1980s, the Hungarian society and its organisational predecessor have never been characterised by significant confrontation or intolerance of one another's views. Naturally, personal conflicts and differences in opinion still exist. Sándor Ferenczi's work and personality have left us a shared heritage that joins all of us.

A significant difference between the Ferenczi and the "Viennese" schools was that Ferenczi's followers attributed much greater importance to the mother-child relationship, while the Viennese practitioners were more likely to follow the fate of the instincts in their analyses. Székács-Schönberger was welcomed by Ferenczi's disciples, but he was not able to meet Ferenczi in person, because by the time he became interested in psychoanalysis, Ferenczi was already seriously ill. To avoid any misunderstanding, Dr Székács-Schönberger always pointed out that Ferenczi had pernicious anaemia.

Dr István Székács-Schönberger was in private psychoanalytic practice between 1934 and 1943. After the Second World War, in 1946, under the leadership of Hermann, an attempt was made to reorganise the Hungarian Psychoanalytic Society. Dr Székács-Schönberger received training analytic status in that year. In the period before, the membership of the Society was vastly reduced owing to the persecution of Jews, war losses, and massive emigration. The attempt to revive the Society did not succeed, and the then new Communist regime forced it to dissolve itself.

Although the cultivation of psychoanalysis and the training model survived – more in the manner of an underground stream – it was not possible to pursue any private psychoanalytic practice. Székács-Schönberger did not specialise beyond his general medical education, unlike other psychoanalysts, who specialised as psychiatrists and were able to use this as a cover for their psychoanalytic and psychotherapeutic activity, so he returned to his original field of biochemistry.

From 1950 to 1953 he was department head at the Biochemistry Institute of the Hungarian Academy of Sciences, where he conducted and directed biochemical research and also participated in the setting up of the organisational structure for the sciences in the new social system. From 1953 to 1970 he worked as a senior member of the Department of Viruses at the National Public Health Institute. Later he worked as the head of the Biochemistry and Isotope Department.

Throughout his career as a biochemist, he followed the main developments in the world of psychoanalysis; he acquired the most important volumes of essay collections and maintained personal contact with foreign analysts.

His gradual return to psychoanalytic practice started in the 1960s. Since he worked with radioactive isotopes and was exposed to radiation hazard, he had reduced working hours, and from the mid-1960s onwards was able to work as an analyst in the afternoons. After his retirement in 1970, he ran sessions for eight hours per day.

From the very beginning, he made an attempt to combine his psychoanalytical knowledge with his views originating from his education in natural sciences. For instance, he could not tolerate the use of vague and redundant concepts and made an effort to use exact definitions and unambiguous terms. On the one hand, he accepted Freud's long-held view that psychoanalysis is the application of natural science methods in the new field of psychology and, furthermore, he also agreed that psychoanalysis is nothing else but the application of scientific research – especially observation – under special circumstances. His approach was later enhanced by recognising and integrating the mutual impact of the observer and the observed in the system.

The model from where this view was incorporated into Székács-Schönberger's thinking was typically rooted in natural sciences: it came from the world of astronomical observations. The notion that the psychoanalytic situation is seen and presented as a "meeting of two subjects" was, of course, still missing from his approach, even though the awareness of the transference-countertransference phenomena, a crucial element of the Budapest tradition, was part of his work right from the outset.

On the other hand, he thought – as many people still do nowadays – that a better understanding of the functioning of the nervous system and the humoral apparatus, as well as the new procedures resulting from it, would, in the future, allow the meeting of biological and psychological systems. It would only be a matter of time before it became possible to influence psychological function by scientific means and thus be used for the treatment of psychic disorders (for example, it would be possible to transform defence mechanisms in this way).

Some of us were sceptical about this kind of a meeting of the two disciplines and argued that it is hard to imagine that an experience, be it from the present or the past, could be induced by chemical means, and could be eliminated or significantly influenced (without side effects). We emphasised that biological and psychological processes take place in tandem and we were unable to fathom their intersection. Biology and psychology are two sides of the same coin; neither can exist without the other, and likewise, one cannot replace the other. The heated debates on these issues were very instructive for us.

The third science theorem which, according to Székács-Schönberger, was also incorporated into psychology, is the law of action and counteraction, which attempts to perceive phenomena as a dynamic interaction of opposing forces. In psychology, this is expressed by urges (e.g., instincts) and their inhibition (defence mechanisms).

Another conceptual principle that originated from natural sciences and was duly emphasised by István Székács-Schönberger is that, in psychoanalysis, too, one should make an effort to see phenomena in the context of their development in order to have a better chance of understanding their complexity.

Finally, he was the one who drew our attention to the significance of statistical relationships, saying that if two or more phenomena occur simultaneously, either always or with a high frequency, then there is likely to be some kind of functional or causal relationship between them, even if we do not know what that relationship might be in the given situation. This is a principle that applies both to natural phenomena and psychology.

After the Soviet occupation, psychoanalytic practice and training were illegal but carried on at a low level under other guises. In many respects, they followed the traditions of the former Hungarian school of psychoanalysis. We had to stay silent. Open discussions about theory, practice, and organisational life were not possible. This particular situation meant that the practice followed the traditions faithfully, and the training of the senior generation differed in some respects from how it is done today or even how it was done internationally at that time.

Training under Dr Székács-Schönberger's guidance took place in the following manner: a few years of personal analysis, followed by control analysis; at the same time his analysands were invited to the seminars that he led. The seminar sessions were open, new participants joined halfway through, and, occasionally, there were guests from the other group to deliberate over some of the topics. Many participants worked for 10–15 years together. They began by processing Freud's cases, followed by *The Interpretation of Dreams*. Next they studied Freud's technical writings.

Later on, members of the seminar discussed Freud's theoretical works and also began to discover the development of psychoanalysis through reading and discussing the works of the most important authors, for example, Ferenczi, Abraham, Reich, Anna Freud, Klein, Racker, Kohut, and Kernberg. The seminar was not divided into a theoretical and a technical part. The review of the literature was occasionally interrupted by the discussion of a case brought up by seminar participants. The sessions had an importance that went far beyond training their participants.

In those years, the so-called "flying universities" were a potential means of transferring knowledge; these were underground intellectual centres that were created and functioned in a semi-clandestine fashion in people's private homes. Székács-Schönberger's Saturday seminar can perhaps be included among these underground educational enterprises. For example, the participants translated a number of essays into Hungarian; these translated texts were circulated widely and gave much to the whole profession. They helped overcome the challenges that arose from the lack of language skills and being isolated from the specialist literature. For instance, Kernberg's book *Borderline Conditions and Pathological Narcissism*, which was published in 1975, was translated in full by the participants of the seminar. Initially, photocopies were distributed, but the text was published as a proper book as soon as it became possible.

By the 1980s, two psychoanalytic groups had emerged in Budapest. These two groups did not establish and maintain formal connections with each other, but informally there were thousands of links connecting them. They had friends and family members in the "other group", as well as respected and highly regarded colleagues.

Some people felt the need for integration and wanted to eliminate the separation. It took several years, but eventually the two groups merged. There was a precondition on behalf of the other group, which had by then achieved IPA's Study Group status. It required that one of their trainers should carry out a supervisory process with members of the Székács-Schönberger group, and this was duly fulfilled.

And so, in 1989, when it became possible to establish independent scientific and social organisations, the Hungarian Psychoanalytic Society was founded, together with the disciples of Székács-Schönberger, as a provisional society of the IPA.

Let us now change our perspective and continue with a personal reminiscence of Zsuzsa Mérei. She writes:

As one of his last disciples, I have reflected extensively about the time that I spent with Dr Székács-Schönberger. I can best illustrate his methods by providing some examples on how he worked at the level of the "basic fault" ...

István Székács-Schönberger was my analyst. I did not go to him because I wanted to learn or get trained – I was his patient. I went to see him because I was in trouble. I didn't know much about him, but based on what my girlfriend said, I assumed that he was a therapist who not only listened to the words but was also following the transference and countertransference feelings. I did not know exactly what all this meant, but I was quite sure I would not be able to make myself understood by words only, so I applied to him. I was afraid of analysis itself, and also of analysts: their stiffness and rigour, and their unquestionable superiority.

Székács-Schönberger was a serious, strong-minded, and gutsy person, a sovereign individual of great calibre. He was also a clear-thinking scientist, who looked for interconnections in emotional relations and worked with objective, rational terms. At the same time, he had an interior compass to the world of what Bálint called the "basic fault": a world before proper words existed. He was able to refrain from interpretation but just be patiently present and provide a safe space. He could alter his working style to fit his analysand's current needs, something that we both needed in order to bridge the age gap of almost 50 years that separated us.

Recalling the analysis and the analyst is like a great trip: there are only flashing memories, the mood, the atmosphere, colours, smells, and images. I liked going to his place, I liked the apartment with its generous affluence where you could hardly find any items of modern design. Books, works of art, fine paintings, a spacious, bright, and clean apartment that often smelled of cakes. I called him the Old Man, even though I did not perceive him as someone terribly old. He was energetic, and I reckon that he might have been in the first years of his second marriage at the time. His sculptor wife, Cathy Michel, who was younger than him, was a Canadian Hungarian.

Her presence could also be felt in the apartment, since we had to walk across it each time in order to get to the consulting room. There were rows of deep-blue, African violets in the corner windows. He raised them, just as he was the one who constructed the elevated analytic couch. It was not unheard of to ask questions of Székács-Schönberger, and he did answer, but he did not dwell on anything and, unfortunately, I never got round to asking what the reason was for increasing the height of the couch. Was it so that he could hear better? Or to reduce the distance? To make it easier to get up? I never found out ...

And above the couch, the large Chagall poster: "Over the town". The lower part of the painting with the lonely little boy, squatting and relieving himself; you can see the fences of no man's land, the village without people, with only a goat in sight – perhaps the biblical scapegoat – and the lovers floating in the air. The image can be found online at https://www.sartle.com/artwork/over-the-town-marc-chagall

Recently, I have contacted several of Székács-Schönberger's disciples and I was happy to hear that others also remembered how he would stand in the doorway when his patients arrived, with a vivid look in his eyes, ready for work, open, but neutral. The atmosphere was neither friendly nor unfriendly. We were in business.

I would like to share three memories of mine.

From the very beginning I tried to let myself go, but for a long time I was still waiting for him to straighten up, clear his throat, and pounce on me with a *Deutung* – some harsh interpretation. My first memory is when I once turned my head and asked him: "Are we always going to just talk like this?" At first, he didn't even understand what I was asking. "Yes, that's what we are going to do", he replied. I can't remember what else he said; I think he just laughed when he eventually understood the question.

As soon as I asked this question, I understood, or rather, I felt, that I could really let myself go, that there was no danger, no ulterior motive, or any expectation. Székács's laughter indicated that he also came to understand something: the fact that I felt and appreciated his method. He didn't want anything from me, he didn't want to teach, educate, didn't even want to heal. Today I would call it a "moment of meeting".

And from then on, we talked for another nine years with occasional interruptions. He never cleared his throat, even though he sometimes croaked. He did not criticise me, and he did not confront me beyond the level that I was just about able to tolerate at that moment. Even so, we had heated arguments, for example, when I wanted to reduce the weekly sessions from four to three – and even below that – or when I started to conduct psychodrama groups.

The second memory is probably from the middle period of the therapy. I had a fantasy, as vivid and detailed as a dream. In my fantasy, I was sitting on his lap, as a little child in a white dress and I could see his face from below. I was two years old when one night the "black car" came for my father: he was arrested. The fantasy took me back to the time before the trauma when I was able to experience safety on my father's lap. I was able to relive the experience in the reverie. The safety of the consulting room brought back the security of early childhood, and Székács-Schönberger allowed me to find and experience the good in myself. All along, he was there with me and let me go into regression, let me be as I was, regressively or not regressively. He let me be myself and allowed me to meet myself.

The third memory is of our last encounter. He had been ill for a while when he called me one evening and asked me to come to the hospital. I was more surprised than frightened by the request. He was 92 years old, quite ill, but he kept his posture and made an effort for our meeting. We did not talk about why he called; we trusted that understanding would come about without words. In this last "session", I could see the little girl whose job was to give strength to adults. It was only much later when I realised that he wanted more than just to say goodbye. He didn't want to leave without saying goodbye; he didn't want to leave me behind suddenly. He didn't want to traumatise me again.

We have both experienced the trauma of someone leaving without saying goodbye. Just as my dad disappeared without saying goodbye when I was two, Székács-Schönberger also had to leave his son behind when the black car came for him in 1953. He was arrested as part of a Stalinist mock trial and was accused of being a spy. He was imprisoned for about nine months and was only released some days after Stalin died.

I think that was the trauma he didn't want to happen again. He didn't want to experience leaving another person in his charge without saying goodbye and neither did he want me to experience that a person whom I trusted would abandon me without bidding farewell.

Székács-Schönberger was unwavering, and he never made any concessions to his consistent value system. This might have seemed like rigidity from the outside, but it was an indisputable, fixed point, a benchmark, or point of origin, relative to which you could locate yourself. It did not make it easy for him to adapt to the changing world. After the war, he became entangled in a serious conflict with Hermann, then with Hermann's disciples, as well as with the Psychoanalytic Society, which was in the process of being re-founded. Ultimately, he decided to join, but mostly at the request and in the interests of his disciples. In actual fact, he did not urge his disciples to join the Society; instead he encouraged them to use their analytical skills where they had the opportunity to do so, for example, in the field of psycho-oncology or art psychology.

I carried on his legacy in my psychodrama practice. My colleague, András Vikár, and I designed a psychodrama method that is largely interconnected with the traditions of the Budapest school. For example, we work so that the participants can meet with themselves, in Bálintian terms. For this to happen, it is essential to have a clear, simple, and stable framework as well as continuous work with the holding function of the group.

In the supportive atmosphere created in this way, we work in tandem with the group and its individual members, paying continuous attention both to their verbal and pre-verbal manifestations. In the process of the psychodrama play, the protagonists externalise their inner world and, as a result, they make it possible for us to monitor contemporaneously inner representations and interpersonal events. This simultaneity helps the protagonists to reach a state of, and act in, what Bálint calls "regression for progression", thereby allowing them to experience the passage between the Bálintian levels, descending to regression and ascending to progression. Whenever there is synchronisation between the inner and outer movements, the protagonist experiences his or her activity and creativity and exists independently and vividly. In the final phase of his or her performance (the psychodrama play), the protagonist reintegrates into the group and the outside world through the principled, mentalizing feedback provided by members of the group.

While remembering him, I read everything I could find from him or about him, I made contact with several of his disciples, and all this gave me an astonishing momentum. In the meantime, I finished my analysis and ended my mourning with a beautiful dream. In the dream, an important object lost its solidity, became transparent, but retained its original structure. In one of his studies, Székács-Schönberger says that creativity is derived from the curiosity to gain insight into the unknown, dark object.

Never speak ill of the dead – so goes the saying echoing the Latin "De mortuis nihil nisi bonum" ("Of the dead say nothing but good"). It may sound a trivial idea but is perhaps the moral basis for the fact that our cemeteries are full of best parents and best spouses. However, it is possible that the saying is more to do with the process of mourning, which, if it does not get stuck, will lead to the creation of the good object. Once we have reached this stage, we are able to remember and speak graciously. This is the fruit of alone-ness below the level of the basic fault.

In this instance, the preparation for this chapter, which simultaneously turned out to be a mourning work, implied going through all three levels of Bálint's object relationships. Recalling the analysis with Dr Székács-Schönberger, and especially the work at the level of the basic fault, has led to the place of creativity and alone-ness under the basic fault. This is where the inner good object and the dream could be born, followed by "shared remembrance", by this stage, at the level of verbalisation.

The process demonstrates that in the course of psychic work, whenever there is penetrability between the three levels and whenever the tools of all three levels are available, a unique, energetic, and fertile state can be brought about, one that allows us to find new beginnings and novel pathways.

Bibliography

Hadas, M. (1995). Beszélgetés Dr. Székács Istvánnal. *Replika*, *19–20*: 11–41.

Schönberger, S. (1939). A dream of descartes: Reflections on the unconscious determinants of the sciences. *International Journal Psycho-Analysis*, *20*: 43–57.

Schönberger, S. (1946). A clinical contribution to the analysis of the nightmare-syndrome. *Psychoanalytic Review*, *33*(1): 44–70.

Schönberger, S. (1948). Disorders of the ego in wartime. *British Journal of Medical Psychology, XXI*: 4.

Székács, I. (1984). Róheim Géza, a pszichoanalitikus. In: G. Róheim (Eds.), *Primitiv Kultúrák Pszichoanalitikus Vizsgálata* (pp. 643–663). Budapest: Gondolat.Székács, I. (1987). Transparency, creativity and interpretation. *International Review of Psycho-Analysis*, *14*(2): 203–219.

Székács, I. (1991). *Pszichoanalízis és Természettudomány* [*Psychoanalysis and Natural Sciences*]. Budapest: Párbeszéd Könyvek.

Székács-Schönberger, I. (2007). *Egy Zsidó Polgár Gyermekkora Analitikus Háttérrel*. Budapest: Múlt és Jövő.

Chapter 11

My debt to Michael Bálint

Kathleen Kelley-Lainé

This chapter may sound more like a testimony than an erudite presentation on Michael Balint.

There are books that change one's life and I have been lucky to come upon a few in my lifetime: one of the important ones was Michael Balint's *Thrills and Regressions*. We all know that for a book to have a transformative effect it has to be at the right time, in the right place, and fit into the psychic state of the reader. A book can open the mind and awaken the reader's interest and engagement in psychoanalysis, or it can close it forever. Why did Balint's book on *Thrills and Regressions* have such a powerful effect on me?

Balint announces outright in the introduction to *Thrills and Regressions* that he wants to go beyond Freudian theory.

Concerning primary object relations, he states that using the term "oral" for everything that is primary is distressingly one-sided and reduces the understanding of primitive phenomena. The oral bias, he feels, fails to extend our theoretical understanding of common human experience. To free himself from the limits of standard theory he proposes to introduce two new terms, "philobat" and "ocnophil", as a novel strategy to understand the dynamic nature of the human psyche. He invites us to look at the first "thrills" that a baby feels when returning to the safety zone that is "mother". This "leaving and returning" to mother in babyhood, as observed by Balint, sets the pattern of human attachment. The ocnophil reaction is a spontaneous reflex to grasp the secure object and hang onto it, whereas the "philobat" needs to be able to let it go. Balint uses the metaphor of the tightrope-walker who hangs onto his rod (secure object) with the purpose of not letting it go. The philobat needs to be alone, relying on his personal resources. The thrill is to move as far and as fast as possible from security, face dangerous situations and survive. Independence is of primary importance.

How does each type experience anxiety? The term ocnophil, inspired by the Greek word *okneo*, means to "hang onto, retract, hesitate, doubt". "The ocnophil world is composed of objects separated by frightful empty spaces", writes Balint. Fear is caused by the separation from objects and tranquility is re-established by the return of their proximity. The object, however, is only partial for the ochnophil, it has no life of its own; only the parts that correspond to specific needs define the

DOI: 10.4324/9781003309826-16

object. The object cannot become a subject of concern for the ochnophil. Balint considers this a pre-depressive state, rendering frustration and ambivalence inevitable since the individual is constantly in danger of being abandoned.

The philobatic world consists of friendly spaces and of avoiding dangerous objects – important is a comfortable distance and sufficient vision to survey the environment. If the ocnophil is defined through the sense of touch, the philobat is defined through sight. The philobat maintains the illusion of not needing an object, since he is self-sufficient. The tendency is being too optimistic – albeit with the need to survey the environment. Convinced that the world will come to him, the philobat feels capable of avoiding dangerous objects through efficient perusal of the environment. The philobat is just as compulsive about surveying as the ocnophil is obsessive about touching.

Balint goes on to test his concept against further aspects of object relations such as "aggression and autoeroticism", love and hate, the reality principle. Aggression is considered as a part of philobatic activity, although the philobat is represented as an independent, courageous, successful hero, but often mistrusted by others.

While philobatic heroism is extremely masculine, it is at the same time childish and never quite adult. Neither ocnophil nor philobat can be deemed more advanced or less regressive.

Concerning "love and hate" Balint points out that both typologies contain the root "phil" which signifies "love", and it would be an error to consider that one needs the love of its objects and the other does not. He states that this kind of opposition was a basic error in the original development of libido theory, when it was considered that sadism and masochism were opposites. He insists that ocnophilism and philobatism are two different attitudes originating from the same root. For example the ocnophil needs an object to relieve fear, but does not necessarily love the object; in fact he can come to hate the object because he feels too dependent. He may have to abandon the object to regain his self-esteem. The philobat can become suspicious or hateful of his objects because of their unpredictability. Both ocnophil and philobat maintain the ambivalence of love and hate towards their "objects". The question is how they both justify their worlds and believe it as "real".

Balint's answer is logical: we incorporate external reality with our internal world because we want to create the world in our own image. The question remains of how we maintain this defective vision of reality even into adulthood. He proposes that the answer is to be found in the primary world of the preverbal child and in regression to infantile narcissism.

I now ask myself, why was I so moved by Michael Balint's book *Thrills and Regressions* written in 1972. My present reading as a psychoanalyst with years of experience is very different from that of the young woman who had emigrated once more as if she had to keep changing countries to counteract having been torn up from her childhood roots and language at a very young age. At least now emigration was by choice.

What probably attracted me most was Balint's desire to go beyond traditional theory of instincts and object relations, and structure knowledge through human experiences of thrills and regression. Like me, he was an immigrant and very sensitive to what is lost in translation of the mother tongue. He adds that the more emotional the communication the more difficult it is to express it in a language other than the mother tongue.

At the time I certainly suffered from the difficulty of expressing myself – emotions were, as he says, mainly in Hungarian, and the logical practical me was in English. The head and the heart were to be joined in the third language, French. It is not surprising that the first and most obvious changes I perceived having started psychoanalysis were the ability to write and to speak in public. I must add that my analysis was in Hungarian and I suppose that the child deep inside was beginning to grow up.

Balint's contribution to psychoanalysis is in understanding the earliest development of the child starting from a pre-anaclitic stage to the beginning of object relations. He tries to describe in detail the emergence of the object. For example, when the investment is excessive and the need is to hang onto the object, the subject tends to neglect the development of an independent ego. This dynamic is "ocnophil". Others, the philobats, react to the same situation by investing in the ego and its personal attributes disproportionately, thereby neglecting to invest in adequate, intimate, and lasting object relations. These are of course extreme examples.

Balint's main purpose was to go beyond the existing "oral" theorising of primary processes such as "instinct", inspired by scientific terminologies and borrowed from biology. He admitted that terms such as "oral destructivity or anal domination, genital-phallic love" etc. have their use, but just as did his teacher Sandor Ferenczi, he believed that the language of psychoanalysis needed to be closer to the stuff of human experience. If it is thanks to Balint that I began psychoanalysis, do I owe him the fact that I became a psychoanalyst? Although my initial training was along traditional Freudian lines, I am very much inspired by the "Hungarian" school of Ferenczi and Balint. Like Balint, I feel that the role of the analyst is to accompany the patient along a transformative journey, wherein by letting go of childhood conditioning, irrational, and false attitudes that lead to failure and breakdown, he/she can find the authentic self with its own desires.

Bibliography

Balint, M. (1959). *Thrills and Regressions*. London: Hogarth.
Balint, M. (1960). Primary narcissism and primary love. *Psychoanalytical Quarterly*, *29*: 6–43.
Balint, M. (1979). *The Basic Fault*. London: Tavistock/Routledge.
Brabant-Gerö, E. (1993). *Ferenczi et l'Ecole Hongroise de Psychanalyse*. Paris: L'Harmattan.
Kelley-Lainé, K. (1997). *Peter Pan the Story of Lost Childhood*. Shaftesbury: Element.

Part 4

Links rediscovered

Introduction to Wladimir Granoff's presentation on Balint at Lacan's seminar

Martine Bacherich[1]

First of all, I wish to express my gratitude to Professor Dany Nobus. It is a rare privilege to introduce an English-speaking readership to the text of a presentation on Michael Balint by Wladimir Granoff at Jacques Lacan's *Séminaire*, on 26 May 1954. This text, which he has translated from the French, has remained unpublished until now, and I would like to thank him for making it available. Relegated for so many years to purgatory, the very existence of this presentation has been ignored by a very large number of people, and this precious piece of a historical and even mythical fresco – Lacan's inaugural teaching – has so far been withheld from both English and French readers. The initiative of Professor Nobus, for whom the notions of history and the archive are not empty words, therefore deserves to be recognised.

The great care Wladimir Granoff himself took to preserve several copies of all the mail he received or sent out, and to secretly compile the minutes of decisive meetings with the authorities of the International Psychoanalytical Association (IPA), at a time when performing such a task was difficult and by no means common practice, shows to what extent the archive, in the noble sense of the word, also occupied a crucial place in his own thought. For him, the archive represented an archaeological fragment that is worthy of the greatest interest, both for future research and for contemporary psychoanalysts. His correspondence from 1972 with Kurt R. Eissler, guardian of the then impenetrable Freud Archives, which Granoff tried to break open, is also quite uplifting in this respect.[2]

During the 1950s, Balint's works had not been translated into French and French psychoanalysts were not especially interested in works written in foreign languages, including the original works by Freud in German, many of which were already available in English thanks to James Strachey. This was obviously not the case for Lacan and Granoff. English was Wladimir Granoff's third language, after Russian and German, and before French. Moreover, Granoff sensed rather quickly that if Freud had discovered psychoanalysis, Ferenczi had been the one to *do* psychoanalysis (Granoff, 1958, p. 85). And so he became interested in and intrigued by Michael Balint, in particular by what Balint epitomised as the crucial link in Ferenczi's lineage, of which Granoff would subsequently quip that he imported it into France. If we add to this that, in 1952, Granoff had read Alice Balint's

DOI: 10.4324/9781003309826-18

"Love for the Mother and Mother Love" (1939), which would inspire him to en-
title his first published article "Desire for Children, Children's Desire: Un désir
d'enfant" (1956) – in an explicit acknowledgement of Balint's influence on him –
everything converged to make him "the right man in the right place" for this presentation on Balint at Lacan's *Séminaire*. Moreover, Lacan was well aware of the
fact that Granoff was not only an English speaker, but above all an Anglophile. His
well-known Anglomania expressed itself in his choice of cars, Gieves & Hawkes
suits, "*bleuet de France*" on his lapel, Blenheim Bouquet, and a wide range of food
products, from Scottish grouse to artisanal sausages. Since Granoff was also the
founder and curator of the Bugatti Museum in Prescott, the society's annual meeting is still held in his country house in the Chevreuse valley, whose listed garden is
inspired by Sissinghurst.

On 26 May 1954, Granoff was not yet 30 years old. He was already a training
analyst and would soon be recognised as a member of the IPA in a personal capacity. He was to all intents and purposes a rising star. The elites of the Société Psychanalytique de Paris had whispered that his future was secure. However, in 1953,
he had taken the lead in the "revolt of the trainees" and had turned his back on
the psychoanalytic establishment and its apparatchiks, following Lacan instead.[3]
On numerous occasions, Granoff has described Lacan's splendid appearance, his
youthfully aristocratic, irresistible emergence in a sclerotic universe that, in his
eyes, would soon be condemned. At his first *Séminaire*, Lacan distributed cards of
elephants to his audience (Lacan, 1975, p. 287). Jean-Claude Lavie has recounted
"this spirit of freedom and enthusiasm that would be hard to imagine nowadays,
where psychoanalysis was not just a practice to be transmitted, but also an adven-
ture to be pursued" (Lavie, 2001, p. 316). A pioneering and fraternal spirit reigned.
Carried away by an ardent exigency, all the participants imagined in their intellectual effervescence that they could change the world. This was the audience and the
room in which Granoff's presentation took place.[4]

Lacan's first seminar inaugurated the period after the split of 1953 and gathered
together on the same stage, on this spring day, the person of Lacan, in all his bril-
liance, Michael Balint (whose text was to be discussed), and Wladimir Granoff.
The seminar is offered as an authentic key for the programmatic approach of an entire swathe of psychoanalysis: theory, technique, its possible downward slides and
its avowed doubts. It still carries within itself the germ of what would happen next:
Westminster 1963, the new break-up, ten years later.[5] At the start of the seminar
session, Granoff wondered what was at stake for Lacan. Was it to assert what one is
supposed to do, or rather what one is not supposed to do in the psychoanalytic treatment? By 1997, he would have answered: back then, it was a question of serving
Lacan in the war he was waging against the governing bodies of psychoanalysis.
And Balint was very much part of the insurgency. Unlike Ferenczi, his aim was
to rearrange things without therefore breaking with Freud, without perishing, and
without the analysand paying the price. In Balint's case, Granoff would speak of
a "current of thought" rather than an established thought process, convinced as he

was that Lacan considered Balint to be a poor theoretician, who was negligible at best. But Balint's swerves could illustrate for the trainees his own personal struggles, because Balint had the merit of casting doubt on the analysts' practice, forcing himself to suspend their certainties and situating them on a slope without hope.

Granoff, for his part, understood that Balint – much like Winnicott, but before him – wanted to replay the same failures, bypass the same resistances. Balint was definitely the first to have opened the abyss in the relationship between theory and practice. As Ferenczi's heir, Balint's deceptive side thus resonated with the dark side of Ferenczi, mocked as such by Ernest Jones. And even if, under the anonymity desired by Lacan, Imre Hermann is entirely plausible as the enigmatic "third man" in the Hungarian trio that is at one point mentioned by Lacan during Granoff's presentation, wouldn't it make sense to say that Hermann also obscured another Hungarian, posted behind the scenes, forever "our master to all" – Sándor Ferenczi? Through Balint's texts, Lacan was the first to direct Granoff towards Ferenczi who, quite ironically, would also become the agency of their separation.[6] Both of them also knew how, shortly before his death, Ferenczi had conceded that Balint picked up where he himself had stopped (Moreau Ricaud, 2007, p. 199; Peeters, 2020, p. 300). They knew that the Ferenczian vacillation had produced effects which, migrating via Balint, had found a space to unfold themselves in London. Balint was also the entirely laudable, generous man, to whom Granoff would address himself in London with a request for personal help. He was the analyst of deadlocks and end points, and the practitioner who allowed Granoff to measure the major role that is to be granted to the dimension of care in the cure (Granoff, 1991).

The reader will notice the sometimes lively tone, without any concession whatsoever, of the exchanges between Lacan and Granoff, which gives a singular flavour to their dialogue. Granoff was definitely not a student like the others, even if he belonged to those who intervened at Lacan's seminar: the group of brilliant disciples who made up "the class of '24", because by a strange coincidence many of them were born in that year. With the exception of Granoff, they also shared the experience of being on Lacan's couch. I am referring, here, to Serge Leclaire and François Perrier, with whom Granoff formed the famous "troika", but also to Jean-Bertrand Pontalis, Jean Laplanche, Jean-Claude Lavie, Octave Mannoni, and many other great psychoanalysts to come.

Reverence is not subjugation. Granoff enjoyed a modality of speech of which he was undoubtedly the sole owner, and the future would prove it. Yet he owed this freedom to the one who opened the windows for him – Lacan himself. Never would he renounce his immense debt to him. Their distinguished *epos* lasted ten years, and 1963 would spell the end of what could be designated as the golden age of psychoanalysis in France: 1953–1963. For Granoff, 1963 would also mark the true level of the bitter failure, the fact that he had not succeeded in introducing all of this to the IPA, because it did not seem impossible to him that everything Lacan had done for him, he could also do for others.

By virtue of this text, readers can now rub shoulders with three towering figures of psychoanalysis who are grappling with the subject, with their expectations and its limits, with the status of love (primary and genital), and with the basic fault, insofar as they constitute the end point, the unsurpassable rock of the treatment for certain patients and their analysts. What else could it really mean for Ferenczi, for Balint, and, after them, for Granoff, than trying to remedy the irremediable (Granoff, 1996)? Whether the debate is finished or infinite, the question still burns and always will.

Notes

1 Text translated by Dany Nobus.
2 The correspondence in question remains unpublished. A selection of letters will be in-cluded, alongside English translations of some of Granoff's key texts, courtesy of Mar-tine Bacherich and myself, in a special issue of the journal *Psychoanalysis and History*, which is scheduled for publication in 2024, to coincide with the centenary of Granoff's birth. (Translator's note.)
3 In May 1953, a group of analysts in training at the Société Psychanalytique de Paris revolted against the statutes of a newly created Training Institute, which resulted in the creation of a new group, the Société française de Psychanalyse (SFP), in which Lacan rapidly established himself as the intellectual figurehead. For a detailed account of this first split in the French psychoanalytic movement, see Roudinesco (1986, pp. 223–276). (Translator's note.)
4 At this point, we can only wonder about the reasons for the omission of Granoff's lecture in the published version of Lacan's *Seminar I*. It is also apt here to compare the miss-ing text of Granoff's lecture in this first seminar with another missing text of his, in the publication of Lacan's 1962–1963 seminar on anxiety. On 20 February, 1963, Granoff was in charge of the session, because Lacan had gone skiing. For that day, Lacan had asked him to present, with François Perrier, the work of some English psychoanalysts again, in this case Barbara Low, Margaret Little, and Lucia Tower. When Lacan returned on 27 February, he immediately opened the debate on countertransference (Lacan, 2004, pp. 146–147).
5 In 1963, members of the SFP were presented with an ultimatum by the IPA: the group would only be granted re-affiliation with the IPA on condition that they agreed to strip Lacan of his position as a training analyst. The motion was passed on 19 November, 1963, which led to the second split in the French psychoanalytic movement. See Roudinesco (1986, pp. 318–359). (Translator's note.)
6 We should also compare two lectures here: Ferenczi's "Confusion of Tongues between the Adults and the Child", which was presented at the Wiesbaden Congress of 1932 (Fer-enczi, 1932), and Granoff's "Ferenczi: faux problème ou vrai malentendu?", presented at the SFP in 1958 (Granoff, 1958). These lectures will mark two ruptures – Freud/ Ferenczi and Lacan/Granoff. For Granoff, the status of the complaint was at the heart of these two ruptures. Both for Freud and for Lacan, the complaint is necessarily that of an adult. Unbearable in adults, it is unsustainable in children. When confronted with this notion, Granoff went so far as to detect a violent policing of it in Freud and a vio-lent contempt for it in Lacan. He envisioned a critical relationship between theorising and the complaint, which made them mutually exclusive. For him, however, theorising would not have existed without drawing an essential part of its driving force from the complaint.

Bibliography

Balint, A. (1939). Love for the mother and mother love. In: M. Balint (Eds.), *Primary Love and Psycho-Analytic Technique* (pp. 109–127). London: Hogarth, 1952.

Ferenczi, S. (1932). Confusion of the tongues between the adults and the child: The language of tenderness and of passion. M. Balint (Trans.). *International Journal of Psycho-Analysis, 30*: 225–230.

Granoff, W. (1956). Desire for children, children's desire: Un désir d'enfant. *La Psychanalyse, 2*: 75–109.

Granoff, W. (1958). Ferenczi: Faux problème ou vrai malentendu? In: *Lacan, Ferenczi et Freud* (pp. 73–114). Paris: Gallimard, 2001.

Granoff, W. (1991). Cure and care. In: *Le Désir D'analyse* (pp. 185–197). Paris: Flammarion, 2007.

Granoff, W. (1996). Remédier à L'irrémédiable. In: *Le Désir D'analyse* (pp. 167–183). Paris: Flammarion, 2007.

Lacan, J. (1975). *The Seminar. Book I: Freud's Papers on Technique (1953–54).* J.-A. Miller (Ed.), J. Forrester (Trans.). Cambridge, MA: Cambridge University Press, 1988.

Lacan, J. (2004). *The Seminar. Book X: Anxiety (1962–63).* J.-A. Miller (Ed.), A. R. Price (Trans.). Cambridge-Malden, MA: Polity, 2014.

Lavie, J.-C. (2001). Un désaccord parfait. In: W. Granoff (Ed.), *Lacan, Ferenczi et Freud* (pp. 315–332). Paris: Gallimard.

Moreau Ricaud, M. (2007). *Michael Balint. Le Renouveau de l'École de Budapest.* Ramonville-Saint Agne, France: Érès.

Peeters, B. (2020). *Sándor Ferenczi. L'enfant Terrible de la Psychanalyse.* Paris: Flammarion.

Roudinesco, É. (1986). *Jacques Lacan & Co.: A History of Psychoanalysis in France 1925–1985.* J. Mehlman (Trans.). London: Free Association, 1990.

Chapter 13

Presentation on Balint at Lacan's seminar *Freud's papers on technique*, 26 May 1954

Wladimir Granoff[1]

The question is whether I should summarise this book.[2] It seems impossible for me to do so, because it's a collection of papers and presentations by Balint, or rather by the first Balint couple – Balint and his first wife Alice – on the occasion of various conferences. The papers span a period from 1930 until 1952, and it's not always easy to identify a guiding thread. There is no commonality, strictly speaking, even in the orientation of these papers, and so I really cannot summarise the book for you. As a result, I think we need to restrict ourselves to extracting some general impressions from it. As to connecting these impressions with the current stage of our seminar, I think I should leave it to Dr Lacan to do this, because otherwise I would run the risk of misinterpreting. Extending this preliminary remark some-what, I should nonetheless point out that this book is extremely funny, because one has the impression that our pioneering work doesn't lose its value and its acuity in it, and that we're actually very far from being alone in pursuing a certain tendency.

In this book, Balint presents a current of thought [*une pensée*]. It's difficult to say this, because I actually think that, ultimately, he manifests a certain mood in it. One may ask, and I've asked myself, about the reasons that prompted you [Lacan] to entrust me with its examination. Is this book meant to be the illustration of what one is supposed to do in analysis, or rather of what one is *not* supposed to do? In the end, the entire book revolves around this question. Because up to a certain point, which shouldn't be closed, and starting from a certain milestone, one definitely shouldn't […]. Now, between us, whenever I shall use the word "correct", it will mean "being in conformity with what we want". The first line of what is extremely correct makes Balint come out on some kind of road which should normally have taken him very far, because it's wide and clear and not very far removed from the place where he's supposed to arrive, yet at the very moment he's about to arrive at his destination, he suddenly turns the steering wheel [*il donne un brusque coup de volant*] and ends up in the ditch.[3] And then he seems to ask himself: "What am I doing here?" This is the pathetic side.[4]

How does Balint conceive of psychoanalysis, his profession, and of what also constitutes the foundation of this book, namely a certain psychology of the ego [*psychologie du moi*]. In short, this is what he says. A certain number of terms and approaches have been brought into circulation by Freud, and for certain reasons

DOI: 10.4324/9781003309826-19

up to a certain date. During a certain period, roughly between 1920 and 1926, this approach was essentially dynamic and functional. Afterwards, it became structural or, more exactly, topic [*topique*].[5] A whole collection of terms have come to us from the first period, yet they have been blunted in their usage. At present, we're faced with a dramatic situation, because on the one hand "we may proudly say that our present-day technique is a very fine, safe and reliable instrument" – Balint will return to this point in order to address certain mental diseases – whereas our theory is totally out of step with this technique.[6] A theory is what we need most of all, because the theory we currently have at our disposal, and which we've been forced to fabricate is – he uses English terms that are really quite strong, although the book is addressed at his colleagues – "badly deficient and hopelessly lop-sided [sic]", "incomplete and lopsided".[7] "There is only one method of psycho-analysis", he says, "that laid down by Freud".[8] However, "there are different ways of achieving that aim" [of applying psychoanalytic technique], as many ways as there are practitioners and patients. In pursuing this course, Balint seems entirely truthful to the spirit in which, at a certain point, we have also placed ourselves. For in strictly adhering to the analytic method itself, he throws our entire daily practice into doubt. This is what constitutes one of his peculiar, and one might even say deceptive sides. At one point, he demands that we suspend all our certainties.[9] This is one of the essential messages of this book. Besides, he admits that he himself is probably having his own little opinion about what we might find when reason has reached its end, but in the meantime we need to suspend our certainties. He even suggests that some things should be dropped altogether.

LACAN:	What's the reference?
GRANOFF [apparently ignoring Lacan's question]:	Why do we find ourselves in these situations? Because, and he says it quite deliberately, Freud chose a biological, or anatomical imagery, and for mere reasons of convenience.[10] This has led us, by weighing down this collection of terms, to find ourselves in a situation where this anatomical schema paralyses the development of our practice, and takes us towards the constitution of a theoretical basis with one body, or towards a "One-Body Psychology", whereas what is most obvious in our practice is that we're not alone, but that there are two of us.[11]
LACAN:	He doesn't say "there are two of us". He says that we need to construct a "Two-Body Psychology", which is a term he borrows from Rickman.[12]
GRANOFF:	It's in a slightly tormented post-script, where he actually identifies – and he draws attention to counter-transference, the group psychotherapies, collective psychoanalyses, etc. – a contemporary movement.
LACAN:	It's in the appendix to "Changing Therapeutical Aims and Techniques in Psycho-Analysis".[13]

GRANOFF: Before I extract some particularly characteristic sentences from these papers, we can try to develop some kind of overarching view of Balint's current position. He says, in an extremely pathetic way, that we're in the process of entering a blind alley, and that we need to do something else, that we need to understand things in a different way.[14] How? Well, if we take what the patient tells us, according to your [Lacan's] expression, at face value, we miss out on the essence of our experience.[15] This is where the switch is situated for him, and where he decides to move towards the ditch, because at that very moment, when he has become sensitive to what we've decided to call the register of the Imaginary, he is incapable, it seems – because he's limited in his own developments – to move towards the register of the Symbolic. And so he gets stuck in a vertiginous misrecognition of the register of the Imaginary. And all of this whilst saying that we need to attribute the greatest importance to language, to the language that is spoken parenthetically by the psychoanalyst.[16] An entire page is devoted to this. He says that because it's not this face value that matters, we need to hunt down the patient as far as possible, so that we can arrive at a state of sniffing each other [subodoration].[17] We need to suss the patient out, monitor him in his tiniest gestures, in his attitudes, his thoughts, his sighs, because it's obvious that we need to find the symbol behind what he says.[18] The problem is that he isn't looking for this symbol in the only register where it can be found, i.e. in the patient's discourse. And that's what drives him towards this blind alley, and what takes him very far, much further than his conception of the ego [moi], in particular that which he has elaborated with his wife and which – had it not been for this dramatic error – should have taken him, it seems, straight towards goals that are correct, in conformity with ours. Indeed, what does he say on the topic of the ego? He doesn't express himself really. And that's what leads him to become tangled up in a pretty inextricable fashion with the notion of character. He borders very closely on the idea of the ego as a function of misrecognition [méconnaissance], yet in the end he remains far removed from this notion.[19] How does he come to conceive of the ego?

In a passage by Alice Balint, auto-erotism is being discussed.[20] I think this is quite an important passage. I think it should be compared to what you [Lacan] wrote about the mirror stage.[21] In one of her papers – and we need to remember from the start that it's called "Love for the Mother and Mother Love", that is to say the love the mother directs towards the child – Alice Balint says the following, after a rather soft introduction [to this section of the paper]:

As is well known, several auto-erotisms may supplant each other when one or the other method of discharge has become impossible. But the dissolution of the instinctual interdependence of mother and child also influences the auto-erotic function. One could even say that it is here that the psychological rôle of auto-erotism really begins. In the next period, rich in relative love-frustrations, auto-erotism assumes the significance of a substitute gratification.[22]

And now a phrase which captures the dissolution of the mirror stage, I think: "In this way it becomes the biological foundation of secondary narcissism, the psychological pre-condition of which is the identification with the faithless object" [*l'objet qui a trahi*].[23] The faithless object is the mother. I think that, in this sentence, Alice Balint comes closest to our views on the constitution of the ego.

BARGUES[24]:   Can you [Granoff] repeat this phrase?

GRANOFF: Auto-erotism "becomes the biological foundation of secondary narcissism, the psychological pre-condition of which is the identification with the faithless object".[25] It's obviously the last proposition that is most important: the faithless object. This phrase is rather abrupt and seems rather surprising for her. But she arrives at it through the exposition of some clinical cases. I cannot repeat them here, but of one particular clinical case she gives a synopsis which, to the best of my knowledge, has a depth and a penetration, indeed a boldness that is seldom found in the literature, unless we were to return to Freud's example of the *Fort!* and the *Da!*, which in the context of Freud's work is the prerogative of the child rather than the adult.[26] Alice Balint talks about a woman who is in analysis with her. It's the first year of the analysis, which she says has basically focused on the analysis of the woman's "masculine feelings".[27] The treatment has made some progress. She developed a capacity for orgasm that was much higher than at the beginning.[28] Everything is going well, but at the same time nothing is moving, because she retained a very strong hatred towards her mother.

LACAN: A very strong attachment it seems.

GRANOFF: In deepening things, Alice Balint obviously discovers that this young woman harbors death wishes towards her mother. And so, she says: "It came to light that the death wishes did not originate in any hatred against her mother. This hatred served only as a secondary rationalization of a much more primitive attitude ...".[29] She's saying things there that one really doesn't read very often:

...according to which the patient simply demanded that her mother 'should be there' or 'should not be there', according to the patient's needs. The thought of her mother's death filled the patient with the warmest feelings, the meaning of which was not repentance but something like 'How kind of you that you did die, how much I love you for that.'[30]

> The deepest layer of her attitude towards her mother is that of a little girl. However, the

Little daughter who is of the opinion that mummy should peacefully die in order that she (the daughter) might marry daddy does not necessarily hate her mother; she only finds it quite natural that the nice mummy should disappear at the right moment. The ideal mother has no interests of her own. True hate and with it true ambivalence can develop much more easily in relation to the father whom the child gets to know right from the beginning as a being who has interests of his own.[31]

> The arrival on the scene of this third character that is the father corresponds, for Alice Balint, to the learning of reality, where the role of the father, and the position of the subject in an Oedipal situation, brings the beginning of its structure and its adherence to reality. That is to say, nothing is formative outside of this Oedipal notion. After this paper, it's difficult to resist the temptation – because it's very persuasive – to talk about the pretty picture that […].

LACAN: (Words and phrases mentioned in English in the original are marked by an asterisk.) Right now, maybe you could articulate a bit better what you've just said. It concerns the notion introduced by Balint and his wife, and a third person, because all three of them were in Budapest.[32] I will mention straight away the pleasure one has in what you earlier referred to as a current of thought [une pensée], and not simply a mood, although this thought obviously asks to be explained. It's the idea of "primary love"*, the primary form of love. And I introduce it here – I apologise for interrupting you – precisely because you're about to approach "genital love"*. Because in the thought [la pensée] of these authors, of the authors of this volume, the opposition is made between two modes of love. There's a mode of love that is the pregenital mode. There's an entire paper called "Pregenital Love"*, which is centered, defined, focused on the fundamental notion that it's a love in which the object has absolutely no interest of its own: "absolute unselfishness"*.[33] The subject doesn't recognise in the object any requirement, any need of its own: "What is good for one …", this is the formula he gives of it, which is the implicit formula where the subject also expresses, by its conduct, its latent requirements, "…is 'right'* for the other also".[34] This is quite naturally what you should do. It's on this notion of a love relationship that is completely linked to an object which is only there to satisfy the subject that the Balints establish the essential difference between "primary love"*, which obviously becomes structured a little bit while advancing, but which is always characterised as being the refusal of all reality, of not recognizing the requirements of the partner, and "genital love"*. At the moment, I'm not in the process of defining the limits of this conception. You'll see that, today or the next time, I will make such massive objections to it that I think some of you are already able to see that this way of composing things literally dissipates everything psychoanalysis has contributed. Other than that, it's nothing! It's nevertheless articulated like that, because that's what it's all about.

GRANOFF: And this is what in the development of their theory is also related to the optical schema O and O', which you put on the blackboard.[35]

LACAN: But precisely it isn't.

GRANOFF: Chronologically, in the construction...

LACAN: It's the centre, yes it is. Carry on!

GRANOFF: ...which leads them to their shipwreck.

LACAN: Don't you want to talk about "Genital Love"*?[36]

GRANOFF: "Genital love"*, that is to say *l'amour génital*.

LACAN: We generally call it "genital maturation" [*maturation génitale*], arriving at genitality, the goal (at least theoretically) of analysis.[37]

GRANOFF: This paper *seems* to be – it certainly isn't – more or less intended as an answer to schemas like those composed by Fliess.[38] It's obvious that they are extremely schematic, whereby eventually everything is resolved very happily, and results in what is the goal of analysis and the touchstone of normality: the subject becomes capable – and this is where it's more or less decided to finally suspend the analysis – of providing proof of his capacity to love in a genital way. This means that he's able to love a partner by satisfying this partner, which in turn satisfies him. It also means that he's able to love a partner in a durable fashion, at the exclusion of all others, and that he's able to love the partner in such a way that the partner's interests are respected, without veiling the partner's interests, i.e. in a certain climate of tenderness, idealization, and with a certain type of identification.[39] These are the characteristics of this "genital love"*, and I hasten to tell you that Balint is writing this paper in order to demolish it.

LACAN: He wrote it in such a way that it's full of humour. One cannot say that he demolishes it. He highlights the issues in a way which simply shows that he doesn't hide for himself the difficulties of realizing this ideal. The article is from 1947.

GRANOFF: He takes up the various characteristics of this love, and he says that, in order to avoid all misunderstandings, he will imagine an ideal case where this post-ambivalence of genital love is fully realised, where no traces of the pre-genital ambivalence of the object-relation are maintained. And so he says: "There should be no greediness, no insatiability, no wish to devour the object, to deny it any independent existence, etc., i.e. there should be no *oral* features".[40] In another paper, he will return to the way in which he makes use of the oral terms.[41] Subsequently, there "should be no wish to hurt, to humiliate, to boss, to dominate the object, etc., i.e. no *sadistic* features".[42] Furthermore, there should be no wish to despise the partner "for his (her) sexual desires and pleasures; there should be no danger of being disgusted by the partner or being attracted only by some of his (her) unpleasant features, etc., i.e. there should be no remnants of *anal* traits".[43] Finally, there "should be no compulsion to boast about the possession of a penis, no fear of the partner's sexual organs... no trace of the *phallic phase* or of the castration complex".[44] "We know", he says, "that such ideal cases do not exist in practice, but we have to get all this negative stuff out of our way before we can start with the proper examination".[45] Already with regard to the elimination of the "negative stuff"*, he doesn't beat around the bush, because it's the first time we read, in this official way, that it's not the case. It's already not that common! He continues: "What then is 'genital love' apart from the absence of all the enumerated 'pregenital' traits? Well, we love our partner (1) because he or she can satisfy us; (2) because we can satisfy him or her; (3) because we can experience a full orgasm together, nearly or quite simultaneously".[46] The English sentence is quite funny: it seems to be quite a tranquil navigation, "very plain sailing"*.[47] One could translate this as "it's very easy going" [*on semble jouer sur du billard*], but unfortunately it's not the case. "Let us take the first condition", Balint says, "that our partner can satisfy us".[48] This condition may occur, but it's completely narcissistic. Here, he employs the word "egotistical".[49] It should also be noted that one of the pitfalls to which their conception leads them is that when they talk about primary love – having not used the vocabulary that we've been taught to use, and which sometimes doesn't seem very simple to us – they arrive at an even more confusing vocabulary. It's that they are, willy-nilly, forced to use a notion in which they include the term ego. They call it "naïve egoism", which is heavy to say the least, and not very operational.[50] And they seem to be led towards the introduction of this term by a sort of fatality from which they cannot escape.

GRANOFF TO	Besides, to please you, on the subject of "successful repres-
HYPPOLITE[51]:	sion", there is a place where Balint says that repression can-
	not be successful. There is nothing more missed than successful
	repression.[52]

So he reviews all these conditions, and he says that in the *Chronique scandaleuse*, or in literature, there are many relationships where, precisely, all these conditions are satisfied –mutual satisfaction, simultaneous orgasm, etc. – and yet we cannot talk about love.[53] These people "find real happiness in each other's arms, where they feel an absolute security", and a certain pleasure. And in passing he quotes a Shakespeare sonnet.[54] In addition, it very often happens that, even after all these conditions have been fulfilled, the two partners, for a certain time at least, have no desire to see each other again any time soon, but are nevertheless not completely disgusted by each other, to the point that they may decide to see each other again later. So he says that there must be "something more".[55] What is this "more"? "We find in addition to genital satisfaction in a true love relation: (1) idealisation; (2) tenderness; (3) A special form of identification".[56] And then, there's some kind of retraction: "As Freud dealt with the problem of idealisation, both of the object and of the instinct, I need only to repeat his findings".[57]

He showed convincingly first that this idealisation is not absolutely necessary, that without any idealisation a good love relation is possible, and second that in many cases idealisation is not a help but a hindrance to the development of a satisfactory form of love.[58]

The least we can say is that, in this little digest he produces of Freud's thought, at that point [...] it has been treated abundantly here. Now, the second phenomenon, of tenderness, may perhaps be interpreted differently. Balint says: "[T]enderness is the result of aim-inhibition: the original urge was directed towards a certain aim, but – for one reason or another – had to content itself with only partial satisfaction".[59] And then, *faute de mieux* – the word is in French in Balint's text – it leads to full satisfaction.[60] According to other views, and as suggested in another paper by Freud, "tenderness is an archaic quality which appears in conjunction with the ancient self-preserving instincts, and has no further aim but this quiet, not passionate gratification. Consequently passionate love must be a secondary phenomenon, superimposed on the archaic tender love".[61] Balint believes that this idea finds support on the basis of subjective data, in anthropology.[62] And he draws up a brief table of courtship love from the Middle Ages, and even of some things that we find in Hindu literature [...] complicated, and which is cut through by sexual poetry, love poetry, prolific, an appreciation of tenderness.[63] This tenderness is presented as an artificial product of civilization, a systematic result of all the frustrations endured during education.[64] And it's really quite funny, because he says: "Etymology, too, seems to support this idea".[65] He then quotes a whole range of English and German terms, with extreme pertinence, whereby he discovers that this tenderness is attached to words which also mean – as for the root where they come from – stupid, gaga, funny, not very serious, fragile, fairly inhibited. And there he stops: "Something is surely wrong here. How has genital love, the mature form of love, got mixed up with this doubtful company of disease, weakness, immaturity, etc.?"[66] And then he kind of plugs into his conclusion: "[M]an resembles the ape embryo …"[67] Normally, the ape embryo only develops itself and acquires its genital maturity at the end of a certain development, whereas human beings acquire this development already at a foetal stage. "There are several more such instances in the animal kingdom", Balint says, "where an embryo acquires truly developed bisexual genital functions; these are called *neotenic* embryos. Genital love is an exact parallel to these forms".[68] The human being is a neotenic embryo, not only anatomically, but also psychologically. Besides, the anatomists discovered this before we did. Thus, what we present as true love, genital love, isn't defined yet. It's quite simply some kind of return to an absolutely primitive form of love, in which the subject and the object of his or her love are confounded by an absolute instinctual reciprocity. So what is genital love? It's an art… It's the fortunate case where there is a confluence between certain instinctual and certain cultural matters. According to him, one might say that true love is in the end the original homosexual love, that which unites the brothers of the horde, whereas heterosexual love was limited to its pure and most simple expression, to a pure and simple act of copulation.[69] And it's from a transportation of this homosexual love onto a heterosexual framework that what we now consider to be the successful case was born.

LACAN: It's very interesting to see that it comes to this!

MANNONI[70]: He cannot avoid the word "successful", which raises all kinds of problems.

GRANOFF: I'm the one who's using it. He doesn't say it like that. According to him, it can almost never be successful.

LACAN: Echoing this theory, you're absolutely right to focus fundamentally on a more than normative and moralizing theory of love.

HYPPOLITE: Normal and not normative.

LACAN: Moralizing, no? It doesn't preclude the fact that what you [Granoff] are in the process of highlighting, here, is that he's led to this question: At the end of the day, is what we consider to be normal a natural state, or an artificial or cultural result, or even what he calls a "happy chance"*, *une chance heureuse*?[71] He transports and transfers this to a question which covers the entire problem for us, namely: What is this "normal", which occasionally he calls "health", with regard to the termination of analysis? "Is the analytical cure a 'natural' or an 'artificial' process?"[72] In other words, Balint poses the question of the ends [of a psychoanalytic treatment process], and he asks whether health is a natural state of equilibrium: "[D]o processes exist in the mind which – if unhampered and undisturbed – would lead the development towards that equilibrium?"[73] Or, by contrast, is "*health* the result of a lucky chance, a rare or even an improbable event, the reason being that its conditions are so stringent and so numerous that the chances are very heavily weighed against it?"[74] This leads Balint to nothing less than to suppose this question, which is evidently significant from the beginning, because the beginning leads to a question of which he says that the ambiguity, in the analytic chorus, is complete. Notably that there are as many people who formulate an answer in the sense of "yes", as there are whose answer is in the sense of "no".[75] The question must instill doubt that perhaps the question hasn't been put very clearly from the start. So, let's continue!

GRANOFF: This leads, towards the end of his message, at the same time to a modification in the goals of the treatment as well as in the technique, and to the end of the treatment. In including this article ["On the Termination of Analysis"], he quite simply ends by saying that the development of the treatment leads to a renaissance, i.e. in nothing does it constitute a reparation or a restitution.[76] Here too, it's difficult to say which.

LACAN: Be more precise.

GRANOFF: Is it a *restitutio in integrum* or not? It's the unblocking of the capacities, of the subject's ability to return without shame and modesty [*honte et pudeur*], and without fear, to "primary love"*, that is to say the "naïve egoism", or precisely the stage where the identity, the reciprocity of the instinctual goals of the subject and his object are confounded. This is what brings him to conceive the end of analysis as something of a brutal dissolution, in full honeymoon, of this state. I'm not sure this tallies with the views you [Lacan] have.

LACAN: It's exactly that.

GRANOFF: And at that point he becomes embroiled in the "character".

LACAN: Go on then. Talk about the way he talks about character.

GRANOFF: For Balint, character inherits part of what we habitually see being devolved onto the ego. Character is what prevents the individual from experiencing the most anxiety provoking demands of reality; it's what prevents the individual from sinking into a love where he could get lost, even where he could destroy himself. It's a fortunate limitation of the subject's abilities.[77] Then he poses the question: Is it justified, or not, to modify the subject's character?[78] And so he comes to the commonplace on analytical amputation.[79]

LACAN: Focus on the passage on character, in which he himself comes to pose the question.

GRANOFF: Is it legitimate or not to change the subject's character? Is it legitimate or not to restrict or increase, that is to say to fortify or weaken? The outline is, roughly, as follows. The strong character turns an individual into someone quite boring, who is neither capable of loving very strongly, nor of hating very strongly. The weak character condemns him to a very unhappy existence, but rich in various possibilities. It's more fun, more poetic, but less interesting for the subject. Fortunately, he says, the subjects who come to analysis ultimately do not have this kind of scruple as to what, in this respect, will become of them.[80] This makes that ultimately – he comes to his conclusion – the character is only the result of the accidental limitations imposed by the "errors of upbringing", and so we're entirely justified in rendering him the service of repairing it under these circumstances.[81]

LACAN: Maybe you're moving a bit fast. I have to say that you probably want to move forward, and finish up, but you're not bringing out something very interesting, namely the definition of character, as what controls the relation of the human being to his objects.[82] "[C]haracter always means a more or less extensive limitation of love and hate possibilities".[83] "Character therefore means", I'm translating everything that is italicised in the book, "a limitation of the capacity 'for love and enjoyment'*", *pour aimer et pour la joie*.[84] The word doesn't seem gratuitous to me. It's introduced there, I believe, in a way that one should spell out. This dimension of enjoyment [*joie*], which is going very far, goes far beyond the category of jouissance. The subjective plenitude that is included in the enjoyment would merit a development in itself. It's being questioned there, and you can't avoid being struck by it! If the paper hadn't been from 1932, I'd say that we almost owe Balint some kind of influence from a certain moral ideal, that I would call "puritan". Because even in Hungary there are Protestant historical traditions, which moreover have quite precise historical ramifications with the history of Protestantism in England. There's a peculiar convergence of the thought of this student of Ferenczi's, who is carried by Ferenczi along the trails which I'm making you follow today, with his destiny, which ultimately allowed him to become so well integrated into the English community. And one cannot fail to see that in his conception, character in its strong form, that which implies all these limitations, is altogether preferable to what he calls a "weak character"*, which is for him basically someone who lets himself be overwhelmed.[85]

GRANOFF: He says that it's preferable, but with regret.[86]

LACAN: The category of the training of individuals according to a very
specialised education is implied in the very text of the most basic
directives of progress. And it's quite striking what he says about
character. Needless to say, this results in total ambiguity between
what he calls "character analysis", and what he does not hesitate
to venture into in the same context, namely logical character.[87] He
doesn't seem to realise that these are entirely different characters:
on the one hand, there's the character as a reaction to the libidinal
development of the subject, as a framework in which this development is caught and limited, and on the other hand there are
its innate elements – just to express the difference I'm pointing
out here – which for the characterologists, divide individuals into
classes that are constitutional. He thinks that the analytic experience will tell us more, because it's closer to experience. This is
undoubtedly true. And even I myself am quite inclined to think
so, but only on condition that the analytic experience allows us
to see from which point, within its limits, we reach this radical
and final sum. In the game in question, namely where the analysis modifies profoundly, or can modify character, it's obviously
something else that's at stake, this something being the construction of the ego. It's at this level that he joins the analytic experience, in the most lively way. Is there anything you want to add?

GRANOFF: How does Balint arrive at article 14?[88] To conduct what he thinks
is a good analysis, it's necessary to place oneself in the perspectives, or rather in the *only* perspective in which one can understand the development of the child. Because if we tried to analyze
primary love in the terms in which we are led to do it, we're not
going to get very far. And besides, being entangled in this anatom-
ical schema, we're forced to realise that "the term 'source of an
instinct' is hardly ever heard or seen in print nowadays".[89] "Even
the once very frequently used term 'aim-inhibited' is definitely re-
ceding".[90] And with regard to the instinctual object, "I have never
seen or heard 'relation to an instinctual object'". "Secondly", he
says, "the well-known terms anal, oral, genital, etc., are less and
less used to denote the source or aim of instincts, but more and
more" – and here he tries to present a structural approach, but
he doesn't succeed – "to denote specific object-relations".[91] And
this is where his great shipwreck is happening: "specific object-
relations, e.g. 'oral greed', 'anal domination', 'genital love', etc.".[92]
"Thirdly", then, "the term 'sadistic' has been gradually going out
of fashion, in my opinion because its implications are much too
libidinous, and relate rather to instinctual aims, gratifications; in

its stead terms like 'hostile', 'aggressive', 'destructive' are used, which have an unmistakable affinity to object-relations".[93]

LACAN: Yes, but maybe you still haven't succeeded in getting your message across. It's entirely fair, what you say though. You highlight the remark Balint makes about the gradual disappearance of certain terms in works and articles that are appearing from a certain period (1938–1940), and which orient the analytic situation towards object-relations.[94] He denotes it, and he points to a certain number of signs. And he recognises in particular – I'm not saying that this is valid as a fact, and we'll see what his interpretation is worth – the disappearance of all the vocabulary of the order of the register, that is to say, of the source, the direction, the satisfaction of the instinct. He denotes it in numerous ways, one of the most salient aspects being that the term "sadist" is almost no longer used. And he adds that its connotation was "much too libidinous".[95] I'd say that, at this point, the admission is significant, because indeed that's what it's all about, a kind of puritanization of the analytic atmosphere, which is indeed quite striking and would be worth highlighting, if only because of the use that I will make of it as a converging sign of a certain evolution. This sentence is really quite significant.

GRANOFF: Were I to be a little bit cheeky, I'd say that what he suffers from is a disorder of the imaginary function.

LACAN: Not him, his theory.

GRANOFF: He finds himself caught in a sort of capture [*captation*]. It's not surprising that he highlights these propositions, because in the next section, in a slightly breathtaking way, at least if we place ourselves in what for him is an object-relation, he tells us: Now, beware, you have to stop for a moment, lest we forget what must be "the analyst's behaviour in the psycho-analytic situation".[96] And first of all he does justice to what we are taught in well-intended seminars, that is to say that the analyst is there, totally out of touch, not as he should really be, but as he still thinks he is. He shows how the analyst is entangled in a dual relationship, whilst denying it, denying that he's there. And, he says, all these questions of "detached friendly understanding", of "well-timed interpreting", all this should not make us forget that if the patient's relation to his analyst is libidinal, "the analyst's relation to his patient is libidinous in exactly the same way".[97] That doesn't stop him, however, in the sense that it doesn't even seem to increase the temptation to talk about a subject-to-subject relationship, even towards the end of his talk. This is yet another *tour de force* that he manages to accomplish – always incidentally, and through misrecognition [*méconnaissance*].

LACAN: To be honest, he fails to avoid it. He doesn't access it. And there we return to our starting point, namely the remark that there must be something that exists between two subjects, since two subjects are there. Since he's completely lacking the conceptual apparatus [...] even widely developed elsewhere, and open more widely to our knowledge, of what constitutes its mediation, and especially on the true function of language [...] to introduce the intersubjective relationship, he is led – and it's not simply a kind of linguistic slip of the lapsus type – to speak of a "Two-Body Psychology"*.[98] It's that it really fits the idea that he has of it. He thinks he's getting out of the "One-Body Psychology"* by saying "We're going to do a 'Two-Body Psychology'"*. But it's obvious that the "Two-Body Psychology"* is still an opposition, that is to say still an object-to-object relationship. And that's the ambiguity of the term object-relation; that's what it means. Theoretically, it wouldn't matter, yet it has technical consequences in the concrete therapeutic exchange with the subject [of the patient]. Because it's not an object-to-object relationship. You expressed it just now when you said "entangled in a dual relationship, whilst denying it". We cannot find a more fortunate formula, and I congratulate you on it for saying how we usually express ourselves, in order to explain what the analytic relationship should be.

GRANOFF: There's an extremely promising sentence though: "[W]e have only some vague idea but no exact knowledge about what distortions happen and how much we miss while describing Two-Body experiences (analytical technique) in a language belonging to One-Body situations".[99]

LACAN: That's exactly what I've just said. And so he doesn't notice that he carries on in the same vein.

GRANOFF: Not only does he continue, but he strengthens it. So what should we do? And since he hasn't found the key that would allow him to escape from the blind alley in which he has thrown himself at a phenomenal pace, he says, and then it becomes a frantic objectification of his patient: first, you [the analyst] have to create an atmosphere; do not close yourself, and do not forget.[100] But then he shoots off. Oral greed, he says, is not just connected to the mouth: "Other aspects equally important are warmth, bodily contact, familiar smells and tastes, or in one word, proper care and nursing".[101] So it's also about the skin, the epidermis, the heat, the friction. It becomes an enumeration. He literally does a tour of the individual in an attempt to broaden, within the framework of object-relations, his position. And contrary to what he said earlier, he ends up by saying: And if it doesn't work, as in our case, just put in a double dose, and it may end up working.[102] That's what he arrives at!

LACAN: I wouldn't qualify this aspect in the same way as you do, that is to say in the objectifying sense.

GRANOFF: He doesn't qualify it in this way either.

LACAN: I wouldn't qualify it like that either. I would consider – I think I will show it to you next time – something that is obviously moving, namely a kind of recourse, strictly speaking, not at all to what I defend and tell you here as the objectifying register. Any progress in knowledge and every technique have an interest in objectifying the parts which *can* be objectified. But it's an objectifying tendency in relation to the subject, that is to say to push, by means of the interventions and the technique itself, the subject to objectify himself, to take himself for an object, which is so problematic. To believe that progress – and he believes it, because that's indeed how analysis progresses for him – is done by an objectification of what he [the subject, the patient] is, is not what it's about.[103] This recourse to a call, as I would designate it, is a recourse to a call upon the real, insofar as it's an erasure by misrecognition, as you said earlier, of this symbolic register. It disappears completely in the object-relation, because it's nowhere, and that's why the objects take on this absolute value, even to the extent that it no longer has the imaginary function as a third term. He tells us what the meaning of our operative function in analysis is now. He says that one needs to create "a proper atmosphere", a suitable atmosphere.[104] That's all he has to say. And it all becomes extraordinarily uncertain; it even verges on the inexpressible. And he then brings all of reality into play, what he calls the event, because analysis isn't exactly made for us to fall into our patient's arms, or for the patient to fall into ours. The limitation of the means the analyst has at his disposal is precisely what raises the question as to the level on which analysis is taking place. But failing to conceive, also in relation to these means, where his experience is defined and limited, Balint is led to make this great call upon the awakening of all the registers of the real. This plane of reality, it's no coincidence that it's there, always in the background, and that I never point it out to you directly in everything we're commenting on here. It's no coincidence that it's precisely excluded, strictly speaking. And Balint won't bring it in any more than anyone else. But this is where his recourse to the call goes, and this is the failure of the theory which corresponds to this inclination of the technique, to this deviation of the technique. Next time, I'll try to allow you [participants] to point out exactly the direction and the meaning of it. Finish, Granoff.

GRANOFF: Just a couple of words. This call upon the real, he's so committed to it that, at another point in his career, as if he'd been sensitive to certain pitfalls in his thinking, he at least wants to say what, according to him, *isn't* part of it, and he gives a unique example in the descriptive literature. I think it's the only time express mention is made of small pieces of tissue paper, cushions, couches, etc.[105] This is at a much earlier time.

LACAN: Yes, in the paper "On Transference and Counter-Transference".[106]

GRANOFF: But it may not be a coincidence that he thought about it. He ends with rather pessimistic considerations about the termination of analysis. It's on this point that we must finish, after having performed in passing, and with sufficient relevance, the trial of our societies at the present time, and whilst also bringing in, as an element of appreciation, the fact that at a historical moment in time (around 1930) a number of analysts came into play whose analyses had obviously not been completed. And so we ended up with two standards, which he calls "Standard A" and "Standard B", that is to say the uncertainty in which one finds oneself as to the judicious moment of launching an analyst into practice.[107] Consideration all the more pessimistic, in that a psychoanalytic treatment ends according to him only in one or two cases out of ten.[108] Since there are a few thousand treatments that end every year, that makes at least a few hundred that really end.[109] We could still go through the trouble of taking a closer look, and find out what happened there. But what seems to me more pessimistic isn't really that, but more his theory. It's that he says: I rarely finish treatments, in one or two out of ten cases.[110] It doesn't even seem that pessimistic to me in itself. But what really strikes me as very scary in what he says is that in the other cases, with hindsight, he says he understood correctly where the error was.[111] But it's perhaps not even there yet that the most distressing part is situated! It's that he says: when I understood, and I may have understood very well, unfortunately there was nothing more that I could do.[112] It's a fucked up situation, once and for all. This seems to me to be the culmination of his perspective, the inevitability of failure once a certain type of mistake has been made.[113]

Notes

1   The text of Granoff's presentation has been established and translated by Dany Nobus from unpublished French notes and transcripts. The title, the endnotes, textual interpolations in square brackets, and the list of references are by the translator. Ellipses in square brackets mark a place where the participants' words were not captured. For the publication of *Séminaire I* (Lacan, 1975a), Jacques-Alain Miller decided to omit Granoff's presentation, presumably with Lacan's consent, much like various other contributions by the participants. Although it is nowhere explicitly stated as such, these omissions have been marked by full dotted lines in the published text of the seminar. In a letter

to John Forrester (the English translator of *Séminaire I*), Miller granted permission for these dotted lines to be glossed with the following note, which was however not retained in the English translation: "Participants' interventions at the seminar have occasionally been abridged by J.-A. Miller; these omissions are signalled by dotted lines" (Miller, 1986). In the published text of *Séminaire I*, Lacan's own interventions have been heavily edited, with various comments omitted and some others added, whilst they have also been collated in four separate "blocks" (Lacan, 1975b, pp. 204–206). For this translation, it was decided to preserve the rhythm of the original exchange, and to come as close as possible to what Granoff, Lacan, and some others actually said, although for the sake of readability it was unavoidable to add punctuation. Throughout the text, Granoff and Lacan quote liberally from Balint's works, often providing their own translations, since a French edition was not available at the time, and without giving precise references. Whenever a direct quote was detected, quotation marks have been added to the text, with a specific reference in the accompanying note. When it came to developing this scholarly apparatus, the option presented itself to simply include page numbers in the text for all the citations from Balint's book, yet this would have diverted the reader's attention away from the individual papers, which deserve to be acknowledged as stand-alone essays by Michael and/or Alice Balint, despite their surplus value as contributions to what Granoff at one point designates as a "current of thought". Source references have also been given for paraphrases of Balint's text, and for other authors mentioned. When they exist, and unless the context requires otherwise, English translations of all sources have been cited; readers should have no difficulty finding the original texts. Words and phrases mentioned in English in the original are marked by an asterisk. For the English edition of the seminar, Forrester silently corrected errors in the French version. Here, it was decided to maintain the errors in the text, but to draw attention to these in a note, and provide a correction. Many transcripts of Granoff's presentation can be found online, yet all of these contain numerous errors in the spelling of names and the attribution of quotations. The most accurate version is to be found in the Wladimir Granoff Papers (Fonds Wladimir Granoff) at the Bibliothèque Nationale de France, Manuscript Division, NAF28972.

2 The book in question is the first edition of *Primary Love and Psycho-Analytic Technique* (Balint, 1952). In 1965, this volume was reprinted with four additional texts, two being added to the first section of the book, and two constituting a new, third section titled "Problems of Training". All page references will be given to the original edition of Balint's book, because this is the version used by Granoff and Lacan. Before giving the floor to Granoff, Lacan opens the session with some introductory observations on why he has chosen to discuss Balint's work, and why he has entrusted Granoff with the task of presenting it (Lacan, 1975b, pp. 203–204).

3 Granoff's metaphor echoes an expression Lacan had used previously, in his discussion of Freud's explanation, in "The Dynamics of Transference" (Freud, 1912a, p. 101), of the patient's resistance at the level of the free associations as a moment of transference:

> If it [the transference] takes on a selective value, it's because the subject himself then feels something like a sharp bend, a sudden turn [*un brusque virage, un tournant subit*] which causes him to pass from one slope of the discourse to the other, from one aspect of the function of speech to another.
>
> (Lacan, 1975b, p. 40)

4 In a postscript to "On Love and Hate", Balint himself refers to "the distressing and pathetic one-sidedness of our theory" (1951, p. 156).

5 The term "topic" is employed by Balint himself in "Changing Therapeutical Aims and Techniques in Psycho-Analysis" (1949a, pp. 222–223). In contemporary psychoanalytic parlance, Freud's distinction between the id, the ego, and the superego is more

commonly referred to as "topographical", a notion Balint employs in "Strength of the Ego and Its Education" (1938), p. 203).

6 Balint (1949a, p. 225).

7 Balint (1949a, p. 230, 1951, p. 156). Elsewhere in "Changing Therapeutical Aims and Techniques in Psycho-Analysis", Balint writes that "our theory is very weak" and that "our theoretical descriptions are rather primitive" (1949a, pp. 226–227).

8 Balint and Balint (1939, p. 220). Granoff uses the third person singular "*il*" (he) and thus ignores the fact that this particular paper was written in collaboration with Alice Balint.

9 To the best of my knowledge, Balint never explicitly states his position like this in *Primary Love and Psycho-Analytic Technique*, yet in the second part of the book, which is entirely devoted to "problems of technique", he intermittently calls for an urgent review of psychoanalytic theory and for a different clinical approach, which considers the patient's object-relations. See, for example, Balint (1949a, p. 229, 1949b, p. 237).

10 In "Changing Therapeutical Aims and Techniques in Psycho-Analysis", Balint calls Freud's persistent theoretical emphasis on the individual – as opposed to a perspective that would also take account of the individual's relationships with the outside world (the objects) – "the physiological, or biological bias", which he attributes to a "self-imposed restriction" (1949a, pp. 223, 226, 228).

11 Balint (1949a, p. 235).

12 Balint (1949a, p. 235). In the addendum to "Changing Therapeutical Aims and Techniques in Psycho-Analysis", Balint himself acknowledges his debt to Rickman:

> I wish to quote here an idea of John Rickman's, of which unfortunately I heard only in April 1950, i.e. only after finishing this paper ["Changing Therapeutical Aims and Techniques in Psycho-Analysis"]. If I had been able to use his ideas, several passages might have been formulated more exactly and more convincingly.
>
> (1949a, pp. 234–235)

In "On Love and Hate", Balint uses the term "two-person-psychology" (*sic*) without reference to Rickman, in order to explain primitive (pre-genital) object-relations as "a relation in which *only one partner is entitled to make demands*, the other is treated as an object, albeit as an instinct or love-object" (1951, p. 146). John Rickman (1891–1951) was a British psychoanalyst who had been in analysis with Sándor Ferenczi (1873–1933) between 1928 and 1930. He is best remembered for his research collaborations with Wilfred R. Bion on leaderless groups at Northfield Hospital (Birmingham) in 1943. Between 1947 and 1950, he also served as the president of the British Psychoanalytical Society (King, 2003; Payne, 1957). Rickman first introduced the idea of one- and two-body psychologies in February 1950 (Rickman, 1950), yet Balint is likely to have heard about it at a meeting of the Medical Section of the British Psychological Society on 26 April 1950, where Rickman reintroduced his terms in a paper titled "Methodology and Research in Psycho-Pathology" (1951a). Shortly before his death, Rickman also referred to "One-Person" and "Two-Person Psychology" in "Number and the Human Sciences" (1951b). Lacan had met Rickman and Bion in person during a trip to England in the late Summer of 1945 (Lacan, 1947, p. 15), and at the start of his seminar on Freud's papers on technique he had described Rickman as "one of the rare souls to have had a modicum of theoretical originality in analytic circles since Freud's death" (1975b, p. 11). The conception of the psychoanalytic treatment as a "Two-Body Psychology", alongside the references to Balint and Rickman, also appears in Lacan's "Rome Discourse" of September 1953 (Lacan, 1953, p. 251).

13 Balint (1949a, pp. 234–235). Unlike the later additions to "Love for the Mother and Mother Love" (Balint, 1939, p. 127), "On Genital Love" (Balint, 1947, pp. 137–140), and "Character Analysis and New Beginning" (Balint, 1932, pp. 172–173), the section of the paper to which Lacan is referring, here, does not carry the heading "Appendix".

However, it is set apart from the rest of the text by a blank line, and its content clearly demonstrates that it constitutes a later addition to the 1949 essay.

14 Balint himself uses the word "blind alley" in Balint (1947, p. 130).

15 The French term is "*valeur faciale*", yet I have not been able to find the expression in any of Lacan's works prior to Granoff's presentation.

16 Balint (1949a, p. 232).

17 Lacan himself had used the term "*subodoration*" in his 1953 "Rome Discourse", notably in the context of a critique of the object-relations movement in psychoanalysis:

> For these are the very people who, making their objective what lies beyond language, react to analysis' 'Don't touch' rule by a sort of obsession. If they keep going in that direction, I dare say the last word in transference reaction will be sniffing each other.
> (1953, p. 221)

18 What Granoff seems to have in mind, here, is Balint's recommendation in "Changing Therapeutical Aims and Techniques in Psycho-Analysis" that the analyst should pay proper attention to "the *formal elements* of the patient's behaviour in the psychoanalytical situation", including "the changing expressions of the patient's face, his way of lying on the couch, of using his voice, of starting and finishing the session, his intercurrent illnesses, even a passing malaise, and especially his way of associating" (Balint, 1949a, p. 224).

19 Lacan had designated the fundamental function of the ego as *méconnaissance* in the seminar session of 10 February 1954. See Lacan (1975b, p. 53).

20 Balint (1939, pp. 122–124).

21 Lacan (1949).

22 Balint (1939, p. 123).

23 Balint (1939, p. 123).

24 René Bargues (1920–1966), French psychiatrist and psychoanalyst, trainee at the Société française de Psychanalyse during the 1950s, and *Analyste de l'École* (AE) of Lacan's *École freudienne de Paris* between 1964 and his death. Whilst pursuing his analysis with Lacan, Bargues worked at the Policlinique Ney of the Bichat Hospital in Paris, where he provided care to young children, and conducted research on the impact of social deprivation on children's mental health.

25 Balint (1939, p. 123).

26 Freud (1920, pp. 14–15).

27 Alice Balint's original phrasing is: "The first years [*sic*] of the analysis were almost completely taken up with a working through of her masculinity complex" (1939, p. 110).

28 In fact, Alice Balint says that there used to be an "absolute frigidity" (1939, p. 110).

29 Balint (1939, p. 110).

30 Balint (1939, p. 110).

31 Balint (1939, p. 111).

32 None of the transcripts I have consulted mention the name of this "third person", yet various passages in *Primary Love and Psycho-Analytic Technique* leave little doubt that it concerns Imre Hermann (1889–1984), the Hungarian neurologist and psychoanalyst whose work on the "clinging instinct" provided the impetus to John Bowlby's theory of attachment. For example, in "Early Developmental States of the Ego. Primary Object-Love", Balint writes:

> Three different trains of thought, independently begun from different angles of approach, have recently led A. Balint, I. Hermann and myself to such converging conclusions that we are practically convinced at least to be moving in the right direction. The common principal stimulus to our trains of thought can be traced back to Ferenczi and beyond him to Freud.
> (1937, pp. 95–96)

See also A. Balint (1939, pp. 126–127). For discussions of Hermann's life and works, see Berner (1996), Harmat (1988, pp. 162–167), Klaniczay (2012), Varga (1989), and Vikár (1999).

33 All the documents I have consulted mention the paper as "Pregenital Love", and this is also how the title appears in the French edition of Lacan's seminar (1975b, p. 228). However, *Primary Love and Psycho-Analytic Technique* does not contain a paper with this title. In the English edition of the seminar, the title has been silently changed to "On Love and Hate" (Lacan, 1975b, p. 204), yet there is no good reason to think that this is the paper Lacan had in mind. Indeed, the discussion that follows seems to suggest that the paper Lacan was thinking of is "On Genital Love", and that he either gave the wrong title, or that the title was transcribed incorrectly. As to "absolute unselfishness", this is the term Alice Balint uses to describe what the child expects from the mother during the archaic, primary stage of the mother-child relationship (1939, p. 110).

34 Balint (1939, p. 120). In using the masculine pronoun, Lacan attributes the phrase to Michael rather than to Alice Balint.

35 Granoff alludes here to the "simplified schema of the two mirrors", which Lacan presented during the seminar session of 5 May 1954 (Lacan, 1975b, p. 165).

36 Balint (1947).

37 In "On the Termination of Analysis", Balint refers in this particular context to "mature genitality", which he defines as

> more than a simple sum-total of all the component sexual instincts; mature genitality is in my opinion a new function emerging about puberty, possibly as the result of a 'natural process' such as I tried to describe in 'Eros and Aphrodite'.
>
> (1949b, p. 236)

In "On Genital Love", he talks about "the mature attitude" (1947, p. 136).

38 Assuming that the notes and transcripts of Granoff's presentation are accurate, this is most likely a reference to a 1948 paper by Robert Fliess (1895–1970), in which he had presented a detailed "ontogenetic table" and "chronological chart" of the development of the human mental apparatus. Fliess was a German-American medical doctor and psychoanalyst, who was the son of Wilhelm Fliess, the Berlin based otorhinolaryngologist with whom Freud maintained an intimate correspondence between 1887 and 1904 (Masson, 1985).

39 Balint (1947, p. 130).

40 Balint (1947, p. 128).

41 The reference is to Balint (1951, pp. 144–146). Granoff himself will return to Balint's broad description of the oral object-relation further on in his presentation.

42 Balint (1947, p. 128).

43 Balint (1947, pp. 128–129).

44 Balint (1947, p. 129)

45 Balint (1947, p. 129). Granoff renders "the proper examination" as "*un examen plus correct*".

46 Balint (1947, p. 129).

47 Balint (1947, p. 129).

48 Balint (1947, p. 129).

49 Balint (1947, p. 129).

50 The essay in which this term appears is "Love for the Mother and Mother Love", and was written by Alice Balint: A. Balint (1939, pp. 114–115, 120–122, 125).

51 Jean Hyppolite (1907–1968), French philosopher, Hegel and Heidegger scholar, responsible for the first French translation of Hegel's 1807 *Phänomenologie des Geistes*, published in two volumes in 1939 and 1941, which was followed by a landmark commentary on the book, titled *Genèse et structure de la* Phénoménologie de l'esprit *de*

Hegel (Hyppolite, 1946). During the 1950s, many French philosophers, including Michel Foucault, Gilles Deleuze, and Jacques Derrida, attended Hyppolite's lectures at the *École Normale Supérieure* in Paris. On 10 February 1954, Hyppolite himself gave an influential presentation on Freud's paper "Negation" (1925) at Lacan's seminar, which Lacan subsequently included as Appendix I in his *Écrits* (Hyppolite, 1954b), and which also features as an Appendix in the English edition of *Séminaire I* (Hyppolite, 1954a), even though it was not included in the original French text.

52 Balint (1932, p. 173).
53 Balint (1947, p. 130). The *Chronique scandaleuse* is a late fifteenth-century illuminated manuscript chronicling life in Paris during the reign of King Louis XI.
54 Balint (1947, p. 130).
55 Balint (1947, p. 130).
56 Balint (1947, p. 130).
57 Balint (1947, p. 130).
58 Balint (1947, pp. 130–131).
59 Balint (1947, p. 131). Granoff translates Balint's "towards a certain aim" as "*vers un certain objet*".
60 Actually, Balint says:

According to this view tenderness is a secondary phenomenon, a faint representative only of the original aim; and because of this quality of *faute de mieux* it never leads to full satisfaction, i.e. it is always and inherently connected with some frustration.
(1947, p. 131)

61 Balint (1947, p. 131). The "other paper" by Freud is (1912b).
62 Balint refers to "suggestive" rather than "subjective" data. This may be a transcription error.
63 Balint himself does not specifically refer to Hindu literature.
64 Balint (1947, p. 132).
65 Balint (1947, p. 132).
66 Balint (1947, p. 132).
67 Balint (1947, p. 133).
68 Balint (1947, pp. 133–134).
69 Balint (1947, pp. 137–139). The expression "brothers of the horde" refers to Freud's myth of the murder of the primal father in *Totem and Taboo*. See Freud (1912–1913).
70 Dominique-Octave Mannoni (1899–1989), French psychoanalyst, author of *Prospero and Caliban* (1956), one of the first psychoanalytic studies of colonisation. Mannoni was in analysis with Lacan during the 1950s, became a member of the Société française de Psychanalyse and subsequently of the *École freudienne de Paris*. He also coined the influential formula "*Je sais bien, mais quand même . . .*" for Freud's psychic mechanism of disavowal. See Freud (1927) and Mannoni (1969).
71 In fact, Balint uses the expressions "lucky chance" and "extremely good luck" (1949b, pp. 239, 242).
72 Balint (1949b, p. 238).
73 Balint (1949b, p. 239).
74 Balint (1949b, p. 239).
75 Balint (1949b, p. 239).
76 What Granoff terms "renaissance", here, is most likely Balint's concept of the end of the analytic treatment as a "new beginning", which runs through many of the papers in *Primary Love and Psycho-Analytic Technique*. Furthermore, in the seminar session of 19 May 1954, the week before Granoff's presentation on Balint, Lacan himself had designated the end of analysis as "the complete integration of his [the patient's] history" (1975b, p. 193).

77 Balint (1932, pp. 168–171).
78 Balint (1932, p. 171).
79 What Granoff seems to have in mind, here, is Balint's belief that psychoanalysis should allow patients to abandon some of their character traits, "which have now become useless and represent an obstacle, only historically justified, to harmless joy" (Balint, 1932, p. 170).
80 Balint (1932, p. 171).
81 Balint (1932, pp. 161, 171). The term 'errors of upbringing' also appears in Balint (1935, p. 197). In both texts, it is associated with Ferenczi's concept of the 'confusion of tongues' between the child and the adult. See Ferenczi (1932).
82 Balint (1932, p. 169).
83 Balint (1932, p. 169).
84 Balint (1932, p. 169).
85 Balint (1932, pp. 167–169).
86 Balint himself does not use the word "preferable" in this context. He writes:

> A man with a strong character is a gain for society, a man with a weak character an everlasting worry, an everlasting danger . . . [O]ur task [as psychoanalysts] is to free the person from his many compulsory rigid conditions of love and hate. In my opinion this is in many cases not only justified but also necessary.
>
> (1932, p. 171)

87 Balint does not use the term "logical character", but refers to the "form-problem of characterology" (1932, p. 168).
88 "Changing Therapeutical Aims and Techniques in Psycho-Analysis" (Balint, 1949a).
89 Balint (1949a, p. 229).
90 Balint (1949a, p. 229).
91 Balint (1949a, p. 229).
92 Balint (1949a, pp. 229–230).
93 Balint (1949a, p. 230).
94 Much like Otto Rank (1884–1939) and his mentor Ferenczi before him, Balint employs "analytic situation" as the standard designation for the clinical psychoanalytic setting "under transference". At this point in his work, Lacan tends to refer to the "analytic experience" instead. See, for example, Balint (1951, p. 152, 1949a, p. 227), Ferenczi (1924, pp. 226–227, 1927), Lacan (1975b, pp. 37, 49), and Rank (1926).
95 Balint (1949a, p. 230).
96 Balint (1949a, p. 231).
97 Balint (1949a, p. 231).
98 Balint (1949a, p. 235).
99 Balint (1949a, p. 235).
100 Balint (1949a, p. 234).
101 Balint (1951, p. 144).
102 Granoff seems to be alluding here to Balint's admission in "Character Analysis and New Beginning" that

> [I]t is very seldom that the analytical work is finished with one single phase of this new beginning. Usually it is only step by step that patients allow themselves to drop the many conditions and formulas on which they made their surrender, their preparedness to love, conditional.
>
> (1932, p. 166)

103 The published transcription of Lacan's words, here, suggests a different perspective: "How does an analysis make progress? – if not through the interventions which impel

the subject to objectify himself, to take himself as object. Balint objectifies the subject, but in a different sense" (1975b, p. 206).

104 Balint (1949a, p. 234).

105 Balint & Balint (1939, pp. 214–215). Again, Granoff attributes the article to Michael Balint (see note 7 above).

106 Balint & Balint (1939).

107 Balint (1949b, p. 241).

108 Balint (1949b, pp. 240, 243).

109 Balint's observation reads:

> Even if we take the cautious view that each member of the International Association who is a practicing analyst finishes only one or two of his cases per year, the sum-total will be 1,000–2,000 per annum. Using my figures quoted in this paper ["On the Termination of Analysis"], according to which at least two out of ten finished cases are truly terminated, we arrive at the figure of 200–400 per annum.
>
> (1949b, pp. 242–243)

110 Balint (1949b, pp. 240, 243).

111 Balint (1949b, p. 240).

112 Balint (1949b, p. 240).

113 At this point, Lacan ends the discussion with some concluding comments, which the reader will find in Lacan (1975b, pp. 206–207).

Bibliography

Balint, A. (1939). Love for the mother and mother love. In: M. Balint (Eds.), *Primary Love and Psycho-Analytic Technique* (pp. 109–127). London: Hogarth, 1952.

Balint, A., & Balint, M. (1939). On transference and counter-transference. In: M. Balint (Eds.) (1932). *Character Analysis and New Beginning. Primary Love and Psycho-Analytic Technique* (pp. 159–173). London: Hogarth, 1952.

Balint, M. (1935). The final goal of psycho-analytic treatment. In: *Primary Love and Psycho-Analytic Technique* (pp. 188–199). London: Hogarth, 1952.

Balint, M. (1937). Early developmental states of the ego. Primary object-love. In: *Primary Love and Psycho-Analytic Technique* (pp. 90–108). London: Hogarth, 1952.

Balint, M. (1938). Strength of the ego and its education. In: *Primary Love and Psycho-Analytic Technique* (pp. 200–212). London: Hogarth, 1952.

Balint, M. (1947). On genital love. In: *Primary Love and Psycho-Analytic Technique* (pp. 128–140). London: Hogarth, 1952.

Balint, M. (1949a). Changing therapeutical aims and techniques in sycho-analysis. In: *Primary Love and Psycho-Analytic Technique* (pp. 221–235). London: Hogarth, 1952.

Balint, M. (1949b). On the termination of analysis. In: *Primary Love and Psycho-Analytic Technique* (pp. 236–243). London: Hogarth, 1952.

Balint, M. (1951). On love and hate. In: *Primary Love and Psycho-Analytic Technique* (pp. 141–156). London: Hogarth, 1952.

Balint, M. (1952). *Primary Love and Psycho-Analytic Technique*. London: Hogarth.

Berner, W. (1996). Hermann's concept of clinging in light of modern drive theory. In: P. L. Rudnytsky, A. Bókay, & P. Giampieri-Deutsch (Eds.), *Ferenczi's Turn in Psychoanalysis* (pp. 189–208). New York: New York University Press.

Ferenczi, S. (1924). Entwicklungsziele der psychoanalyse: Zur Wechselbeziehung von theorie und praxis. In: *Bausteine zur Psychoanalyse. Bd. 3: Arbeiten aus den Jahren 1908–1933* (pp. 220–244). Bern, Switzerland: Verlag Hans Huber, 1964.

Ferenczi, S. (1927). Zur kritik der rankschen "technik der psychoanalyse". In: *Bausteine zur Psychoanalyse. Bd. 2: Praxis* (pp. 116–128). Bern, Switzerland: Verlag Hans Huber, 1964.

Ferenczi, S. (1932). Confusion of the tongues between the adults and the child: The language of tenderness and of passion. M. Balint (Trans.). *International Journal of Psycho-Analysis, 30*: 225–230.

Fliess, R. (1948). An ontogenetic table. A chronological chart of the principal stages in the development of the psychic apparatus. In: R. Fliess (Ed.), *The Psychoanalytic Reader: An Anthology of Essential Papers with Critical Introductions* (pp. 285–290). New York: International Universities Press.

Freud, S. (1912a). *The Dynamics of Transference*. S. E., 12: 97–108. London: Hogarth.

Freud, S. (1912b). *On the Universal Tendency to Debasement in the Sphere of Love* (contributions to the psychology of love, II). S. E., 11: 177–190. London: Hogarth.

Freud, S. (1912–1913). *Totem and Taboo*. S. E., 13: 1–161. London: Hogarth.

Freud, S. (1920). *Beyond the Pleasure Principle*. S. E., 18: 1–64. London: Hogarth.

Freud, S. (1925). *Negation*. S. E., 19: 233–239. London: Hogarth.

Freud, S. (1927). *Fetishism*. S. E., 21: 147–157. London: Hogarth.

Harmat, P. (1988). *Freud, Ferenczi und die Ungarische Psychoanalyse*. Tübingen, Germany: Diskord.

Hegel, G. W. F. (1807a). *La Phénoménologie de L'esprit. Vol. 1*. J. Hyppolite (Trans.). Paris: Aubier-Montaigne, 1939.

Hegel, G. W. F. (1807b). *La Phénoménologie de L'esprit. Vol. 2*. J. Hyppolite (Trans.). Paris: Aubier-Montaigne, 1941.

Hyppolite, J. (1946). *Genesis and Structure of Hegel's Phenomenology of Spirit*. S. Cherniak & J. Heckman (Trans.). Evanston, IL: Northwestern University Press, 1974.

Hyppolite, J. (1954a). Appendix: A spoken commentary on Freud's *Verneinung*. In: J. Lacan & J.-A. Miller (Eds.), *The Seminar. Book I: Freud's Papers on Technique (1953–54)* (pp. 289–297). J. Forrester (Trans.). Cambridge, MA: Cambridge University Press, 1988.

Hyppolite, J. (1954b). Appendix I: A spoken commentary on Freud's *Verneinung*. In: *Écrits* (pp. 746–754). B. Fink (Trans.). New York: W. W. Norton, 2006.

King, P. (2003). Introduction: The rediscovery of John Rickman and his work. In: P. King (Ed.), *No Ordinary Psychoanalyst: The Exceptional Contributions of John Rickman* (pp. 1–68). London: Karnac.

Klaniczay, S. (2012). Imre Hermann: Researching psyche and space. In: J. Szekacs-Weisz & T. Keve (Eds.), *Ferenczi and His World: Rekindling the Spirit of the Budapest School* (pp. 139–155). London: Karnac.

Lacan, J. (1947). British psychiatry and the war. P. Dravers & V. Voruz (Trans.). *Psychoanalytical Notebooks of the London Circle, 4*: 9–33.

Lacan, J. (1949). The mirror stage as formative of the *I* function as revealed in psychoanalytic experience. In: *Écrits* (pp. 75–81). B. Fink (Trans). New York: W. W. Norton, 2006.

Lacan, J. (1953). The function and field of speech and language in psychoanalysis. In: *Écrits* (pp. 197–268). B. Fink (Trans). New York: W. W. Norton, 2006.

Lacan, J. (1975a). *Le Séminaire. Livre I: Les Ecrits Techniques de Freud (1953–54)*. Texte établi par J.-A. Miller. Paris: du Seuil.

Lacan, J. (1975b). *The Seminar. Book I: Freud's Papers on Technique (1953–54)*. J.-A. Miller (Ed.), J. Forrester (Trans.). Cambridge, MA: Cambridge University Press, 1988.

Mannoni, O. (1956). *Prospero and Caliban: The Psychology of Colonization*. P. Powesland (Trans.). Ann Arbor, MI: University of Michigan Press, 1991.

Mannoni, O. (1969). "I Know Well, but All the Same ..." G. M. Goshgarian (Trans.). In: M. A. Rothenberg, D. A. Foster & S. Žižek (Eds.), *Perversion and the Social Relation* (pp. 68–92). Durham, NC: Duke University Press, 2003.

Masson, J. M. (Ed.) (1985). *The Complete Letters of Sigmund Freud to Wilhelm Fliess, 1887–1904.* J. M. Masson (Trans.). Cambridge, MA: The Belknap Press of Harvard University Press.

Miller, J.-A. (1986). *Letter to John Forrester of 20 June 1986.* John Forrester Papers, unlisted collection. Colchester: Albert Sloman Library, University of Essex.

Payne, S. M. (1957). Foreword. In: J. Rickman (Ed.), *Selected Contributions to Psycho-Analysis* (pp. 9–16). London: Hogarth.

Rank, O. (1926). *Technik der Psychoanalyse. I. Die Analytische Situation.* Leipzig, Germany: Franz Deuticke.

Rickman, J. (1950). The factor of number in individual- and group-dynamics. In: *Selected Contributions to Psycho-Analysis* (pp. 165–169). London: Hogarth, 1957.

Rickman, J. (1951a). Methodology and research in psycho-pathology. In: *Selected Contributions to Psycho-Analysis* (pp. 207–217). London: Hogarth, 1957.

Rickman, J. (1951b). Number and the human sciences. In: *Selected Contributions to Psycho-Analysis* (pp. 218–223). London: Hogarth, 1957.

Varga, E. (Ed.) (1989). *Memorial Conference on the Centennial of Imre Hermann's Birth.* Budapest: Sokszorosító.

Vikár, G. (1999). Die Problematik der Aggression in der Auffassung von Imre Hermann und der "Budapester Schule". *Luzifer-Amor: Zeitschrift zur Geschichte der Psychoanalyse,* *23*: 84–96.

Lacan's Balint

Synergies and discords in a professional friendship

Dany Nobus

Exactly when and where Michael Balint first encountered Jacques Lacan may never be fully established with any degree of certainty. In early August 1936, both men travelled to Marienbad (Mariánské Lázně) for the 14th congress of the International Psychoanalytic Association (IPA). For 35-year-old Lacan, who was still in training at the "Société Psychanalytique de Paris" (SPP) (Roudinesco, 1997[1994], p. 73), the event marked his first presentation at an international conference outside France, and his first contact with the international psychoanalytic community. Five years his senior, Balint arrived in Marienbad as an already well-known and highly respected member of the Berlin and the Budapest psychoanalytic societies who, after the untimely death of his mentor Sándor Ferenczi in 1933, was widely regarded as one of the key flag-bearers of Hungarian psychoanalysis (Moreau Ricaud, 2007, pp. 94–97). Lacan's paper had been scheduled for the afternoon of 3 August, the first full day of the conference (Glover, 1937), yet his contribution on "The Looking-Glass Phase" was allegedly cut short after exactly ten minutes by Ernest Jones, the then president of the IPA, who insisted that it was time for the next speaker (Edoardo Weiss) to take the stage (Lacan, 1946, p. 150; Roudinesco, 1994, p. 113). Undoubtedly disgruntled by the fact that his first formal appearance at an IPA event had unexpectedly crystallised into a frustratingly short session, Lacan packed his bags the next day, eager "to get a feeling for the spirit of the time – a time full of promises – at the Olympics in Berlin" (Lacan, 1958, p. 501). He thus hurriedly exchanged the psychoanalytic stage for another stage, whose deeply uncanny atmosphere of carefully choreographed excitement would subsequently be immortalised in Leni Riefenstahl's universally acclaimed *Olympia*. By the time Balint delivered another version of his Ferenczi Memorial Lecture "Eros and Aphrodite", on 7 August (Balint, 1936, p. 73; Haynal & Hudon, 2003, p. 260), Lacan could definitely have been back in Marienbad, although I like to believe that, having abandoned the psychoanalytic scene, he probably spent a few days witnessing and absorbing Goebbels's formidable propaganda machine, and then took the first train back to Paris.[1]

There is no record of Lacan having attended the next International Psychoanalytic Congress, which was notably held in Paris in early August 1938, where Balint presented a paper on the strength of the ego and its education (Balint, 1938,

DOI: 10.4324/9781003309826-20

p. 200; Haynal & Hudon, 2003, p. 260). At that time, Nazi Germany had already annexed Austria, Freud had emigrated to London, the status of the Hungarian Jews was extremely precarious owing to Hungary's coalition with the Axis powers, and Balint and his wife (and close collaborator) Alice Székely-Kovács were seriously considering emigrating to London as well, despite Ernest Jones's conviction that London was already too full (of psychoanalysts), and that they should move to Australia instead (Moreau Ricaud, 2007, p. 125). In the end, and largely by virtue of the intervention of John Rickman, the Balints agreed to settle in Manchester in January 1939 (Moreau Ricaud, 2007, pp. 125–126). Following the sudden death of his wife in August that year, and Britain's declaration of war in early September, Balint's clinical and research activities stagnated – between 1940 and 1945 his bibliography includes just one book review and one short paper (Haynal & Hudon, 2003, pp. 260–261; Moreau Ricaud, 2007, pp. 131–140). Geographically removed from the London battlefields, he nonetheless played an active role in the infamous "Freud-Klein controversies", which ravaged the British Psychoanalytical Society (BPS) from 1941 until 1945 (King & Steiner, 1991). Throughout these acrimonious debates on the "true nature" of psychoanalysis, Balint committed himself neither to the orthodox path of Anna Freud, nor to the purportedly deviant psychoanalytic orientation represented by Melanie Klein, but (much like Sylvia Payne, Ella Sharpe, Ronald Fairbairn, Donald Winnicott, and various others) campaigned for the installation of a clinical and theoretical "middle ground", which eventually led to the creation of the "Independent Group" in British psychoanalysis (Moreau Ricaud, 2007, pp. 149–152; Rayner, 1991). During those years, Balint's sister-in-law Olga Székely-Kovács lived with her husband Ladislas Dormandi in Paris – they had emigrated to France in 1938 – yet there was little or no contact between Balint and his relatives on the other side of the Channel, if only because the Vichy regime of Maréchal Pétain had effectively placed them in enemy territories (Dupont, 2015, pp. 30–42). However, after the liberation, personal contacts resumed, and Balint regularly spent time in Paris. In this way, he became more acquainted with the work of the SPP, partly because his mother-in-law Vilma Kovács (née Prosnitz) had also been an influential psychoanalyst in Hungary and had become close friends with Princess Marie Bonaparte, one of the founding members of the SPP (de Mijolla, 2010, p. 358), partly because his niece (strictly speaking, his niece-in-law) Judith Dupont (née Dormandi) had decided to train as a medical doctor and soon developed an interest in psychoanalysis herself (Dupont, 2015, pp. 42–50).

Much like Balint, Lacan did not publish anything noteworthy between 1940 and 1945 (Dor, 1994, p. 53). During World War II, when France was divided into two zones, he alternated between his work as a medical doctor in occupied Paris and leisure time in the unoccupied south of France, where his new partner Sylvia Maklès (who was Jewish) had found refuge. On both sides of the demarcation line, Lacan frequented gatherings of artists and philosophers, which brought him into contact with such renowned intellectuals as Jean-Paul Sartre, Albert Camus, and Michel Leiris. Yet as the SPP, of which he was now a full member, had interrupted all its activities, and practising the "Jewish science" of psychoanalysis in Paris would have been virtually impossible, also owing to a persistent lack of patients, his psychoanalytic career had come to a halt (Roudinesco, 1994, pp. 153–170). However, in September 1945, just weeks after the end of the war, Lacan decided to visit England, where he met Rickman and Wilfred Bion (Lacan, 1947, p. 15). There is no evidence that he had also arranged to see Balint, who had moved to London by now, or anyone else from the British Psychoanalytical Society.

Did the two men meet during the first International Psychoanalytic Congress after World War II? Held in Zürich in August 1949, this 16th Congress offered Lacan another opportunity to expose his ideas on the mirror stage (1949), prematurely cut as they had been 13 years earlier by presidential decree. Although still presiding over the proceedings, Jones was either absent when Lacan delivered his talk, or Lacan himself was altogether less garrulous, but to all intents and purposes this second session seems to have followed its intellectual course towards the desired end. Unlike many of the other conference papers, Lacan's "Mirror Stage" was not published in *The International Journal of Psycho-Analysis*, but it was at least dutifully summarised in its bulletin (A. Freud, 1949). In Zürich, Balint presented his "Changing Therapeutical Aims and Techniques in Psycho-Analysis" (1949a), which contained more than a few critical comments on the deplorable state of contemporary psychoanalytic theory, and which would not have been appreciated by Anna Freud and her followers, not least because Balint explicitly proclaimed in it that "Mrs Klein's contributions... [and] theoretical ideas go a long way to meet the demands" he had articulated (1949a, p. 230). Unphased by the recent debates in the BPS and unquestionably conscious of his contentious reputation in the IPA as the undisputed keeper of Ferenczi's legacy, Balint designated contemporary psychoanalytic technique as "a very fine, safe and reliable instrument", but also argued that the theory supporting this clinical technique was unfortunately "very weak", "rather primitive", and distinctly "incomplete and lopsided" (pp. 225–230). In his view, psychoanalysts had never succeeded in extending their conceptual reach beyond the "physiological or biological bias", that is, the strictly individualistic perspective Freud himself had imposed upon his theoretical elaborations (pp. 225–230). In no uncertain terms, he called for a fundamental review of some of the most cherished psychoanalytic principles, in order to bring the theory back in line with the state of clinical technique. The latter, he would write in a later addendum to the paper, was already attuned to what his friend (and saving grace) Rickman had designated as a "Two-Body Psychology!, which accounts for the dynamic interplay between the analyst and the patient, whereas the former was still hopelessly mired in clinically inadequate "One-Body" constructions (Balint, 1949a, pp. 234–235; Rickman, 1950, p. 166, 1951a, pp. 207–208, 1951b, pp. 219–220).

On the surface, Lacan's contribution to the Zürich congress could also have been dismissed as another staple of "One-Body" reasoning, given its central preoccupation with the formation of the "I" or ego-function, were it not for the fact that any attentive listener would also have heard how Lacan posited that the development of the ego is crucially conditioned by the child's (imaginary) identification with the reflection of himself as a "similar ideal other" in the mirror.[2] In 1949, neither Lacan nor Balint employed Rickman's nomenclature, for the simple reason that Rickman himself did not introduce it until the year after, yet Lacan's invocation of a formative developmental schema involving the relationship between the child and the specular image of himself *qua* object, without his therefore having recourse to Klein's theories, could have easily resonated with the type of relational model Balint had in mind when he called for a substantial revision of contemporary psychoanalytic thinking. Were Balint to have attended Lacan's presentation in Zürich, he would certainly have been charmed by his French colleague's intermittent recourse to biological, more specifically ethological observations, not to mention Lodewijk Bolk's infamous foetalisation theory (Bolk, 1926), on which he himself had drawn since 1930 and most recently in an essay "On Genital Love" (Balint, 1930, 1947a, pp. 133–134).[3] And were Lacan to have attended Balint's paper, he may not only have been enthused by his Hungarian-British colleague's admirably courageous indictment of the dominant psychoanalytic theory as an outdated conceptual paradigm, and by his palpable predilection for the early (functional or dynamic) Freud, that is, before the introduction of the second topography, but also and perhaps most intensely by his insistence on the need to examine the role of language in the psychoanalytic situation. "[E]very language", Balint averred, "must be examined in order to discover how much conscious or unconscious gratification it affords the analyst, and how much it contributes to the building and shaping of the psychoanalytic situation" (1949a, p. 232). What Balint proposed as a cardinal critical task, here, involuntarily echoed Lacan's phenomenological description of the psychoanalytic experience from 1936, in which he had noted that "The psychoanalyst, in order not to detach analytic experience from the language of the situation that it implies, the situation of the interlocutor, comes upon the simple fact that language, prior to signifying something, signifies to someone" (1936, p. 66).

Towards the end of the 1940s, and possibly catalysed by his own frequent travels between London and Paris, Balint undertook the initiative to enhance the cooperation between the British and the French psychoanalytic societies, starting with an exchange programme of lectures at the scientific meetings. In a letter to Balint dated 30 June 1951, Daniel Lagache, member of the SPP's executive committee and professor of psychology at the Sorbonne, complimented his colleague on the results that had been obtained by virtue of this new Franco-British alliance, and expressed his hope that it might lead to the organisation of a new "Regional Congress" (1951a). Apart from Balint himself, who delivered a paper to the SPP in June 1951 on "The Problem of Discipline", two other members of the BPS had already presented their work in Paris, whereas Lagache and Lacan had already been invited to London, on 4 April and 2 May 1951 respectively.[4] At these meetings, Lagache shared his thoughts on the vexed issue of transference (Lagache, 1951b), while Lacan delivered "Some Reflections on the Ego" (Lacan, 1951b). For Lagache, the lecture was not only an excellent opportunity to test a draft outline of a much more substantive report on transference he had been asked to prepare for the 14th Annual Conference of Francophone Psychoanalysts (ACFP) of 1 November 1951 in Paris (Lagache, 1952), but also a good occasion to demonstrate to his colleagues in the

BPS the French psychoanalytic endorsement of Rickman's and Balint's calls for the development of a "Two-Body Psychology" (Lagache, 1951b, p. 122). Lacan, for his part, steered well clear from taking sides in the "Freud-Klein controversies", emphasising the legitimacy of Klein's contributions as well as the fact that "Miss Anna Freud has enumerated, analysed and defined once and for all the mechanisms in which the functions of the ego take form in the psyche" (Lacan, 1951b, pp. 307, 314).[5] Yet apart from this dual *captatio benevolentiae*, his paper was a highly condensed and unapologetically abstract summa of his own theoretical trajectory since his first, prematurely interrupted presentation at the Marienbad conference. And so it featured quite a few references to Hegel, carefully distilled from his tenacious participation in Alexandre Kojève's seminar on the "Phenomenology of Spirit" during the 1930s (Hegel, 1807; Kojève, 1933–1939), intermittent invocations of ethological studies, and above all another recapitulation of the mirror-stage concept, including its biological foundation in Bolk's foetalisation theory.

I would be extremely surprised if Balint, as the initiator of the exchange programme, had not attended Lagache's and Lacan's lectures. There is no trace of the two events in Balint's published works or in his correspondence, and so we can only speculate about his response to them. Much like the majority of his colleagues in the BPS, he probably greatly appreciated Lagache's didactic approach to the subject matter and his remarkable clarity of style, not to mention the explicit commendation of the "Two-Body" perspective. But Lacan's exceedingly arcane "wisdom" would not necessarily have been lost on him, as it would subsequently be on the American psychoanalyst Henry Harper Hart, who wrote a scathing review of the published version of Lacan's talk for *The Psychoanalytic Quarterly*, in which he revealed that the Frenchman just rambled "from Hegel to grasshoppers", sliding back into complete intellectual chaos, and throwing the honourable members of the BPS into a state of complete "neo-confusionism" (*sic*) (Hart, 1954).[6] Unlike Lacan, Balint had not painstakingly unpacked Hegel's *The Phenomenology of Spirit*, but he was by no means afraid of grasshoppers. If anything, his 1930 paper "Psychosexual Parallels to the Fundamental Law of Biogenetics" pullulated with demandingly detailed descriptions of the sexual reproduction cycles of non-human animals, so much so that he even gave those "readers not particularly interested in biology" explicit permission to ignore those parts of it (pp. 17–24). And even though he would have vehemently disagreed with Lacan's claim (1951b, p. 316) that it is not exactly "psychologically advantageous to have a strong ego", Balint also shared Lacan's interest in foetalisation and the human prematurity of birth. In short, Balint's response to Lacan's lecture at the BPS may not have been markedly different from that which he shared with Lagache almost three years later, on 4 January 1954, having read Lacan's "Rome Discourse" (1953f), the lengthy theoretical report on the status of language in psychoanalysis he was supposed to have presented at the 16th ACFP:

I am still battling with Lacan's paper. I find it very interesting and stimulating, but, if I may use the word, too longwinded and rambling. It is apparently very difficult for him [Lacan] to resist the temptation of a happy bon mot or well-sounding phrase. Still, what he has to say is worth saying, and he has done a service in saying it.[7]

(Balint, 1954a)

Meanwhile, during the first half of 1953, the SPP had entered a state of organisational crisis in the aftermath of the proposed creation of a training institute, and the articulation of a series of statutes governing the selection and "education" of new psychoanalytic trainees. Modelled on the Berlin Psychoanalytic Institute, which had been founded by Karl Abraham, Max Eitingon, and Ernst Simmel in 1920 (Fuechtner, 2011, p. 9), the SPP had already inaugurated its own Institute back in January 1934 (de Mijolla, 2010, p. 607), mainly by virtue of Marie Bonaparte's generous financial assistance, yet it had ceased all activities in the spring of 1940 (Miller, 1976, p. 37). Four years after the end of World War II, the project had been reactivated, which had not only required the identification of new funding streams for the acquisition of a suitable building for the teaching and practising of psychoanalysis, including a research library and administrative offices, but also (and more contentiously) the agreement over a set of principles regulating the format and management of the psychoanalytic training process. Cutting a long and exceedingly complex story short, between January and May 1953, both Nacht (as director of the Institute) and Lacan (as president of the SPP) drew up their own rival statutes for the Institute, Nacht's being much more succinct than Lacan's, but also significantly more formalistic and prescriptive.[8] For example, in Nacht's version, it was stipulated that psychoanalytic trainees would be expected to pursue a training analysis with a frequency of four to five sessions per week, each session lasting 45 minutes, and the average duration of the entire process being between 250 and 300 sessions (Miller, 1976, p. 68). Nacht also proposed that all trainees, both current and newly registered, should sign a declaration that they would not call themselves psychoanalysts and practise psychoanalysis without the authorisation of the Training Committee (Miller, 1976, p. 71). As could have been expected, many of the trainees saw Nacht's statutes as an authoritarian imposition of empty, arbitrary rules that did not take account of each candidate's individual circumstances, and so they started to campaign against them (Miller, 1976, pp. 72–82). However, despite the grassroots opposition, Nacht's statutes were passed by a majority of members of the SPP's executive board, as a result of which those who had voted in favour of Lacan's statutes resigned from the SPP on 16 June 1953, setting up a new psychoanalytic organisation called Société française de Psychanalyse (SFP), which Lacan himself joined immediately, alongside a sizeable majority of the former SPP trainees (Miller, 1976, pp. 90–98). What the resigning members of the SPP had not expected was that their departure would be considered by the IPA executive as a *de facto* abdication of their IPA membership and that the SFP would be effectively operating outside the one and only international psychoanalytic professional body (Miller, 1976, p. 99). Hazardous as it already was for psychoanalysts without a medical degree to engage in clinical practice, the removal of professional protection by the main governing body thus potentially put more practitioners at risk of being accused of illegally providing (mental) health care services to supposedly vulnerable members of the general public.[9]

Why is all of this relevant for Lacan's engagement with Balint? First of all, during the early days of June 1953, Lacan (in his capacity as president of the SPP) asked Balint's permission for his paper "On the Psycho-Analytic Training System" (Balint, 1947b), which he had first delivered to the British Psychoanalytical Society on 5 November 1947, to be translated into French and circulated among the members of the SPP (Balint, 1953a).[10] In this extraordinary text, which remains as relevant today as it was 75 years ago, Balint unequivocally presented himself as the heir of the "Hungarian system" (*sic*) in psychoanalysis, and took aim at all the representatives of the so-called "Eitingon model" of psychoanalytic training – because it had been advanced by Eitingon under the auspices of the Berlin Psychoanalytic Institute during the 1920s – and thus at the vast majority of the most respected psychoanalysts in the IPA. Not pulling his punches, Balint argued that the Eitingon model, which requires all psychoanalytic trainees to receive theoretical education, followed by a training analysis, and subsequently by supervised practice, required a fundamental revision, because it was too authoritarian, inherently dogmatic, and unjustifiably rigid in its rules and regulations. Balint realised all too well that in questioning the dominant regulatory framework for psychoanalytic training, he also questioned the quality of the training that many of the senior analysts in the BPS had received, but it did not stop him from breaking the institutional silence, calling his colleagues to the witness stand, and saying what many people in the BPS (and further afield) had known for a long time, but what few if any had ever dared to expose. Repeating a principle Ferenczi had defended more than 20 years earlier (1927, p. 376), Balint opined that a training analysis should not be conceived differently from any other type of analysis, with the caveat that it should even go further and deeper than the psychoanalytic treatment being offered to the "mainstream" patient. Most provocative, however, was his declaration that the dominant training system in the IPA, in which a candidate's training analyst plays a major part in the decision as to when and whether the training analysis has been completed and the candidate can be admitted to the psychoanalytic profession, inevitably leads to intellectual obedience, clinical conformism, and institutional tribalism. Instead of training well-qualified psychoanalysts, Balint posited, the training system's implicit aim is "to train the new generation to identify themselves with their initiators, and especially with the analytic ideas of their initiators" (1947b, p. 267). "[E]ach school of thought", he continued, "tries hard to win more candidates to itself and to educate them to be safe, trustworthy and loyal followers" (p. 268). In his view, which could only have been heard as a massive bombshell, candidates were not being trained to be "honestly critical", but to be deeply respectful of "their master's words", without which they would inevitably run the risk of never being allowed by the ruling authorities to finish their training analysis, and never being given formal access to their chosen profession (p. 271). "What we need", Balint concluded,

Is a new orientation of our training system which must aim less at establishing a new and firm superego and more at enabling the candidate to free himself and to build up a strong ego which shall be both critical and liberal at the same time.

(p. 269)

And the best way to achieve this would be "to decrease – at least in name – the unnecessary weight of authority" (p. 270).[11]

In the age of open connectivity and social media, one is often being told that a message forwarded is not tantamount to a message endorsed, yet in this case I think it is safe to say that, when Lacan distributed copies of Balint's paper to the members of the SPP in June 1953, he wholeheartedly agreed with Balint's critical analysis of psychoanalytic training practices, and wanted his colleagues to know that at least one senior member of the BPS had called for a less dogmatic and more egalitarian, less rigid and more open-ended, less authoritarian and more democratic system of training. Balint's paper may very well have been read by the members of the SPP, but in the end it was another version of the Eitingon model that prevailed.

The second reason as to why my earlier, succinct reconstruction of the internal conflict in the SPP during the winter and spring of 1953 is directly relevant for a critical evaluation of the connections between Lacan and Balint relates to Balint's professional stance in the subsequent IPA debate concerning the institutional status of the SFP. On 24 June 1953, Balint informed Lagache that he had been told by Pierre Marty, who acted as the SPP secretary, that some members of the SPP had decided to resign, and that members of the BPS had all been "very perturbed about the news" (Balint, 1953b). He also disclosed that Marie Bonaparte (who had rather unexpectedly voted in favour of Nacht's statutes) had asked the executive of the BPS to put forward a motion at the forthcoming 18th Congress of the IPA for the International Training Committee (ITC) to be re-convened.[12] I have not been able to locate Lagache's response to Balint's letter, yet on 14 July 1953 – Bastille day, and eight days after the executive of the SFP had been informed that, in resigning from the SPP, they had effectively also forfeited their IPA membership (Eissler, 1953, p. 99 – Lacan himself contacted Balint about the "situation", in what was simultaneously an expression of gratitude for his colleague's previously agreeing to the French translation of his paper on psychoanalytic training. "Bien cher ami", he wrote, "I put high hopes in your paper... but my attempt [to resolve the dispute] failed, much like all the others I had made before" (1953d, p. 119). Nonetheless, he continued, "<ds><ds>. . . </ds></ds>the Société française de psychanalyse was born under the most favourable auspices, those of soulfulness [*réaction de cœur*] and of audacity, and without us having to reproach ourselves in any way" (p. 119). "Till soon, dear friend", he concluded, "and let it be known to you that in my teaching I have always reserved a large place for the spiritual line of Ferenczi <ds><ds>. . . </ds></ds>" (p. 119). Exaggerated as it may have been, Lacan's last admission was probably not entirely disingenuous, although it was no doubt also as much of a *captatio benevolentiae* as his acknowledgements of Anna Freud and Melanie Klein in his 1951 lecture at the BPS.[13] Lacan also suggested to Balint that he provide a more detailed explanation of the circumstances in a personal meeting before the London Congress, but it remains unclear whether the two men did indeed sit down together to discuss the background and the repercussions of the split.[14] Either way, when the central executive of the IPA considered the SFP's status at the London Congress on 26 July 1953, Balint categorically opposed the IPA's unilateral decision to immediately withdraw the SFP's institutional recognition, as well as its proposal to postpone its full reinstatement pending the outcome of an investigative inquiry into its clinical standards (Hartmann, 1954, p. 74). Not unlike his having advocated a "middle ground" during the Freud-Klein controversies, Balint offered the executive three alternative, more positive solutions to the crisis: "membership at large; provisional recognition of the whole group; or individual membership in other Component Societies" (Hartmann, 1954, p. 74). Despite Balint's best efforts at reconciliation, the executive eventually decided that a committee should be appointed to examine the SFP's practices and procedures. When a member of the audience asked about the status of the new French group in the meantime, Anna Freud responded: "The status is the one they created themselves by resignation" (Hartmann, 1954, p. 74).

What took most people, including Lagache and Lacan, by surprise during these discussions, is that the original source and origin of the dispute – the disagreement over the formal regulation of psychoanalytic training – was almost instantly shifted towards another bone of contention: Lacan's clinical technique, especially in the case of training analyses. For example, at the very start of the debate, Marie Bonaparte claimed:

[T]he split occurred because of divergence in technique… [T]he question of technique [is] a fundamental one in analysis in general, and in the training of analysts in particular… [A] careful examination of the technique used by the members of the new group is required, particularly in view of the fact that one of these members [Lacan] two years ago promised to change his technique, but did not keep his promise.

(Hartmann, 1954, p. 72)

The "divergent technique" Bonaparte was alluding to, here, concerned Lacan's routine replacement of the standard, 50- or 45-minute psychoanalytic session with sessions of variable length, and not infrequently with consistently short sessions, whereby he would actively, yet not arbitrarily, interrupt the patient's discourse after ten or 15 minutes by telling him or her that the session would end there. Judging by records of meetings published in the *Revue française de Psychanalyse*, Lacan had endeavoured to explain and justify this controversial technical innovation to his colleagues in the SPP in a series of three lectures titled "Dialectical Psychoanalysis" (*Psychanalyse dialectique*), which were held between December 1951 and February 1953.[15] Yet quite a few of his fellow psychoanalysts remained unconvinced that it was a good idea, afraid as they were that it might give the analyst too much power and control over the treatment process, that it might lead to analysts deliberately cutting short their patients' sessions for financial reasons, and (most worrying of all) that it might result in poorly trained psychoanalytic practitioners in the case of training analyses. Knowing all too well that the words of "la Princesse" at the IPA executive meeting in London would not fall on deaf ears, Lacan realised immediately that the SFP's prospective re-alliance with the IPA would become *his* problem, in every sense of the expression. And so he set out to defend himself, first and foremost to his friend Balint, who had been unreservedly sympathetic to the cause of the SFP, in a lengthy missive of 6 August 1953.[16] Accusing Bonaparte of having lied to the IPA executive about his clinical technique, Lacan wrote:

> They've tried to make people believe that I not only conducted short sessions, but also truncated, "facile" analyses, leaving large periods of time between sessions. This is false. My analyses are well-known for being rather long (3 to 4 years) and it's funny to see how some of my colleagues are hiding their own, rather questionable behaviour on this topic behind these accusations (in some cases, analyses of less than a year). The frequency of my sessions is in keeping with practices that are in place everywhere – in any case, in our entire society. As to the experiments to which I was led with regard to the duration of the sessions, I explained my reasons for them at the time, that is to say at the very moment when I tested them out, and they seemed plausible to many, if not to all in our society. But let's leave the matter for what it is, because I have now abandoned this practice for professional reasons, and in its entirety since January.[17]
>
> (1953c)

In a 1985 interview with Antoine Vergote and Francis Martens, Wladimir Granoff, who had been in analysis with Marc Schlumberger before the 1953 split, and who became one of the most active members of the SFP after it had been established, admitted without restraint that whatever Lacan may have said at the time, to friends and foes alike, about his having relinquished his controversial technique, he was lying through his teeth. "Everyone lying on Lacan's couch", Granoff stated, "testified that short sessions were the norm" (1985, p. 123). It should be noted, here, that Granoff did not reject Lacan's approach in principle, but that he thought it had been foolish of Lacan to think that he would not be found out (Figure 14.1).

In his response to Lacan's letter of 6 August, Balint showed himself once again to be the strident individualist and conciliatory diplomat he had always been:

> Thank you very much for your kind words about my unsuccessful attempt to prevent the Association [the IPA] making fools of themselves. I still think that the only sensible solution is to have two French societies, at least for a few years until the emotions have calmed down.
>
> (Balint, 1953c)

As regards Lacan's technical experiments, he was more prudent and reserved, yet also curious about his colleague's rationale:

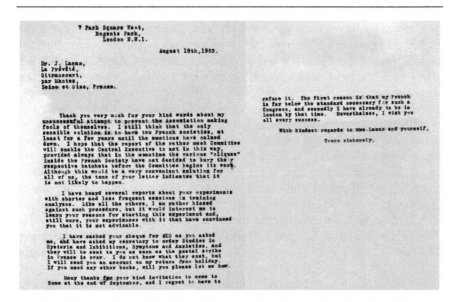

Figure 14.1 Letter from Balint to Lacan, 18 August 1953. With permission of Judith Dupont and the Institute of psychoanalysis

I have heard several reports about your experiments with shorter and less fre-quent sessions in training analyses. Like all the others, I am rather biased against such procedure, but it would interest me to learn your reasons for starting this experiment and, still more, your experiences with it that have convinced you that it is not advisable.

(1953c)

Undoubtedly keen to consolidate Balint's support for the SFP, and eager to re-juvenate the Franco-British alliance under its patronage, Lacan invited Balint to come to Rome in September, where Lacan had now been officially barred from delivering his theoretical report on language in psychoanalysis at the 16th ACFP, but where the SFP had decided to organise their own "shadow conference" two days after the end of the ACFP, on 26 and 27 September (Lacan, 1953c). "As you know", Lacan wrote, "your popularity amongst us is immense" (1953c). Balint po-litely declined the offer, stating that his French was too sub-standard for him to be able to speak at the event and that he also had to be in London at that time (1953c).[18]

In many ways, the first congress of the SFP in Rome contained *in nuce* all the elements that would come to mark the society's intellectual profile and institutional functioning over the next ten years. Since Lacan's long report had already been dis-tributed to the members of the SFP in advance, he presented a largely improvised synopsis of it, which was significantly shorter than the written text, but equally erudite, provocative, and challenging (Lacan, 953f). If it was by no means the start of Lacan's notoriously hermetic style, because it had already transpired in many of his previous contributions, it was definitely the beginning of his ascendancy as the intellectual figurehead of the new French psychoanalytic society. Add to this that Lacan's report did not just offer a critical panorama of psychoanalytic approaches to language, but constituted a veritable theoretical manifesto, which would come to inform, permeate, and typify virtually each and every aspect of the SFP's work. However, when Lagache, in his capacity as president of the SFP, was the first to formally respond to his colleague's presentation, he did not let the opportunity go by to highlight the fact that Lacan's text had occasionally been rather difficult, but that at least for once the speaker's discourse had avoided the highly poetic, yet largely impenetrable language of the French symbolist Stéphane Mallarmé (Lagache, 1953b).[19] Lagache's little sneer echoed the way in which he had introduced Lacan on the occasion of the very first scientific meeting of the SFP, which had been held in the large amphitheatre of Sainte-Anne Hospital in Paris on 8 July 1953, and where Lacan had given a lecture on "the Symbolic, the Imaginary and the Real":

> We've asked our friend Lacan to speak, because you all know our admiration for and attachment to him, despite his little flaws, and he's always ready to put himself on the line [*payer de sa personne*] for some interesting scientific talk.[20]
> (Lagache, 1953c; Ohayon, 1999, p. 374)

Until 19 November 1963, when a majority of SFP members voted in favour of Lacan's demotion as a training analyst in exchange for the group's renewed, official recognition by the IPA (Miller, 1977, p. 85), Lagache and Lacan would become increasingly rivalrous, hostile, and antagonistic – Lacan being unquestionably envious of Lagache's admirable position as a professor at the Sorbonne, despite his ostensibly mediocre intellect, Lagache feeling indubitably sidelined by Lacan's widely acknowledged position as the main *maître-à-penser* of the SFP, despite his incorrigible propensity for obscurantism.

However, during the first (academic) year of its activities, the SFP celebrated its newly established independence from the reactionary, orthodox strands of thought running through the psychoanalytic establishment, and its members worked hard to prove the institution's legitimacy and respectability, efforts in which they probably felt encouraged by the allegiance of Angelo Hesnard and René Laforgue, two first-generation French psychoanalysts who had been instrumental in creating the SPP back in 1926 (de Mijolla, 2012, pp. 412–417; Laforgue, 1953a, 1953b).[21] During that year, Balint maintained a regular correspondence with Lagache, and he at one point informed him that he had heard, from a reliable source, that the IPA's central executive was minded not to recognise the SFP for psychoanalytic training purposes. The issue not only bothered him owing to his sympathy for the French group's institutional plight, but also owing to the fact that his niece Judith Dupont was about to start her training analysis with Lagache (Balint, 1954c; Dupont, 2015, p. 49). As it turned out, the IPA executive did not present the SFP with an ultimatum until the summer of 1963, and Lagache reassured his colleague that, although his niece would evidently remain free to change her mind about her choice of training analyst, the lack of IPA recognition would have no direct impact on her being able to practise as a psychoanalyst, if only because she had already trained as a medical doctor (Lagache, 1954a). On Sunday 25 April 1954, Balint also became the first member of the BPS to present a paper for the SFP (Lagache, 1954b). Although he knew that his recent volume *Primary Love and Psycho-Analytic Technique* had already received some attention at Lacan's first public seminar, on "Freud's Papers on Technique" (Lacan, 1975), Balint decided to deliver, or at least to ask someone from the SFP to read, a French version of "Training General Practitioners in Psychotherapy", the paper in which he first conceived what would later become known as "Balint groups", and which had recently been published in the *British Medical Journal* (Balint, 1954b).[22]

During the first five years of his public seminar, that is, between the autumn of 1953 and the summer of 1958, Lacan would develop his own conception of the object-relation – which Balint had initially captured under the heading of a "Two-Body Psychology" – in a close critical engagement with Balint's views on the dynamics of primary love. In fact, over and above their personal and professional synergies, the intellectual confluence between Balint and Lacan during this period can be detected in at least four different areas of psychoanalytic investigation: 1. the ongoing issue of the principles governing psychoanalytic training, which also continued to feature highly on the agenda of the IPA until well into the 1950s; 2. the ethical question as to the end of the psychoanalytic treatment, which Balint had first broached in a paper presented at the 13th IPA Congress at Lucerne in 1934, and which he would designate alternately as the "final goal" (1935) and the "termination" (1949b) of analysis; 3. the controversial matter as to the versatility – or, as Ferenczi dubbed it, the "elasticity" (1927–1928) – of psychoanalytic technique, which Balint had inherited and absorbed from his second analyst and intellectual mentor, and which covered the nature of the analyst's position within the treatment, as well as the temporal parameters within which a psychoanalytic process can unfold; 4. the mainly theoretical topic of the status of the object within the successive stages of libidinal development, first adumbrated by Karl Abraham in a landmark essay from 1924 and subsequently taken up by Klein in a series of contributions that would lead to the emergence of the object-relations tradition in psychoanalysis.

Within the space of this chapter, I cannot possibly undertake a thorough examination of each of these four areas of psychoanalytic inquiry, which oriented Lacan's engagement with Balint's ideas during the 1950s, and which to some extent continued to underpin Lacan's views until well into the 1960s. For mainly pragmatic reasons, for example, because it is in many ways the least contentious issue, I shall restrict myself to a brief critical unpacking of Lacan's commentaries on Balint's theory of primary love, which the latter had developed collaboratively with his first wife Alice during the late 1930s, and which raises the question concerning the status of the object in the psychosocial organisation of the libido. Remarkably, these aspects of Lacan's intellectual trajectory have hardly received any attention, neither in the Lacanian field nor in the object-relations tradition, although the same is true for the other areas of confluence between Balint and Lacan I have identified above – the issue of psychoanalytic training, the question of the end (goal, direction, termination) of the psychoanalytic process, and the matter of psychoanalytic technique.[23] Although Lacan devoted no less than three entire sessions of his first public seminar (Lacan, 1975, pp. 201–233) to a discussion of Balint's *Primary Love and Psycho-Analytic Technique* (1952), and would intermittently return to Balint's work until the late 1960s, it is almost as if Balint has been erased from the Lacanian memory, his only place being that of yet another devoted object-relations theorist identified and singled out by Lacan as a prime example of how the theory and practice of Freudian psychoanalysis had slowly degenerated into a proto-educational doctrine of psycho-sexual, libidinal genitalisation.

Should it still be unclear by now, my overall argument has been rather different. Unacknowledged and all but ignored, Balint had a significant influence on the "early Lacan", personally as well as professionally, clinically as well as theoretically, and he therefore deserves to be restored to his rightful place as a major source of inspiration and a key sparring partner for Lacan during the years of his famous "return to Freud" (Lacan, 1955). My point should not be understood, here, as an index of Lacan's unequivocal agreement with Balint's clinical, theoretical, and technical conceptions of psychoanalysis, but rather as Balint being a kindred spirit, an esteemed partner, and a strategic ally to Lacan during those difficult years following the first schism in the French psychoanalytic movement, when Lacan gradually started to come into his own, and his purportedly Freudian revisionism steadily came to fruition. In addition, if there are few if any traces of Lacan's impact on Balint's work, then the respect was by all means mutual, Balint continuing to support Lacan and the SFP in their long, arduous, and troublesome project of obtaining re-affiliation with the IPA, and his gladly creating the space for Lacan's viewpoints to become known in the Anglo-American psychoanalytic community.

The most telling indication and, in my humble opinion, indisputable proof that Lacan highly valued both Balint the man and the psychoanalyst, and his manifold contributions to psychoanalytic theory and practice, is contained in Lacan's first public seminar, on Freud's technical papers, which was held at Sainte-Anne Hospital during the 1953–1954 academic year, under the auspices of the SFP's newly launched psychoanalytic training programme (Lacan, 1975). Towards the end of an in-depth discussion of various technical essays included in Balint's recently released *Primary Love and Psycho-Analytic Technique*, whose presentation he had entrusted to Wladimir Granoff, one of his most loyal and treasured *compagnons de route* (Granoff, 1954), Lacan proclaimed: Balint "is not an idiot" ("*il n'est pas un imbécile*") (Lacan, 1975, p. 228). To anyone operating in the vicinity, in the margins or even outside Lacan's circle, to be designated as being not totally stupid, or not a complete fool was tantamount to the highest form of praise, nothing less than an intellectual badge of honour. However, Lacan did not stop there. Throughout his seminar, and for a long time afterwards, Lacan heaped oodles of praise on his "dear friend Michael Balint" (Lacan, 1975, p. 139). For example, earlier on in the seminar, he said that "Balint is one of the rare souls who know what they are saying" (1975, p. 175), "one of the most self-aware of analysts", whose description "of what he does is extremely lucid" (p. 180),

> Someone who is, in lots of ways, close, even congenial to us [the members of the SFP], and who without question has an orientation which converges with some of the demands we are here making explicit as to what the intersubjective relation in analysis must be.
>
> (p. 203)

As to Balint's *Primary Love and Psycho-Analytic Technique*, he thought it was "a very interesting book, extremely pleasurable to read, clear, lucid, often bold, full of humour" (p. 204), a robust collection of measurably disparate papers that is nonetheless "characterised by a remarkable unity" (p. 209), compiled by someone who is "subtle,... refined, [and] as delicate a practitioner, as admirable a writer" (p. 226).

As I highlighted at the start of my essay, it remains unclear when and where Lacan first came to appreciate Balint, and which factors precipitated and perpetuated his persistent admiration. Lacan knew, of course, that Balint belonged to what he termed "the Hungarian tradition" (p. 208) in psychoanalysis, and that psychoanalysts within this tradition – Ferenczi first and foremost – had often rallied against the formation of a rigid psychoanalytic orthodoxy, both in terms of theory and practice, technically as well as conceptually, in matters of training and with regard to the professionalisation of the discipline. As I pointed out earlier, Lacan would have also decided to circulate Balint's 1947 essay "On the Psycho-Analytic Training System" (1947b) – an unusually trenchant exposition of the painful shortage of relevant literature on a question so crucial to the preservation of the psychoanalytic profession, and a candid condemnation of the existing standards and practices on both sides of the Atlantic – to the members of the SPP in 1953, precisely because he had fully endorsed Balint's perspective that training procedures should not be adopted uncritically, without careful consideration of their rationale and implications, merely on the pragmatic grounds that they had already been in existence in various parts of the world for many years. Lacan may also have known in advance that when the executive committee of the IPA would discuss the renegade SFP's position within the IPA during its administrative session of 26 July 1953, Balint would be one of the very few participants arguing that the (members of the) SFP should not lose their recognition by the IPA, purely by virtue of their secession from the SPP. Finally, on a theoretical level, Lacan would have greatly appreciated Balint's outlook on the clinical psychoanalytic setting as a specific type of dynamic relationship between the analyst and the patient, rather than as a mere clinical encounter or therapeutic meeting, as Otto Fenichel (1941) had suggested in his *Problems of Psychoanalytic Technique*.

This is effectively where Lacan commenced his discussion of Balint in his seminar on Freud's technical papers. "[T]he elaboration of the notion of the relation between analyst and analysand [*l'analysé*]", he posited, "represents the most fertile line of thought traced out since Freud's death" (1975, p. 11). Lacan ascertained this conceptualisation of the psychoanalytic setting as a specific relationship in Balint's call for a "Two-Body-" or "two-person-" psychology in the addendum to "Changing Therapeutical Aims and Techniques in Psycho-Analysis" (1949a, pp. 234–235) and in "On Love and Hate" (1951c, p. 146). As Lacan reminded his audience, Balint had borrowed this term from Rickman (1950, p. 166, 1951a, pp. 207–208, 1951b, pp. 219–220), who also featured prominently in his highly restricted pantheon of psychoanalytic luminaries, into which he was inducted without irony as "one of the rare souls to have had a modicum of theoretical originality in analytic circles since Freud's death" (Lacan, 1975, p. 11).

However, much as Lacan commended Balint's conception of the analytic relationship as a "two-person psychology", this is also where the agreement ended. Putting aside several critical observations on Balint's standpoints about the end of the psychoanalytic treatment, which were primarily brought out by Granoff in a critical presentation of *Primary Love and Psycho-Analytic Technique* (Balint, 1952; Granoff, 1954), Lacan devoted three entire sessions of his seminar to a meticulous critique of Balint's concept of primary love, which Miller (presumably with Lacan's acquiescence) combined under the heading "Michael Balint's Blind Alleys" (Lacan, 1975, p. 201). Intermittently expressing his surprise at Balint's seemingly contradictory constructions, and going so far as to explicitly apologising for debunking Balint's theoretical positions, given "the wonderful character he is" (Lacan, 1975, p. 227), Lacan ruthlessly uncovered the inconsistencies running through Balint's work, although often with a little help from Granoff, who dutifully cleared the ground for Lacan's exposition and acted as the mediator between the two men (as he would do again a few months later, in the context of Balint's commissioned book chapter on fetishism) (Lacan & Granoff, 1956).

Lacan's forceful and protracted critique of Balint's conception of the object-relation and primary love can be summarised along three distinct lines. First, Lacan argued that Balint's notion of primary love, which had emanated as much from Balint's own mind as it was rooted in Alice Balint's contributions, is but an illusory representation of the mother-infant relationship, because the latter is never characterised by a harmonious, symbiotic complementarity of needs, but always already embedded in a conflictual and fractured pattern of exchanges, on account of the symbolic system of speech and language by which this relationship is governed. In other words, whereas Balint would subsequently understand the "basic fault" as a relatively common, yet nonetheless accidental epiphenomenon of the mutually enriching, reciprocal satisfaction of primary love (Balint, 1968), Lacan would regard it as an intrinsic, insuperable feature of the mother-infant relationship, which cannot be repaired and which is carried over into all the subsequent stages of libidinal development. In a sense, Lacan's critique of Balint, here, is reminiscent of Rickman's own critical reflections on the usefulness of the two-person template for capturing the analytic setting and the mother-infant relationship, in "Number and the Human Sciences" (1951b). Without referring to what Lacan would term "the function and field of speech and language" (1953g), Rickman averred:

Investigations in this seemingly closed two-person relationship [the analytic situation], however, disclose that it is not in fact closed... Thus a *Three-Person Psychology*, which goes by the name of the Oedipus complex, is forced on the observer under the condition of the transference situation in analysis. A more direct observation of this kind of psychology, based however on the findings of analysis is recorded by Dr. Winnicott, when he makes his clinical examination of babies seated on the mother's lap.

(1951b, pp. 219–220)

Second, Lacan admonished Balint for taking the object, in all its manifestations and irrespective of the type of relation in which it partakes, always as an object of satisfaction, that is to say, as an object whose power to satisfy is never in doubt. By contrast, Lacan designated the object as an inherently lacking, and therefore fundamentally dissatisfying manifestation, which is forever taken up in an endless cycle of displacement, and with which the subject can only have some form of satisfying relation by virtue of the intercalation of the fantasy. Lacan's argument, here, drew in equal measure, although implicitly, on Freud's assertion, in the final essay of his *Three Essays on the Theory of Sexuality*, that the finding of an object is only ever the refinding of it, in other words, that an object is never to be found in its original state but only as a replacement (Freud, 1905a, p. 222), and on Abraham's idea of the partial object (and an associated partial love), in his comprehensive and hugely influential study of the developmental history of the libido (1924). In 1956–1957, Lacan would devote a year-long seminar to the study of object-relations, in which this conceptualisation of the object as an inherently lacking entity would be redistributed along the three registers of "the Real, the Symbolic and the Imaginary", and his entire construction, which effectively comes down to Lacan arguing that there is no such thing as a satisfying object-relation, would eventually crystallise in his promotion of the (abject) object *a*, as the object (cause) of desire (1994).

Third, Lacan acknowledged Balint's theorisation of the genital object-relation as a genuinely intersubjective bond, in which one partner is not just concerned with the satisfaction of the other partner and vice versa, but which also entails the mutual recognition of the partner-object *qua* subject and therefore as someone who does not merely exist as an object of satisfaction. Yet he underscored how Balint was incapable of explaining how this intersubjectivity could ever have been installed, given his ongoing reliance on the closed system of primary love. If, as Balint had posited, intersubjectivity is present at the end of libidinal development, then Lacan concluded it must have somehow always already been there from the beginning, unless something exogenous interfered with the harmonious complementarity of primary love. Lacan's point, here, is significant, because it also includes a critique of the maturational paradigm he detected in Balint's work, and which constitutes a staple of virtually all accounts of human ontogenetic progress in developmental psychology. Against this chronological perspective, Lacan reinstated what he believed to be the "proper" psychoanalytic way of looking at temporal processes. Instead of evaluating how object-relations develop chronologically, over time, from a postulated beginning to a projected moment of accomplishment, one needs to consider how previous experiences, historical stages of development, are shaped and situated retroactively, by deferred action, from a certain point in the present, if not from an anticipated moment in the future.

The three axes of Lacan's critique of Balint's primary love, and the specific theory of libidinal development in which it was embedded, would in themselves warrant an in-depth evaluation of their validity and justification. In other words, the question remains to what extent each of Lacan's three distinct criticisms of Balint's object-relations theory is not only persuasive or plausible, but valid and justified with reference to the substance of Balint's outlook on the psychosocial organisation of the libido during the early 1950s. This assignment would be neither futile nor merely academic, because it would prompt a more exhaustive analysis of Balint's work, and Lacan's interpretation of it, whilst also informing a more precise review of its clinical implications. If I shall leave this task to others, or for another occasion, it is only because its complexity and richness cannot be over-estimated. Nonetheless, I can already disclose that some of Lacan's criticisms of Balint's primary love were already anticipated, or at least identified, by Alice and Michael Balint themselves, which probably helps explain why Lacan felt he could call Balint "one of the most self-aware of analysts" in the international psychoana-lytic community (1975, p. 180).[24]

Bringing my essay to a conclusion, I would like to add a simple clarification. In choosing to present it under the title "Lacan's Balint", my intention was not just to document how, over a period possibly spanning more than ten years, Lacan had engaged closely with Balint's works – an engagement which, as I outlined, can be tabulated across four distinct areas of psychoanalytic investigation – but also to emphasise how Lacan's own theory came into existence by virtue of oth-ers, in the context of personal and professional object-relations he himself enter-tained with psychoanalysts whom he considered to be at the creative forefront of theoretical and clinical innovation. There is no doubt that during the 1950s Lacan required strategic allies outside the SFP in order to facilitate the group's readmission to the IPA, yet he also needed intellectual brothers-in-arms, prac-titioners who were not afraid to disclose their own failures, figures who did not shy away from laying bare the fallacies of the formalistic rules and regulations pervading the psychoanalytic establishment, people who did not adhere to any type of doctrinal orthodoxy but were prepared to carve out their own path, warts and all – in short, Hungarians. It would be nonsensical to claim that in his theory and practice Lacan was once a Balintian, yet it would definitely be no exaggera-tion to say that he was Ferenczian in his technical experimentation, Balintian in his opposition to pragmatism and rigidity, and Hungarian in his profoundly sceptical attitude to the gatekeepers of the institutionalised psychoanalytic faith. Something of the Hungarian tradition lived on in the spirit of Jacques Lacan. Something of the French psychoanalytic rebellion probably lived on in the spirit of Michael Balint as well.

Notes

1 Until this day, no one has ever found the original manuscript of Lacan's presentation on the mirror stage at the Marienbad conference. The closest approximation of this "obliterated archive" (Roudinesco, 2001, pp. 26–39; 2003) is a set of notes taken by Françoise Dolto when Lacan delivered a lecture on the mirror stage at the SPP on 16 June 1936, that is, some six weeks before he went to Marienbad (Dolto, 1936). However, Lacan clearly included various aspects of his work on the mirror stage in subsequent essays on the reality principle (1936), on the family (1938), and on the question of psychical causality (1946).

2 Or, as Lacan had put it in his 1946 "Presentation on Psychical Causality": "It is in the other that the subject first identifies himself and even experiences himself" (p. 148).

3 With his foetalisation theory, Bolk argued that human beings are essentially born too soon, because they enter the world long before they are capable of surviving independently.

4 Lagache's letter to Balint does not mention the two other British psychoanalysts by name, and the records of the SPP's scientific meetings, as published in the *Revue française de psychanalyse*, do not provide any further details. The information pertaining to Balint's own presentation is derived from a letter he sent to Lagache on 20 May 1951, in which he announces his forthcoming lecture, and also includes a copy of the abridged English version of his paper on discipline (1951a), so that it can be translated into French prior to the meeting (1951b). The full text of the essay would subsequently be included in Balint's 1957 volume *Problems of Human Pleasure and Behaviour* (pp. 34–48), although without mention of its having been presented at the SPP. I have not been able to ascertain which member of the BPS had extended invitations to Lagache and Lacan, and why it had been decided for these two members of the SPP to come to London, rather than any of the other prominent figures in the French psychoanalytic society, such as Sacha Nacht, Angelo Hesnard, Maurice Bouvet, Francis Pasche, or indeed Marie Bonaparte herself, although she was recovering from hip surgery at the time (Bertin, 1983, p. 236). In 1951, both Lagache and Lacan were members of the SPP's executive committee, yet so were Nacht (who was the president), Pasche, and Bouvet. Both Lagache and Lacan were able to read English fluently, yet neither could speak the language well (Pick, 2001, p. 4; Roudinesco, 1994, p. 159). Between 1947 and 1950, Rickman was the president of the BPS (King, 2003, p. 3) and, as mentioned above, he had met Lacan in September 1945, yet by the time the invitations would have been extended Rickman's tenure had come to an end and he had been replaced by William Gillespie (King, 2003, p. 3). In an August 2001 interview with Daniel Pick, the British Kleinian psychoanalyst Hanna Segal stated that Lagache and Klein were good friends (Pick, 2001, p. 3), yet in 1951 Klein's position in the BPS would not have been sufficiently consolidated for her to be capable of persuading the executive to invite her friend to come and give a lecture. In light of the fact that the Franco-British exchange had been Balint's initiative, and Balint had clearly befriended Lagache when he started visiting Paris more often after World War II – the letters between the two men from 1951 invariably start with "Cher ami" or "Mon cher ami" – it is difficult to resist the temptation to hypothesise that it was effectively Balint who had suggested that Lagache should be invited to the BPS, and that Lagache, when asked about other possible speakers, had proposed Lacan.

5 In his paper at the Zürich conference, Lacan had endorsed Anna Freud's *The Ego and the Mechanisms of Defence* (1936) on two separate occasions (1949, pp. 79–80), yet in reality he was much closer to Klein than to Anna Freud, personally as well as professionally. In her acclaimed biography of Klein, Phyllis Grosskurth quotes a letter dated 28 January 1948 from Klein to her former Canadian trainee W. Clifford M. Scott, in which she mentions how she has had a discussion with Lacan about the programme of

the first World Congress of Psychiatry, which was being launched by Lacan's friend Henri Ey, and had been scheduled to take place in Paris from 18 until 27 September 1950 (1986, p. 377). In an addendum to this letter, Klein disclosed to Scott that Lacan, whom she considered "the most progressive member" of the SPP, had also told her that "the progressive point of view in psychoanalysis", meaning her own, should have been included at the forthcoming International Conference on Child Psychiatry, which had been planned for London from 11 until 14 August 1948, rather than the conservative psychoanalytic perspective on child development that was being promoted by Anna Freud (1986, p. 377). In her interview with Pick, Segal said that she did not know whether Klein had ever met Lacan in person, but that Klein had definitely read his early works. From Grosskurth's biography, however, it can be inferred that Lacan asked Klein in person at the Zürich conference whether she would kindly agree to him undertaking a French translation of her book *Die Psychoanalyse des Kindes* (1932) (Grosskurth, 1986, p. 377; Quinodoz, 2013, pp. 15–16; Roudinesco, 1994, p. 196). Although Lacan's project never materialised, and it has been claimed that Klein subsequently fell out with Lacan over the botched translation (Kristeva, 2000, p. 227; Roudinesco, 1994, p. 197), Lacan's offer must have been driven by a genuine interest in Klein's work, as well as by a desire to make it better known among Francophone psychoanalysts.

6 In the absence of a publicly accessible Lacan archive, it is impossible to compare the published version of Lacan's 1951 lecture to its original presentation, yet in a long letter to Marie Bonaparte of 28 August 1951 Lacan wrote that he had spent two whole Sundays revising his BPS paper for publication (Lacan, 1951a). Interestingly, in this letter Lacan also stated that, whilst in London, he had spoken at a few other places as well ("[je] causai dans quelques autres lieux"), but details of these "other speaking engagements" seem to have disappeared in the creases of history. Lacan's letter to Bonaparte was nothing short of sycophantic. Little did he know that earlier that year, in one of her regular letters to Rudolph Loewenstein, who had been Lacan's analyst during the 1930s, she had called him a madman (Bertin, 1983, p. 236).

7 For all its conceptual complexity and its rhetorical pyrotechnics, the rules of French grammar often being bent to breaking point, Lacan's essay could not really be criticised for its size, because as the main theoretical report on the conference theme, a critical, comprehensive, and exhaustive treatment of the subject matter is what would have been expected from the person assigned to the report. If anything, Lagache's theoretical report on transference for the 14th ACFP (1952) had been even longer than Lacan's examination of language in psychoanalysis.

8 The reader will find the detailed story of the SPP's organisational crisis, which led to the first secession in French institutional psychoanalysis, in Roudinesco (1986, pp. 223–276) and de Mijolla (2012, pp. 279–432).

9 In 1950, Margareth Clark-Williams, an American-born lay analyst who was working as a psychoanalytic psychotherapist at the Centre pédagogique Claude Bernard had indeed been accused of illegally practising medicine. First acquitted, she was eventually found guilty and ordered to pay a fine (de Mijolla, 2012, pp. 137–138, 151–154, 185–186, 380).

10 After its first publication in *The International Journal of Psycho-Analysis'*, the paper was only included in the second edition of Balint's *Primary Love and Psycho-Analytic Technique*, in which it featured alongside "Analytic Training and Training Analysis" (1953d), Balint's presentation at the 18th IPA Congress in London, in a separate final section entitled "Problems of Training". In an introductory note to his publication of archival documents relating to the expulsion of SFP members from the IPA, Jacques-Alain Miller points out that Lacan's archives contain a great many copies of the paper, although he does not mention whether and by whom the text was translated into French (1976, p. 93). If it was, it definitely was not published at the time, because the first

French translation of it was not officially released until 1972, on the occasion of the complete French translation of the second edition of *Primary Love and Psycho-Analytic Technique* (Balint, 1965).

11 It would take a separate essay to gauge the extent to which Balint's scathing exposure of the IPA's authoritarian training system still applies to established training practices in contemporary psychoanalytic institutions, within as well as outside the IPA, but it is fair to say that his ardent call for a fundamental revision of institutional training standards was not heard at all, and that quite a few contemporary psychoanalytic schools still operate with the unspoken principle of conformity as the gold standard for the end of psychoanalytic training. I shall never forget the day when, while being in training at a Lacanian psychoanalytic organisation, I delivered a rather critical paper on Lacan, and an esteemed member of the Lacanian community came up to me afterwards to say, without irony, that I clearly had not finished my analysis.

12 The 18th Congress of the IPA was scheduled to take place at Bedford College, London, from 26 until 30 July 1953. Instead of giving the reader my own summary of the historical development of the ITC, I shall hopefully be forgiven for extensively quoting Balint's version of it in his essay "On the Psycho-Analytic Training System". Apart from the fact that it is generally accurate, this synopsis also relays Balint's serious misgivings as to its relevance: "[T]he history of the International Training Committee is full of critical situations and its end is truly melancholy [*sic*]. Organised originally at the Hamburg? Congress, 1925, practically as the extension of the joint Berlin and Vienna Institutes, it almost disintegrated two years later at the Innsbruck Congress. At that time the apparent source of strife was the question of lay analysis, or what was called officially "conditions for the admission of candidates". This remained the main topic of the discussions till it died a well-deserved death after the Wiesbaden Congress, 1932. Instead of settling down to proper work, there came the American problem at the Marienbad Congress, 1936 [the fact that the American psychoanalytic associations opposed the idea of training standards being controlled centrally, by a relatively small committee], which soon led to a new Declaration of American Independence and to an almost complete paralysis of what was once a proud and powerful organisation. Really, one does not know whether the I.T.C. still exists in reality, or on paper only, or even at all. Existing from 1925 to 1938, during the years of perhaps the most rapid expansion of psycho-analysis, the International Training Committee, the congregation of the pick of the whole analytical world, was not able to produce anything in print save records of most futile disputes" (Balint, 1947b, pp. 263–264).

13 Transcripts of Lacan's year-long seminars on Freud's case studies of Dora (Freud, 1905b), the Rat Man (1909), and the Wolf Man (1918), which were held at his home in Paris between 1950 and 1953, and various other lectures he delivered at the SPP after World War II, have not been preserved or made accessible to researchers, save a small set of notes from the Wolf Man seminar (Lacan, 1951–1952). However, the seminars on Dora and the Rat Man would definitely have informed the contemporaneous texts "Presentation on Transference" (Lacan, 1951c) and "The Neurotic's Individual Myth" (Lacan, 1953e). In none of these texts and transcripts does Lacan explicitly refer to (the spiritual line of) Ferenczi. Indeed, even though Ferenczi would intermittently appear on his radar, and generally in a complimentary sense, *after* 1953, none of his publications until then contain references to Ferenczi and/or the Hungarian tradition in psychoanalysis. For discussions of Lacan's engagement with Ferenczi's works, the reader will benefit from various papers included in Gorog (2009), and sections of Lugrin (2016). The very same day Lacan sent a letter to Balint, he also wrote an exceptionally long letter to his former analyst Loewenstein, in which he presented his own detailed summary of the events leading up to the creation of the SFP (1953a). And seven days later, he sent a much shorter missive to Heinz Hartmann, the then IPA president, in which he petitioned

him to let reason prevail: "I am counting on your authority in order that the genuine labour ... that is ours be respected ..." (1953b).

14 In her 2001 interview with Pick, Hanna Segal mentioned that at the London Congress Lacan and Lagache had been given ten minutes to make their case for the continued IPA membership of the SFP: "I met Lagache at tea at Mrs Klein's house, and he was worried that neither of them [Lagache and Lacan] had good enough English to do it. My husband and I invited Lagache over to translate the paper for him. But instead of Lagache, Lacan turned up, and kept us up all night over his 10 minute paper!" (Pick, 2001, p. 4). Lagache and Lacan thus definitely came to London some time before the conference, but whether Lacan also managed to speak to Balint in person is still a question. In a long letter Lacan wrote to Balint on 6 August 1953, and thus after the IPA central executive had reached its decision, he said: "I didn't see you very much in London, out of fear that I might be seen to solicit the sympathy that you have always accorded to me" (1953c).

15 Much like the manuscript of Lacan's original, 1936 paper on the mirror stage, the text of these lectures has never been found, although it may very well sit in Jacques-Alain Miller's private Lacan archives.

16 For a brief summary of the letter, which remains unpublished, see Beck (1991, pp. 171–172).

17 As if he had anticipated that the issue of his technical experiments, especially in the context of training analyses, might come up at the London Congress, Lacan had written in a similar vein to Loewenstein in his long letter of 14 July – indicating, on the one hand, that he had explained and justified his approach to his colleagues on various occasions, and confirming, on the other hand, that he had by now given up on it (1953a, p. 63).

18 A letter Balint sent to Ernest Jones on 26 September 1953 (Brabant, 2004, p. 177) indeed proves that Balint was in London on that day, but whether he really had to be there is a different matter.

19 When Miller decided to reprint Lacan's presentation in Rome for the centenary volume *Autres Écrits*, he included Lacan's responses to his respondents, but not the words of the respondents themselves (Lacan, 1953f, p. 146).

20 Here too, Lagache's introduction was omitted by Miller for the first official publication of Lacan's talk (Lacan, 1953h), yet it was included in Miller (1976, p. 100).

21 Laforgue's resignation from the SPP was in a sense less surprising than the SFP's decision to welcome him into their cenacle, as Lagache's letter to Balint of 26 November 1953 indicates (1953a). After the war, Laforgue had been accused, notably by some of his colleagues in the SPP, of having collaborated with the Germans, in particular via his professional contacts with Matthias Göring – the cousin of Hermann Göring, one of the most powerful members in the Nazi party – who had set up the (aryan) German Institute for Psychological Research and Psychotherapy, as a replacement for the (primarily Jewish) German Psychoanalytic Society (Cocks, 1997; Lockot, 1994). Laforgue was cleared of all charges in the spring of 1946, but he was no longer welcome in the SPP, and initially moved to Casablanca. When he was given the opportunity to speak again at Henri Ey's first World Congress of Psychiatry in Paris in 1950, he took revenge on his former colleagues by publicly excoriating the fanaticism pervading the psychoanalytic societies (Roudinesco, 1986, pp. 156–163).

22 The French version of Balint's paper had been prepared by Lagache and would subsequently be published in the SFP's flagship journal *La psychanalyse* (Balint, 1956). The note at the bottom of the translation indicating the date when the paper was delivered erroneously states that the lecture took place on 25 May 1954. In September 1954, Balint would return the favour by inviting Lacan to contribute to a book on perversion he was co-editing with Sandor Lorand (Balint, 1954d; Lorand & Balint, 1956). Since Lacan's written English was rather poor, the invitation resulted in Granoff writing a paper in

English about Lacan's ideas on fetishism (Granoff, 1986; Nobus, 2003), which would eventually be published as a co-authored chapter (Lacan & Granoff, 1956).

23 And so I cannot compensate for my own shortcomings by referring the reader to a large body of secondary source materials. Nevertheless, some aspects of Lacan's engagements with Balint's ideas have been addressed in Benoit (1971), Cléro (2017, pp. 232–242), Granoff (1997, pp. 20–24), Harrison Bowen (1994), Kelley-Lainé (2012), Laurent (1977), Lugrin (2016), Mélèse (2002), Moreau Ricaud (2007, pp. 184–191), Turnheim (1992), and Zafiropoulos (2003, pp. 87–92).

24 For example, in an appendix to her extraordinarily insightful paper "Love for the Mother and Mother Love", Alice Balint categorically opposed the suggestion that primary love is a dual unity (1939, p. 127).

Bibliography

Abraham, K. (1924). Versuch einer Entwicklungsgeschichte der libido auf grund der psychoanalyse seelischer störungen. In: J. Cremerius (Ed.), *Psychoanalytische Studien I* (pp. 113–183). Frankfurt am Main, Germany: S. Fischer Verlag, 1971.

Balint, A. (1939). Love for the mother and mother love. In: M. Balint (Ed.), *Primary Love and Psycho-Analytic Technique* (pp. 109–127). London: Hogarth, 1952.

Balint, M. (1930). Psychosexual parallels to the fundamental law of biogenetics. In: *Primary Love and Psycho-Analytic Technique* (pp. 11–41). London: Hogarth, 1952.

Balint, M. (1935). The final goal of psycho-analytic treatment. In: *Primary Love and Psycho-Analytic Technique* (pp. 188–199). London: Hogarth, 1952.

Balint, M. (1936). Eros and aphrodite. In: *Primary Love and Psycho-Analytic Technique* (pp. 73–89). London: Hogarth, 1952.

Balint, M. (1938). Strength of the ego and its education. In: *Primary Love and Psycho-Analytic Technique* (pp. 200–212). London: Hogarth, 1952.

Balint, M. (1947a). On genital love. In: *Primary Love and Psycho-Analytic Technique* (pp. 128–140). London: Hogarth, 1952.

Balint, M. (1947b). On the psycho-analytic training system. In: *Primary Love and Psycho-Analytic Technique* (pp. 253–274). New and enlarged edition. London: Tavistock, 1965.

Balint, M. (1949a). Changing therapeutical aims and techniques in psycho-analysis. In: *Primary Love and Psycho-Analytic Technique* (pp. 221–235). London: Hogarth, 1952.

Balint, M. (1949b). On the termination of analysis. In: *Primary Love and Psycho-Analytic Technique* (pp. 236–243). London: Hogarth, 1952.

Balint, M. (1951a). The problem of discipline. *New Era, 32*: 104–110.

Balint, M. (1951b). Letter to Daniel Lagache of 20 May 1951. Michael Balint Papers. Archives of the British Psychoanalytical Society.

Balint, M. (1951c). On love and hate. In: *Primary Love and Psycho-Analytic Technique* (pp. 141–156). New and enlarged edition. London: Tavistock, 1952.

Balint, M. (1952). *Primary Love and Psycho-Analytic Technique*. London: Hogarth.

Balint, M. (1953a). Letter to Jacques Lacan of 8 June 1953. Michael Balint Papers. Archives of the British Psychoanalytical Society.

Balint, M. (1953b). Letter to Daniel Lagache of 24 June 1953. Michael Balint Papers. Archives of the British Psychoanalytical Society.

Balint, M. (1953c). Letter to Jacques Lacan of 18 August 1953. Michael Balint Papers. Archives of the British Psychoanalytical Society.

Balint, M. (1953d). Analytic training and training analysis. In: *Primary Love and Psycho-Analytic Technique* (pp. 275–285). New and enlarged edition. London: Tavistock, 1965.

Balint, M. (1954a). Letter to Daniel Lagache of 4 January 1954. Michael Balint Papers. Archives of the British Psychoanalytical Society.

Balint, M. (1954b). Training general practitioners in psychotherapy. *British Medical Journal, 1*: 115–131.

Balint, M. (1954c). Letter to Daniel Lagache of 6 April 1954. Michael Balint Papers. Archives of the British Psychoanalytical Society.

Balint, M. (1954d). Letter to Jacques Lacan of 29 September 1954. In: M. Augé (Ed.), *L'objet en Psychanalyse. Le Fétiche, le Corps, L'enfant, la Science* (p. 50). Paris: Denoël.

Balint, M. (1956). Formation des omnipraticiens à la psychothérapie. D. Lagache (Trans.). *La Psychoanalyse, 2*: 221–242.

Balint, M. (1957). *Problems of Human Pleasure and Behaviour*. London: Hogarth.

Balint, M. (1965). *Amour Primaire et Technique Psychanalytique*. J. Dupont, R. Gelly, & S. Kadar (Trans.). Paris: Payot, 1972.

Balint, M. (1968). *The Basic Fault: Therapeutic Aspects of Regression*. New edition. London: Tavistock, 1979.

Beck, M.-C. (1991). Correspondances de Michael Balint au sujet de Sándor Ferenczi et de la technique psychanalytique. *Le Bloc-Notes de la Psychanalyse, 10*: 157–174.

Benoit, P. (1971). De la démarche balintienne auprès des médecins à la technique des psychanalystes lacaniens. In: *Le Corps et la Peine des Hommes* (pp. 55–72). Paris: L'Harmattan, 2004.

Bertin, C. (1983). *Marie Bonaparte: A Life*. London: Quartet.

Bolk, L. (1926). *Das Problem der Menschwerdung*. Jena, Germany: Gustav Fischer.

Brabant, E. (Ed.) (2004). Correspondance Ernest Jones/Michael Balint. Avril 1938–janvier 1958. *Le Coq-Héron, 177*: 25–88.

Cléro, J.-P. (2017). *Lacan et la Langue Anglaise*. Toulouse, France: Érès.

Cocks, G. (1997). *Psychotherapy in the Third Reich: The Göring Institute*. Second edition, revised and expanded. New Brunswick, NJ: Transaction.

de Mijolla, A. (2010). *Freud et la France (1885–1945)*. Paris: Presses Universitaires de France.

de Mijolla, A. (2012). *La France et Freud. Tome 1: Une Pénible Renaissance (1946–1953)*. Paris: Presses Universitaires de France.

Dolto, F. (1936). Notes de Françoise Dolto à la S.P.P. le 16 juin 1936. In: G. Guillerault (Ed.), *Le Miroir et la Psyché. Dolto, Lacan et le Stade du Miroir* (pp. 267–272). Paris: Gallimard, 2003.

Dor, J. (1994). *Nouvelle Bibliographie des Travaux de Jacques Lacan*. Paris: E.P.E.L.

Dupont, J. (2015). *Au Fil du Temps... Un Itinéraire Analytique*. Paris: CampagnePremière.

Eissler, R. (1953). Lettre du secrétaire général de l'IPA à Jacques Lacan. In: J.-A. Miller (Ed.), *La Scission de 1953. La Communauté Psychanalytique en France – 1* (p. 99). Paris: Navarin, 1976.

Fenichel, O. (1941). *Problems of Psychoanalytic Technique*. Albany, NY: The Psychoanalytic Quarterly.

Ferenczi, S. (1927). Das Problem der beendigung der analysen. In: *Bausteine zur Psychoanalyse. Band III: Arbeiten aus den Jahren 1908–1933* (pp. 367–379). Bern, Switzerland: Verlag Hans Huber, 1964.

Ferenczi, S. (1927–1928). Die elastizität der psychoanalytischen technik. In: *Bausteine zur Psychoanalyse. Band III: Arbeiten aus den Jahren 1908–1933* (pp. 380–398). Bern, Switzerland: Verlag Hans Huber, 1964.

Freud, A. (1936). *The Ego and the Mechanisms of Defence.* C. Baines (Trans.). London: Hogarth, 1937.

Freud, A. (1949). Report on the sixteenth international psycho-analytical congress. *Bulletin of the International Psycho-Analytical Association* in *the International Journal of Psycho-Analysis, 30*(1): 178–208.

Freud, S. (1905a). *Three Essays on the Theory of Sexuality.* S. E., 7: 123–243. London: Hogarth.

Freud, S. (1905b). *Fragment of an Analysis of a Case of Hysteria.* S. E., 7: 7–122. London: Hogarth.

Freud, S. (1909). *Notes Upon a Case of Obsessional Neurosis.* S. E., 10: 151–249. London: Hogarth.

Freud, S. (1918). *From the History of an Infantile Neurosis.* S. E., 17: 1–122. London: Hogarth.

Fuechtner, V. (2011). *Berlin Psychoanalytic: Psychoanalysis and Culture in Weimar Republic Germany and Beyond.* Berkeley, CA: University of California Press.

Glover, E (1937). Report on the Fourteenth International Psycho-Analytical Congress. *Bulletin of the International Psycho-Analytical Association* in *The International Journal of Psycho-Analysis, 18*(1): 72–107.

Gorog, J.-J. (Ed.) (2009). *Ferenczi Après Lacan.* Paris: Hermann.

Granoff, W. (1954). Presentation on Balint at Lacan's Seminar *Freud's papers on technique,* 26 May 1954. D. Nobus (Ed. & Trans.). In: R. Soreanu, J. Szekacs, & I. Ward (Eds.), *The Balints and Their World* (this volume), 2023.

Granoff, W., Bacherich, M. & De Sauverzac, J.F. (1985). Des années de très grand bonheur… In: *Le Désir D'analyse* (pp. 117–143). Paris: Flammarion, 2007.

Granoff, W. (1986). D'un fétiche en forme d'article. In: M. Augé (Ed.), *L'objet en Psychanalyse. Le Fétiche, le Corps, L'enfant, la Science* (pp. 33–49). Paris: Denoël.

Granoff, W. (1997). Propos sur Jacques Lacan. In: *Lacan, Ferenczi et Freud* (pp. 11–58). Paris: Gallimard, 2001.

Grosskurth, P. (1986). *Melanie Klein: Her World and Her Work.* London: Hodder & Stoughton.

Harrison Bowen, D. (1994). Entre la relation d'objet et la relation intersubjective. In: S. G. Lofts & P. Moyaert (Eds.), *La Pensée de Jacques Lacan: Questions Historiques – Problèmes Théoriques* (pp. 65–82). Louvain-Paris: Peeters.

Hart, H. H. (1954). International journal of psychoanalysis, XXXIV, 1953: Some reflections on the ego. Jacques Lacan (Review). *The Psychoanalytic Quarterly, 23*: 608.

Hartmann, H. (1954). XVIIIth congress of the international psycho-analytical association. Report from the president. In: J. Lacan & J. Copjec (Eds.), *Television/A Challenge to the Psychoanalytic Establishment* (pp. 71–74). J. Mehlman (Trans.). New York: W. W. Norton, 1990.

Haynal, A., & Hudon, M. (2003). Multilingual bibliography of the works of Michael Balint. *American Journal of Psychoanalysis, 63*(3): 257–273.

Hegel, G. W. F. (1807). *The Phenomenology of Spirit.* T. Pinkard (Trans.). Cambridge, MA: Cambridge University Press, 2018.

Kelley-Lainé, K. (2012). Thalassa to the ocean: From Sandor Ferenczi to Françoise Dolto. In: J. Szekacs-Weisz & T. Keve (Eds.), *Ferenczi for Our Time: Theory and Practice* (pp. 43–56). London: Karnac.

King, P. (2003). Introduction: The rediscovery of John Rickman and his work. In: P. King (Ed.), *No Ordinary Psychoanalyst: The Exceptional Contributions of John Rickman* (pp. 1–68). London: Karnac.

King, P., & Steiner, R. (1991). *The Freud-Klein Controversies 1941–45.* London: Brunner-Routledge.

Klein, M. (1932). *Die Psychoanalyse des Kindes.* Leipzig, Germany: Internationaler Psychoanalytischer Verlag.

Kojève, A. (1933–1939). *Introduction to the Reading of Hegel.* A. Bloom (Ed.), J. H. Nichols Jr. (Trans.). New York: Basic Books, 1969.

Kristeva, J. (2000). *Melanie Klein.* R. Guberman (Trans.). New York: Columbia University Press, 2001.

Lacan, J. (1936). Beyond the "reality principle". In: *Écrits* (pp. 58–74). B. Fink (Trans.). New York: W. W. Norton, 2006.

Lacan, J. (1938). Les complexes familiaux dans la formation de l'individu. Essai d'analyse d'une fonction en psychologie. In: *Autres Écrits* (pp. 23–84). Paris: du Seuil, 2001.

Lacan, J. (1946). Presentation on psychical causality. In: *Écrits* (pp. 123–158). B. Fink (Trans.). New York: W. W. Norton, 2006.

Lacan, J. (1947). British psychiatry and the war. P. Dravers & V. Voruz (Trans.). *Psychoanalytical Notebooks of the London Circle, 4:* 9–33.

Lacan, J. (1949). The mirror stage as formative of the *I* function as revealed in psychoanalytic experience. In: *Écrits* (pp. 75–81). B. Fink (Trans.). New York: W. W. Norton, 2006.

Lacan, J. (1951a). Letter to Marie Bonaparte of 28 August 1951. Marie Bonaparte Papers. Library of Congress, Washington, DC.

Lacan, J. (1951b). Some reflections on the ego. *Journal for Lacanian Studies, 2*(2): 306–317.

Lacan, J. (1951c). Presentation on transference. In: *Écrits* (pp. 176–185). B. Fink (Trans.). New York: W. W. Norton, 2006.

Lacan, J. (1951–1952). Seminario su "L'uomo dei lupi". A. Turolla (Trans.). *La Psicoanalisi, 6:* 9–12.

Lacan, J. (1953a). Letter to Rudolph Loewenstein. In: J. Lacan & J. Copjec (Ed.), *Television/A Challenge to the Psychoanalytic Establishment* (pp. 53–67). J. Mehlman (Trans.). New York: W. W. Norton, 1990.

Lacan, J. (1953b). Letter to Heinz Hartmann. In: J. Lacan & J. Copjec (Ed.), *Television/A Challenge to the Psychoanalytic Establishment* (pp. 69–70). J. Mehlman (Trans.). New York: W. W. Norton, 1990.

Lacan, J. (1953c). Letter to Michael Balint of 6 August 1953. Michael Balint Papers. Archives of the British Psychoanalytical Society.

Lacan, J. (1953d). Lettre de Jacques Lacan à Michael Balint. In: J.-A. Miller (Ed.), *La Scission de 1953. La Communauté Psychanalytique en France – 1* (p. 119). Paris: Navarin, 1976.

Lacan, J. (1953e). The neurotic's individual myth. M. N. Evans (Trans.). *Psychoanalytic Quarterly, 48*(3): 405–425.

Lacan, J. (1953f). Discours de Rome. In: J. A. Miller (Ed.), *Autres Écrits* (pp. 133–164). Paris: du Seuil, 2001.

Lacan, J. (1953g). The function and field of speech and language in psychoanalysis. In: *Écrits* (pp. 197–268). B. Fink (Trans.). New York: W. W. Norton, 2006.

Lacan, J. (1953h). The symbolic, the imaginary, and the real. In: *On the Names-of-the-Father* (pp. 1–52). B. Fink (Trans.). Malden, MA: Polity, 2013.

Lacan, J. (1955). The Freudian thing, or the meaning of the return to Freud in psychoanalysis. In: *Écrits* (pp. 334–363). B. Fink (Trans.). New York: W. W. Norton, 2006.

Lacan, J. (1958). The direction of the treatment and the principles of its power. In: *Écrits* (pp. 489–542). B. Fink (Trans.). New York: W. W. Norton, 2006.

Lacan, J. (1975). *The Seminar. Book I: Freud's Papers on Technique (1953–54)*. J.-A. Miller (Ed.), J. Forrester (Trans.). Cambridge, MA: Cambridge University Press, 1988.

Lacan, J. (1994). *Le Séminaire. Livre IV: La Relation D'objet (1956–57)*. Texte établi par J.-A. Miller. Paris: du Seuil.

Lacan, J., & Granoff, W. (1956). Fetishism: The symbolic, the imaginary and the real. In: S. Lorand & M. Balint (Eds.), *Perversions: Psychodynamics and Therapy* (pp. 265–276). New York: Gramercy.

Laforgue, R. (1953a). Lettre ouverte à Monsieur le Secrétaire de la Société psychanalytique de Paris, 22 octobre 1953. Michael Balint Papers. Archives of the British Psychoanalytical Society.

Laforgue, R. (1953b). Letter to Michael Balint of 11 November 1953. Michael Balint Papers. Archives of the British Psychoanalytical Society.

Lagache, D. (1951a). Letter to Michael Balint of 30 June 1951. Michael Balint Papers. Archives of the British Psychoanalytical Society.

Lagache, D. (1951b). Some aspects of transference. In: *The Work of Daniel Lagache: Selected Writings* (pp. 109–128). E. Holder (Trans.). London: Karnac, 1993.

Lagache, D. (1952). Le problème du transfert. *Revue Française de Psychanalyse, 16*: 5–122.

Lagache, D. (1953a). Letter to Michael Balint of 26 November 1953. Michael Balint Papers. Archives of the British Psychoanalytical Society.

Lagache, D. (1953b). Intervention du Pr Lagache. *La Psychanalyse, 1*: 211.

Lagache, D. (1953c). Première réunion scientifique de la SFP. In: J.-A. Miller (Ed.), *La Scission de 1953. La Communauté Psychanalytique en France – 1* (p. 100). Paris: Navarin, 1976.

Lagache, D. (1954a). Letter to Michael Balint of 8 April 1954. Michael Balint Papers. Archives of the British Psychoanalytical Society.

Lagache, D. (1954b). Letter to Michael Balint of 15 April 1954. Michael Balint Papers. Archives of the British Psychoanalytical Society.

Laurent, É. (1977). Sur Michaël Balint. *Ornicar?, 10*: 33–38.

Lockot, R. (1994). *Die Reinigung der Psychoanalyse. Die Deutsche Psychoanalytische Gesellschaft im Spiegel von Dokumenten un Zeitzeugen (1933–1951)*. Tübingen, Germany: Diskord.

Lorand, S., & Balint, M. (Eds.) (1956). *Perversions: Psychodynamics and Therapy*. New York: Gramercy.

Lugrin, Y. (2016). Ferenczi: Lacan's missed rendez-vous? In: A. Wm. Rachman (Ed.), *The Budapest School of Psychoanalysis: The Origin of a Two-Person Psychology and Emphatic Perspective* (pp. 26–57). London: Routledge.

Mélèse, L. (2002). Balint after Lacan… and after. *American Journal of Psychoanalysis, 62*(1): 65–81.

Miller, J.-A. (Ed.) (1976). *La Scission de 1953. La Communauté Psychanalytique en France – 1*. Paris: Navarin.

Miller, J.-A. (Ed.) (1977). *L'excommunication. La Communauté Psychanalytique en France – 2*. Paris: Navarin.

Moreau Ricaud, M. (2007). *Michael Balint. Le Renouveau de l'École de Budapest*. Ramonville Saint-Agne, France: Érès.

Nobus, D. (2003). Transference in writing: Some notes on "Fetishism: The Symbolic, the Imaginary and the Real". *Journal for Lacanian Studies*, *1*(2): 309–316.

Ohayon, A. (1999). *L'impossible Rencontre. Psychologie et Psychanalyse en France 1919–1969*. Paris: La découverte.

Pick, D. (2001). *Memories of Melanie Klein: An Interview with Hanna Segal*. Available from: http://melanie-klein-trust.org.uk/wp-content/uploads/2019/06/Memories_of_Melanie_Klein_Hanna_Segal-1.pdf (last accessed 30 September 2022).

Quinodoz, J.-M. (2013). *Melanie Klein and Marcelle Spira: Their Correspondence and Context*. London: Routledge, 2015.

Rayner, E. (1991). *The Independent Mind in British Psychoanalysis*. London: Free Association.

Rickman, J. (1950). The factor of number in individual- and group-dynamics. In: *Selected Contributions to Psycho-Analysis* (pp. 165–169). London: Hogarth, 1957.

Rickman, J. (1951a). Methodology and research in psycho-pathology. In: *Selected Contributions to Psycho-Analysis* (pp. 207–217). London: Hogarth, 1957.

Rickman, J. (1951b). Number and the human sciences. In: *Selected Contributions to Psycho-Analysis* (pp. 218–223). London: Hogarth, 1957.

Roudinesco, É. (1986). *Jacques Lacan & Co.: A History of Psychoanalysis in France 1925–1985*. J. Mehlman (Trans.). London: Free Association, 1990.

Roudinesco, É. (1994). *Jacques Lacan*. B. Bray (Trans.). New York: Columbia University Press, 1997.

Roudinesco, É. (2001). *L'analyse, L'archive*. Paris: Bibliothèque nationale de France.

Roudinesco, É (2003). The mirror stage: An obliterated archive. B. Bray (Trans.). In: J.-M. Rabaté (Ed.), *The Cambridge Companion to Lacan* (pp. 25–34). Cambridge, MA: Cambridge University Press.

Turnheim, M. (1992). Balint et la fin d'analyse. *Revue de l'École de la Cause Freudienne*, *20*: 40–45.

Zafiropoulos, M. (2003). *Lacan and Lévi-Strauss, or The Return to Freud (1951–1957)*. J. Holland (Trans.). London: Karnac, 2010.

Contributors

Martine Bacherich is a psychoanalyst in private practice in Paris and a member of the Société de Psychanalyse Freudienne. She is the author, inter alia, of *Edouard Manet. Le regard incarné* (Olbia 1998), *Qu'est-ce qui vous amène?* (Gallimard 2006) and *La passion d'être soi. Cinq portraits* (Gallimard 2008). She has also edited a collection of essays by Wladimir Granoff titled *Le désir d'analyse. Textes cliniques* (Flammarion 2004) as well as the *Œuvres littéraires* of Jean-Bertrand Pontalis (Gallimard-Quarto 2015). She has recently completed editing the complete works of Françoise Dolto, to be published by Gallimard in the Quarto collection.

Antal Bókay is Professor of Modern Literature and Literary Theory in the Department of Modern Literature at the University of Pécs, Hungary. He is also co-founder of the Psychoanalysis PhD Programme, in which he lectures. He is a founding member of the Hungarian Ferenczi Association and Imago Society Budapest. He has an interest and publications in the theory and history of psychoanalysis, the life and work of Sándor Ferenczi, psychoanalysis and literature and the psychoanalytic poetics of modern poetry.

Anna Borgos is a psychologist and women's historian, working as Research Fellow in the Institute of Cognitive Neuroscience and Psychology, Budapest. Her last book, *Women in the Budapest School of Psychoanalysis: Girls of Tomorrow*, came out in 2021 at Routledge. She is the editor-in-chief of Hungarian psychoanalytic journal, *Imágó Budapest*.

Antonella Bussanich is a contemporary Italian artist. She creates artworks that combine video, photography, installation and performance. She has exhibited widely, including at the Uffizi Museum in Florence, where her video work is in the permanent Collection of Self-portraits, and also at the Oberdan Space in Milan; the Modern Art Museum in Troyes, the CCC (Centre de Création Contemporaine) in Tours and Le Cube in Paris; the CCCB (Centre de Culture Contemporània) in Barcelona and the Fondation Bancaja in Valencia; the John Spoor Broome Art Gallery, California; and the Moscow Museum of Modern Art. A television broadcast was dedicated to her work by the Franco-German TV channel ARTE Télévision. After many years in the USA and France, she now lives and works in Florence.

Ferenc Erős   (1946–2020) studied psychology and literature at the ELTE University in Budapest and graduated in 1969. He was professor emeritus in the Department of Social Psychology at the Faculty of Humanities of the University of Pécs. In cooperation with Antal Bókay, he founded the doctoral programme in psychoanalytic studies and directed it between 1997 and 2017. The focus of his research included the social and cultural history of psychoanalysis in Central Europe, and psychoanalytic theory and its application to social issues. He is the author of several scientific books and articles in his areas of research in English, Hungarian, German and French. He edited the Hungarian psychoanalytic review *Thalassa* (1990–2010), and from 2011 he was one of the editors of *Imágó Budapest*. He edited the Hungarian translation of the Freud-Ferenczi correspondence and edited (with Judit Szekacs-Weisz and Ken Robinson) *Sándor Ferenczi – Ernest Jones: Letters 1911–1933* (Karnac 2013).

Gábor Flaskay   graduated as clinical psychologist. He completed his psychoanalytic training in 1990 and became a training analyst six years later. He was elected president of the Hungarian Psychoanalytic Society for two terms. Later he was president of the Training Committee for four terms running seminars for psychoanalytic candidates. Now he is training and supervising analysts in private practice.

Wladimir Granoff   (1924–2000) was one of the most prominent French psychoanalysts of the 20th century. Trained as a psychiatrist, he was a member of the *Société française de Psychanalyse* and, from 1964, of the *Association Psychanalytique de France*. During the 1950s, he was also instrumental in introducing the work of Sándor Ferenczi in France. Among his numerous publications are *Filiations. L'avenir du complexe d'Œdipe* (Minuit 1975), *La pensée et le féminin* (Minuit 1976) and *Le désir et le feminine*, with François Perrier (Aubier-Montaigne 1979). A special issue of the journal *Psychoanalysis and History* including English translations of some of Granoff's essays, as well as previously unpublished archival documents is currently being prepared by Martine Bacherich and Dany Nobus and scheduled for publication in 2024, to coincide with the centenary of Granoff's birth.

André Haynal   (1930–2019) was a philosopher, physician, psychoanalyst (IPA, Swiss Society) and Professor at the University of Geneva (Switzerland). He was the author of more than a dozen books and hundreds of other publications, scientific editor of the Freud/Ferenczi correspondence and a Sigourney Award recipient for his life's work. His publications include *The Technique at Issue. Controversies in Psychoanalysis from Freud and Ferenczi to Michael Balint* (Karnac 1988); *Disappearing and Reviving. Sándor Ferenczi in the History of Psychoanalysis* (Karnac 2002); and *Encounters with the Irrational* (IPBooks, NY 2017).

Kathleen Kelley-Lainé   is a tri-lingual psychoanalyst working in private practice in Paris. She is a member of the Societé Psychanalytique de Paris, European and International Psychoanalytical Associations and the International

Sándor Ferenczi Society. She is also a writer, well known for the successful book *Peter Pan ou l'enfant Triste* (Calmann-Levy 2005), translated into English, Hungarian and Greek. A revised English version, *Peter Pan: The Lost Child* is published by Phoenix (October 2022).

Zoltan Kőváry,   PhD, is a clinical psychologist, existential consultant (SFTR), Litterateur & Linguist Associate Professor at Eötvös Loránd University, Budapest, in the Department of Clinical Psychology and Addiction. He was born in 1974 in Hungary and lives in Budapest. After graduation as a litterateur and linguist and a clinical psychologist he gained his PhD in theoretical psychoanalysis, including the psychobiographical study of eminent artistic creativity. Besides this he is interested in existential psychology and ecopsychology. He also has a private practice, working within the frames of existential psychology. He has published four books, and also edited four books (including *New Trends in Psychobiography* with Claude Helene Mayer, published by Springer) and 70 articles in Hungarian and English.

Zsuzsa Mérei   is a clinical psychologist, a psychoanalytic psychotherapist, and a training and supervising psychodramatist. She runs a private practice and leads psychodrama groups in Paris and Budapest. Her main professional interest is identifying the interface between psychodrama and psychoanalysis.

Dany Nobus   is Professor of Psychoanalytic Psychology at Brunel University London, former Chair and Fellow of the Freud Museum London and Founding Scholar of the British Psychoanalytic Council. He has published numerous books and papers on the history, theory and practice of psychoanalysis, most recently *Thresholds and Pathways Between Jung and Lacan: On the Blazing Sublime* (edited with Ann Casement and Phil Goss, Routledge 2021) and *Critique of Psychoanalytic Reason: Studies in Lacanian Theory and Practice* (Routledge 2022).

Raluca Soreanu   is Professor of Psychoanalytic Studies in the Department of Psychosocial and Psychoanalytic Studies, University of Essex, UK. She is a psychoanalyst and a member of the Círculo Psicanalítico do Rio de Janeiro, Brazil and the author of *Working-through Collective Wounds: Trauma, Denial, Recognition in the Brazilian Uprising* (Palgrave 2018) and the co-author (with Jakob Staberg and Jenny Willner) of *Ferenczi Dialogues: On Trauma and Catastrophe* (Leuven University Press 2023). Between 2015 and 2019, she studied the archive of psychoanalyst Michael Balint, held by the British Psychoanalytical Society, with the support of a Wellcome Trust grant. Between 2022 and 2027, she is leading an interdisciplinary research project *FREEPSY: Free Clinics and a Psychoanalysis for the People: Progressive Histories, Collective Practices, Implications for Our Times* (UKRI Frontier Research Grant), aiming to produce a new global figuration of psychoanalysis as a progressive discourse and practice. She is Academic Associate of the Freud Museum, Editor of the *Journal of the Balint Society* and Editor of the *Studies in the Psychosocial* series at Routledge.

Judit Szekacs-Weisz,   PhD, is a bilingual psychoanalyst and psychotherapist – a double citizen both in her professional and private life. Born and educated (mostly) in Budapest, Hungary, she has taken in the way of thinking and ideas of Ferenczi, the Balints, Hermann and Rajka as an integral part of a "professional mother tongue". She is a founding member of the Sàndor Ferenczi Society, Budapest. The experience of living and working in a totalitarian regime and the transformatory years leading to the fall of the Berlin Wall sensitised her to the social and individual aspects of trauma, identity formation and strategies of survival. In 1990, she moved to London, where, with a small group of psychoanalysts, therapists, artists and social scientists, she founded Imago East-West and later the Multilingual Psychotherapy Centre (MLPC) to create a space where diverse experiences of living and changing context and language in different cultures can be explored and creative solutions found. In 2001, she organised, together with Kathleen Kelley-Lainé and Judith Mészáros, the Lost Childhood Conferences in Budapest, London and Paris. She writes about body-and-mind, trauma, emigration, changing context and social dreaming.

Julianna Vamos,   PhD, is a psychoanalyst with the Société Psychanalytique de Paris (SPP) and a Perinataliste at the progressive Bluets maternity hospital in Paris. She is a founding member and trainer of the Association Pikler-Lòczy de France. She is the co-author of *Devenir Maman pour les nuls* (2018) and *From Budapest to Psychoanalysis: Three Portraits and Their Analytical Frames* (Routledge 2022).

Ivan Ward   is Head of Learning Emeritus at the Freud Museum London and former manager of the museum's conference programme. He is the author of a number of books and papers on psychoanalytic theory and the application of psychoanalysis to social and cultural issues. Recent publications include 'Everyday Racism: Psychological Effects' in *The Trauma of Racism: Lessons from the Therapeutic Encounter*, edited by Michael Slevin and Beverly Stoute (Routledge 2022). He is an Honorary Research Fellow at UCL Psychoanalysis Unit.

Index

Note: *Italic* page numbers refer to figures and page numbers followed by "n" denote endnotes.

Abraham, Karl 150, 157
aggression 43, 97, 110
Aichhorn, August 27
Alexander, I. 82
Anna, Édes 75
anxiety 76, 96, 109, 118n4, 129
"applied psychoanalysis" 75
Arató, Anna 91, 92
"Archive Fever" (Derrida) 18
Association of Socialist Physicians 21
Atwood, George 77
Austro-Hungarian monarchy 92
Autobiography (Csontváry-Kosztka) 80, 82–83
auto-erotism 110, 122, 123

Balazs, Bela 4
Bálint, Alice (Michael Bálint wife) 3, 5, 11, 18, 19, 46–47, 49n25, 56, 101, 120, 123, 124, 146, 160; in analysis 40–46, *44*; biography of 32–35, *33*; child analytical and pedagogical research 61; complex feelings and repressed passions towards mother 45; diaries 39–40; "Love for the Mother and Mother Love" 115–116, 122, 167n24; oeuvre and reception 35–39, *36*; *The Psycho-Analysis of the Nursery* 19, 21, 38, 39; *The Psychology of the Nursery* 36, 38; thoughts on sexuality 46
Bálint Archives 18
Bálint, Enid (Michael Bálint wife) 5, 13, 17, 39, 47n2
"Balint groups" 12, 13, 157

Bálint, János (Michael Bálint son) 34, *36*
Bálint, M. 3, 4, 18, 19, 32, *36,* 39, 40, 47n2, 48n23, 100, 115, 120, 128, 132, 134, 140n60; *The Basic Fault* 5, 14, 65, 76; case of Tivadar Csontváry-Kosztka 80–84; "Changing Therapeutical Aims and Techniques in Psycho-Analysis" 57, 120, 136n5, 137n10, 137n12, 138n18, 147, 160; contribution to psychoanalysis 111; on creativity 76–78; "Early Developmental States of the Ego. Primary Object-Love" 138n32; "Eros and Aphrodite" 145; in history of psychoanalytic thought 11–15; human being in culture 9–11; ideas of "ocnophilic" and "phylobatic" character 7; letter to Lacan 154, *155*; "Love and Hate" 65; love structures 60–62; metapsychology based on love 59–60; "Notes on the Dissolution of Object-Representation in Modern Art" 76; object relations theory 55; "On Love and Hate" 136n4, 137n12, 139n33, 160; "On the Psycho-Analytic Training System" 151, 159, 165n12; "On the Termination of Analysis" 139n37; primary harmony (*see* primary harmony); *Primary Love and Psycho-analytic Technique* 14, 47, 55, 136n2, 137n9, 138n32, 139n33, 140n76, 158–160, 164n10;

"The Problem of Discipline" 148; themes and writings 5; theories and views 6; therapy-based theory of psychoanalysis 56–59; *Thrills and Regressions* 14, 76–77, 109, 110
Bálint, Mihály *44*
Bargues, René 123, 138n19
The Basic Fault (Bálint) 5, 14, 65, 76
Bergler, Edmund 79
Berlin Ethnographic Museum 34
Berlin Psychoanalytic Society 33
Bernfeld, Siegfried 20, 27
Bick, Esther 64
Bion, Wilfred 9, 147
Black Hamlet (Sachs) 38
Blum, Harold 74
Bolk, Lodewijk 148
Bólyai, János 79
Bonaparte, Marie 79, 150, 153, 154
Borderline Conditions and Pathological Narcissism (Kernberg) 104
Bowlby, John 78, 138n32
BPS *see* British Psychoanalytical Society (BPS)
Brandchaft, Bernard 77
British Independent Group 6
British Psychoanalytical Society (BPS) 14, 16–18, 34, 36, 48n2, 146, 147, 151, 163n4, 164n6
Budapest: concentration on childhood and education 19; global perspective of 10
"Budapest School in England" 7
Budapest School of Psychoanalysis 84; role of 75–76
Bussanich, Antonella 65, *71–73*

Camus, Albert 146
"Changing Therapeutical Aims and Techniques in Psycho-Analysis" (Bálint) 57, 120, 136n5, 137n10, 137n12, 138n18, 147, 160
children: consultancy for psychopathic 22; psychoanalytic ideas about 21
Clark-Williams, Margareth 164n9
"clinging instinct" 78, 81, 138n32
comparative psychology 78
"Confusion of Tongues between the Adults and the Child" (Ferenczi) 62, 62n4, 118n6
Coppie (Couples) *72*, 72–73, *73*
countertransference 57, 58, 60, 105
creativity: Imre Hermann on 78–79; Michael Bálint on 76–78

Csáth, Géza: *Egy elmebeteg nő naplója* 75–76
Csontváry-Kosztka, Tivadar 80–84; *Autobiography* 80, 82–83

Dalí, Salvador 81
Danto, Elizabeth 20
Darwin, Charles 79
Dénes, Anni 100
"depth psychology" 74
Derrida, Jacques: "Archive Fever" 18
desire 14, 38, 46, 59, 111
"Desire for Children, Children's Desire: Un désir d'enfant" (Granoff) 116
"divergent technique" 153
Dormandi, Ladislas 146
"dream drawing" technique 95
"A Dream of Descartes" (Székács-Schönberger) 101
Dubovitz, M. 22, 23
Dupont, Judith 11, 14, 37, 146, 156
"The Dynamics of Transference" (Freud) 136n3

"Early Developmental States of the Ego. Primary Object-Love" (Balint) 138n32
education 145–146; psychoanalytic ideas about 21
ego 145–146; fundamental function of 138n19
The Ego and the Mechanisms of Defence (Freud) 163n5
ego-psychology 14, 57, 61
Egy elmebeteg nő naplója (Csáth) 75–76
Eissler, Kurt R. 18, 115
Eitingon, Max 41, 150
"Eitingon model" of psychoanalytic training 151
emigration 12
"Eros and Aphrodite" (Balint) 145
Erős, Ferenc *30*, 30–31
'errors of upbringing' 130, 141n81
existential-humanistic psychology 77
experimental/general psychology 78
"Exposing Behaviour as a Method in Psychoanalysis" (Rajka) 94
Ey, Henri 164n5, 166n21

Fairbairn, Ronald 6, 55
Famiglie (Families) *71*, 72
Farkas, Erzsébet 18, 24, 26, 27
fascism, into Central Europe 5
Fechner, Gustav Theodore 79

Fenichel, Otto 20, 48n23; *Problems of Psychoanalytic Technique* 159
Ferenczi Archives 18
Ferenczi–Balint archives 17
Ferenczi, S. 3, 4, 6, 7, 11–13, 18, 22, 23, 31–33, 35, 36, 38, 40, 43, 46, 49n29, 55, 58, 61, 62n2, 68, 75, 76, 81, 84, 91, 92, 100–102, 111, 116–118, 130, 141n81, 141n94, 145, 147, 151, 152, 157, 159; "Confusion of Tongues between the Adults and the Child" 62, 62n4, 118n6; defined idea of love 59–60; "motherly" intersubjectivity 41; "On introjection and transference" 19; "Psychoanalysis and education" 19; *A Psychoanalyst Unlike Any Other* 14; psychoanalytic position 57; "Stages in the development of the sense of reality" 19
Vth International Congress of Psychoanalysis 19
First World War 11, 91, 92
Fliess, Robert 139n38
Fliess, Wilhelm 139n38
"flying universities" 104
Földházi, Ágnes 48n2
Forrester, John 136n1
Fourteenth International Psycho-Analytical Congress 24
14th Annual Conference of Francophone Psychoanalysts (ACFP) 148–149
French Revolution (1789–1794) 10
Freud, Anna 19, 27, 35, 36, 39, 48n16, 146, 147, 149; *The Ego and the Mechanisms of Defence* 163n5
Freud-Klein controversies 146, 149, 153
Freud, S. 14, 15, 18, 22, 34, 35, 57, 60, 74, 78, 81, 83, 92, 103, 118n6, 120, 121, 123, 127, 137n12, 146, 159, 160, 165n13; "The Dynamics of Transference" 136n3; *The Interpretation of Dreams* 75, 104; *Leonardo da Vinci and a Memory of His Childhood* 74; "Lines of advance in psycho-analytic therapy" 20; "On Narcissism: An Introduction" 61; "On the Universal Tendency to Debasement in the Sphere of Love" 61–62; *Three Essays on the Theory of Sexuality* 59, 161; *Totem and Taboo* 11, 33
Freund, Anton von 18, 20
Füst, Milán 75

Gaál, Emmy 25
Gadoros, Julia 96
genital love 60–62, 124, 125, 128; post-ambivalence of 126
Gereblyés, László 22
Glover, Edward 24
Goldberger, Lajos 25
Göring, Hermann 166n21
Gorog, J.-J. 165n13
Graf Apponyi Poliklinik 22
Granoff, Lacan: "Rome Discourse" 138n17
Granoff, W. 55, 56, 62n3, 115–118, 118n2, 118n4, 118n6, 121–123, 125–136n1, 136n2, 138n18, 139n35, 139n38, 140n76, 141n79, 141n102, 154, 160, 166n22; "Desire for Children, Children's Desire: Un désir d'enfant" 116
Grosskurth, Phyllis 163n5
Guinzbourg, Boris 72
Gyömrõi, Edit 25

Haag, Geneviève 64
Haag, Michel 64
Hajdú, Lilly 27, 38
Hári, Pál 100
Harlow, Harry 78
"harmonious interpenetrating mix up" 65, 66
Hart, Henry Harper 149
Hartmann, Heinz 165n13
hate 58, 110, 124
Haynal, André 4, *16*, 16–17, 47n2
Hegel, G. W. F. 139n51; *The Phenomenology of Spirit* 149
Heidegger, Martin 77, 78, 139n51
Hermann, Alice 24, 38
Hermann, Imre 35, 36, 48n6, 56, 61, 76, 81, 84, 84n1, 93, 100–102, 117; case of Tivadar Csontváry-Kosztka 80–84; on creativity 78–79
Hesnard, Angelo 156
Hódos, Mária 26, 27
Hollós, István 75
Horthy (Admiral) 12, 20
Hug-Hellmuth, Hermine 19
human links 71–73, *71–73*
Hungarian Israelite Patronage Association 25
Hungarian Psychoanalytic Association 18, 21
Hungarian Psychoanalytic Society 34, 100–102, 105, 107

Hungarian tradition in psychoanalysis 55, 56, 159, 162, 165n13
Husserl, Edmund 77
Hyppolite, Jean 127, 128, 139n51

Illés, Endre 38
Illyés, Gyula *22*
infantile hopes 65
instincts 57, 102, 111, 131; "clinging instinct" 78, 81, 138n32; partial 78, 81
Institute of Psychoanalysis 11–12
International Conference on Child Psychiatry 164n5
The International Journal of Psycho-Analysis 101, 147, 164n10
International Psychoanalytic Association (IPA) 101, 115, 117, 145, 151, 153, 154, 156, 157, 159, 164n10, 165n11, 165n12
International Psychoanalytic Congress 145, 147
International Training Committee (ITC) 152
The Interpretation of Dreams (Freud) 75, 104
intersubjectivity 58–59
IPA *see* International Psychoanalytic Association (IPA)
Isaac, Susan 27
István, Szent 92
ITC *see* International Training Committee (ITC)

Jaspers, Karl 97
Jewish immigrants 10, 11
Jones, Ernest 5, 12, 34, 101, 117, 146, 147
Joseph II (Emperor) 10
József, Attila 21, *22*

Karinthy, Frigyes 75
Kernberg, O. F. 55; *Borderline Conditions and Pathological Narcissism* 104
Keve, Tom 4
Klein, M. 19, 20, 55, 61, 81, 83, 101, 148, 149, 157, 163n4, 163n5, 164n5, 166n14
Koestler, Arthur 11
Kohut, Heinz 77
Kojève, Alexandre: "Phenomenology of Spirit" 149
Korczak, Janusz 27

Korda, Alexander 11
Kosztolányi, Dezső 75
Kovács, Frigyes 32
Kovács, Vilma 32, 34, 40, 46, 101, 146
Kretschmer, Ernst 82

Lacan, J. 49n25, 55, 56, 58, 59, 62, 62n1, 62n4, 62n5, 116, 117, 118n4, 120–125, 128–136n1, 136n2, 136n3, 137n12, 138n17, 138n19, 138n24, 139n33, 139n35, 140n70, 140n76, 141n94, 141n103, 142n113, 145, 152, 154, 158, 162, 165n13, 166n15, 167n23; clinical technique 153; critique of Balint 160, 162; letter from Balint to 154, *155*; "The Looking-Glass Phase" 145; "Mirror Stage" 147; "The Neurotic's Individual Myth" 165n13; "Rome Discourse" 149; *Séminaire* 115–118; "the Symbolic, the Imaginary and the Real" 156
Laforgue, R. 156, 166n21
Lagache, D. 148, 156, 163n4, 166n20, 166n22
"language of dreams" 74
"the language of symptoms" 74
"languages of the unconscious" 74
Laplanche, Jean 117
Lavie, Jean-Claude 116, 117
Leclaire, Serge 117
Leirism, Michel 146
Leonardo da Vinci and a Memory of His Childhood (Freud) 74
Lévy, Kata 18, 20, 24, 26, 27
Lévy, Lajos 18, 100
"Lines of advance in psycho-analytic therapy" (Freud) 20
"Living Archives Project" 18
Loewald, Hans 81, 83
London Freud Museum 18
"The Looking-Glass Phase" (Lacan) 145
Lorand, Sandor 166n22
love 110; characteristics of 126; genital 60–62, 124–126, 128; metapsychology based on 59–60; pregenital 58, 60–62, 124; primary 125, 126, 129, 131, 157, 160, 162
"Love and Hate" (Balint) 65
"Love for the Mother and Mother Love" (Balint) 115–116, 122, 167n24
Lugrin, Y. 165n13

Lukács, Georg 4, 11

Mahler, Margaret 84n1
Mallarmé, Stéphane 156
Mannoni, Dominique-Octave 117, 128;
    Prospero and Caliban 140n70
Mária Valéria settlement 92
Marienbad conference 149, 163n1
Martens, Francis 154
Maslow, Abraham 80
Maternité Des Bluets 64, 65
Meerloo, Joost A. M. 48n19
Memoirs of my Nervous Illness (Schreber)
    96–97
Mérei, Zsuzsa 105
metapsychology 55; based on love 59–60
*Michael Balint: Object Relations Pure and
    Applied* (Stewart) 6
Miller, Alice 80
Miller, Jacques-Alain 135–136n1, 160,
    164n10, 166n15, 166n19, 166n20
"Mirror Stage" (Lacan) 147
Möbius, Paulus 74
mother-infant relationship 13, 36, 41, 58,
    74, 160
Mother Nature 80–83

Nacht, Sacha 150
naïve egoism 126, 129
narcissism 61–62, 74, 76; secondary 123
Neill, A. S. 27
neotenic embryos 128
Neumann, John von 11
"The Neurotic's Individual Myth" (Lacan)
    165n13
"new beginning" 58, 140n76
Nietzsche, F.: *Thus Spake Zarathustra* 92
Nobus, Dany 115, 118n1, 135n1
"Notes on the Dissolution of Object-
    Representation in Modern Art"
    (Bálint) 76
"Number and the Human Sciences"
    (Rickman) 160
nyelvujtás ("Language learning")
    movement 10
Nyugat ("West") 75

object-relations 109–111, 133, 134, 160,
    162; pre-genital ambivalence of
    126; theory 55; tradition 157, 158
object-to-object relationship 133
obsession 80, 96

ocnophilia 76, 78, 109–111
Oedipus complex 76
"One-Body Psychology" 121, 133, 137n12,
    147
"On introjection and transference"
    (Ferenczi) 19
"On Love and Hate" (Balint) 136n4,
    137n12, 139n33, 160
"On Narcissism: An Introduction" (Freud)
    61
"On the Psycho-Analytic Training System"
    (Balint) 151, 159, 165n12
"On the Termination of Analysis" (Balint)
    139n37
"On the Universal Tendency to Debasement
    in the Sphere of Love" (Freud)
    61–62
"On Transference and Counter-
    Transference" 135

Pákozdy, Ferenc *22*
Pálos, Elma 41
partial instincts 78, 81
Patronage Association 25, 27
"pedagogical experiment" 27
Perrier, François 117, 118n4
Pertorini, Rezső 80, 82
Pest 10; culture of 11
phenomenological-existential approaches
    77
"Phenomenology of Spirit" (Kojève) 149
The Phenomenology of Spirit (Hegel) 149
philobatism 76–78, 110, 111
Picasso, Pablo 80
Pick, Daniel 163n4, 164n5, 166n14
Pikler, Emmi 24, 27, 64, 68
Pikler Loczy Institute 64
Polányi, Laura 27
Polányi, Michael 34
Pontalis, Jean-Bertrand 117
"post-Cartesian psychoanalysis" 77, 78
pregenital love 58, 60–62, 124
Premier regard (First gaze) 72, *72*
"premorbid psychopathy" 80–81
primary harmony 64–65, 68–69; clinical
    vignette 66; consultation 66–67;
    infantile hopes 65; object taken for
    granted 65–66; partnership 68
primary love 125, 126, 129, 131, 157, 160,
    162
*Primary Love and Psycho-analytic
    Technique* (Bálint) 14, 47, 55,

136n2, 137n9, 138n32, 139n33, 140n76, 158–160, 164n10
"The Problem of Discipline" (Balint) 148
Problems of Psychoanalytic Technique (Fenichel) 159
professional hypocrisy 58
"progression for regression" 76, 84
Prospero and Caliban (Mannoni) 140n70
psychoanalysis 13, 42, 74, 120; Balint's contribution to 111; cultivation of 102; evolution of 75; and existential-humanistic psychology 77; and experimental/general psychology 78; "Jewish science" of 146–147; object-relations movement in 138n17; object-relations tradition in 157; post-WW2 history of 100; therapy-based theory of 56–59
"Psychoanalysis and education" (Ferenczi) 19
Psychoanalysis and History 118n2
The Psycho-Analysis of the Nursery (Bálint) 19, 21, 38, 39
psychoanalysts, generation of 95–96
A Psychoanalyst Unlike Any Other (Ferenczi) 14
Psychoanalytic Association 21, 24
psychoanalytic creativity research, birth of 74–75
psychoanalytic education 11
psychoanalytic ideas 21, 93; about children and education 21
The Psychoanalytic Quarterly 149
psychobiography 74, 79, 82
psychodrama method 100, 107
psychological saliency 81–84
The Psychology of the Nursery (Bálint) 36, 38

Rajka, Tibor 91, 100; analyst as young man 92; clinician 94–95; "Exposing Behaviour as a Method in Psychoanalysis" 94; history 93; mental case 96–97; research as tool in analytical enquiry 95–96
Rank, Otto 141n94
Reich, Wilhelm 20, 21
Révész, László 92
Rickman, John 12, 34, 137n12, 146–148, 160, 163n4; "Number and the Human Sciences" 160

Róheim, Géza 35, 38, 100, 101
"Rome Discourse" (Lacan) 138n17, 149
Rope, Michael 20

Sachs, Wulf: *Black Hamlet* 38
Sandler, Anne-Marie 13
Sandler, Joseph 13
Sándor Ferenczi Society 30
Sartre, Jean-Paul 146
Schiele, Egon 81
Schmidt, Vera 27
Schreber, D. P.: *Memoirs of my Nervous Illness* 96–97
secondary narcissism 123
Second World War 9, 24, 27, 93, 102, 146, 150
Segal, Hanna 163n4, 164n5, 166n14
selfobjects 77
Séminaire (Lacan) 115–118
Semmelweis, Ignác 79
"sense of reality" process 61–62
separation-individuation theory 84n1
sexuality 14, 21, 42, 43, 46; theory of drive and 59
SFP *see* Société française de Psychanalyse (SFP)
Simmel, Ernst 20, 150
Sklar, Jonathan 39
Social Democratic Party 21
Société française de Psychanalyse (SFP) 118n3, 118n5, 150, 152–158, 162, 164n10
Société Psychanalytique de Paris (SPP) 116, 118n3, 145, 150–153, 163n4, 164n5
solicitude 65–66
Soreanu, Raluca 7
Spitz, René 78
"Stages in the development of the sense of reality" (Ferenczi) 19
Stewart, Harold: *Michael Balint: Object Relations Pure and Applied* 6
Stolorow, Robert 77, 78
Strachey, James 115
sublimation 76–78, 81, 83, 84
Swerdloff, Bluma 21
"the Symbolic, the Imaginary and the Real" (Lacan) 156
Szántó, Imre 22
Székács-Schönberger, István 99, 99–108; "A Dream of Descartes" 101; law of action and counteraction 103;

multi-faceted relationship with analytical society 100; private psychoanalytic practice 102
Székács-Weisz, Judit 18
Székely, Béla 21, *22*
Székely-Kovács, Olga 146
Székely, Zsigmond 32
Szilard, Leo 11

Teller, Edward 11
theory of attachment 138n32
"The Theory of the Parent-Infant Relationship – Contributions to Discussion" 64–65
therapy-based theory, of psychoanalysis 56–59
Three Essays on the Theory of Sexuality (Freud) 59, 161
Thrills and Regressions (Bálint) 14, 76–77, 109, 110
Thus Spake Zarathustra (Nietzsche) 92
Totem and Taboo (Freud) 11, 33

transference 56–58, 105, 136n3
"triple artist" 75
"two-body psychoanalysis" 56, 58
"Two-Body Psychology" 121, 133, 137n12, 147, 149, 157, 160

Vajda, Zsuzsanna 35
Vajna, Éva Sára *25*
Vamos, Julianna 72, 73
Vergote, Antoine 154
Vikár, András 107

Wagner, Lilla 79
Warsaw Ghetto 27
Wartime Manchester 5
Weiss, Alfonz 25
Weiss, Elisabeth 25
"Where Are You, My Sons?" 24
Winnicott, Donald 9, 55, 117, 161
Winthuis, Josef 38

Zürich conference 163–164n5

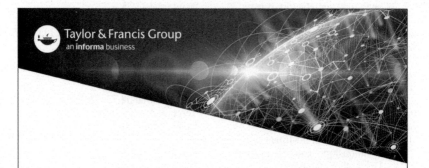